A WALK IN

HIS SHOES

Enjoy! Dustin John

DUSTIN JOHN & DALLAS JOHN

COLLABORATION AND EDITS BY KIMBERLY FLACK

This book is dedicated to my late
father Dallas.
He was such a wonderful man.

I love you dad.

Acknowledgements

A warm and loving thank you to my wife Maiju, who has been an exceptional supportive anchor in my recovery. She was also irreplaceable with her excellent knowledge of computers/Photoshop in building the artwork for this book. I want to also give a special thanks to my family for supporting this 6-year project. Without their cheers of consistent encouragement, this book wouldn't have been possible. A big thanks to Kimberly Flack. Her editing abilities and her understanding of the English language is phenomenal. Without her correcting our prattle-scat-twaddle-yammers', this book would have fallen far short of its intended goal. I also want to thank my blog followers, friends and co-workers who have shown care, connection and interest in my story.

Preface

Dallas

T he scenarios you will read about in this book are mere sprouts of a deeply rooted, long-standing weed. Its roots are nourished and spreading in an underground, unseen world by thousands of drug-addicted people who – through their need for drugs – would just as soon slit your throat as look at you.

Despite all efforts, the supply and consumption of illegal drugs kills more individuals each year than those who suffer vehicular fatalities. Instead of repairing this disheartening trend, the opposite is taking place as a staggering 8,100 new Americans begin tampering with illicit substances daily. That works out to an estimated 3.1 million new drug users annually according to the Center for Disease Control. This is not just a passing phase. Drug use and addiction is an increasing trend that is ravishing this country. It is so prevalent that our story will resound with every American because they either know an addict or have experimented with drug use themselves. If neither of these scenarios fit, it is only a matter of time according to the statistics. Addiction, in some format or another, is slinking its way into every home and into every family structure in this country seeking to extend its roots and spread its devastation.

Although the majority of us would like to believe that drugs, drug trafficking, and drug addiction can only be found on big city streets and in states and neighborhoods outside our own – that is simply not the case.

Sadly enough, accepting that these dangerous drugs do exist and that each of us is fair game to addiction's out-stretched arms is not enough. We must educate ourselves to recognize its many faces and – more importantly – to know when this monster has attached itself within the family structure.

Although we do follow some chronological order, our story does not detail the beginning of Dustin's demise, rather several vignettes encapsulating some of the most atrocious aspects of the addiction we as parents were

1

exposed to. We have chosen to present this story following Dustin's life timeline. Dustin will detail a chapter of his life from his perspective, then I, Dallas, will write a response to Dustin's experiences from my point of view on the same situation. I will share with you specific accounts of a Christian family and of a young man raised in a Christian community who has - and will always - be battling the forces of drug addiction.

From the gripping experiences detailed throughout this book, it might appear to some as though our family had always known, or should have always known, of Dustin's drug addiction. Unfortunately, we were just as blind and naive as the majority of you. Raising our family in a small, comparatively sheltered town, Dustin being the youngest of our four children, we never imagined the most destructive predator lurked so close to our door. Although our family had suspicions, hard evidence of his actions did not surface for more than a year after our son had begun using. Validation to this statement and the above mentioned time frame is based solely on our son's recollection and collaboration in the sharing of this tragic story.

I ask readers to withhold their judgments as they stare into the deepest, most sacred crevices of my and my family's souls. I plead with you to take the experience of my family and learn from our sorrows and triumphs. I pray that you may never have to know personally of the anguish associated with these trials, but if you are harrowed up with this sort of situation or know someone who is, our intent is to educate and motivate you to either repair, prevent, or at least better endure the ordeal should it come knocking at your door.

As I prepare to share the devastation, madness, and sorrow for which my family has to this day endured, I would propose there is one of two paths we can choose to walk on in life. There may be variations to these paths, but they all stem from one of two options. The first path has many great things to offer. This passageway rewards individuals with happiness, self-worth, success, and often contributes to one's good health. By this same token, it's counterpart, the second path reeks of disappointment, failure, obliteration of self-worth, depression, poor health, and more often than not addiction.

It has been my experience as a parent that we must accept responsibility for our children and the eventual path they will follow. For it is through our examples, commitment, guidance, and our willingness to educate our children that they just might stand some chance of receiving those rewards I have mentioned from the first path.

By this same token, I must submit that we as individuals are all responsible for our own actions. The glory and/or sadness which follows is the direct result of those choices we, and only we alone, have made.

Regardless of this fragile balance, I still question whether or not I was there for Dustin in his hour of need. Had I fallen short of my parental duties and responsibilities? If not, why then did our son find it necessary to turn to drugs?

Although I do not have any professional credentials for dealing with addicts, I share the following thoughts and suggestions based on my own real-life battle to save my son from heroin and other mind-altering substances.

1

DROP DEAD

DUSTIN

SPRING 2005

Cars zoom past me as if late for an important meeting. I stand alone on the faded yellow curb. A local transit bus squeals to a sudden stop to my right. Potential passengers' hustle their way towards me as the bus platform lowers to the curb. The sounds of leaky hydraulics radiate from under the frame as the bus driver opens the scissor-style doors. As the passengers' board and fight their way to an empty seat, I notice a young boy staring at me through the scratched window of the bus. He is all alone. He is wearing a blue and yellow mask that he probably made at school. The eyeholes are cut out as well as a small slice for his mouth. For some reason I can't break my focus from this little boy. As I stare in bewilderment, he gives me what looks to be a half smile that is projecting an unspoken message. He slowly shakes his head side to side. Is he telling me no? What is he trying to say? Why is this bothering me? I feel a shiver forming through my body. I continue to stare at the boy as the bus pulls away. He raises his hand in the shape of a pistol and puts it to his temple. He pulls the trigger and drops his head down on an angle so that I can see his mask as the bus pulls away.

The exhaust is still billowing into the air as I walk across the street to a local gas station. My thoughts are still turning the odd visuals of the little boy, his mask, and the bus. As I approach the station, my attention is diverted to a man on a Harley Davidson. He is wearing a worn black leather jacket that looks like it has seen its share of highway miles. His Levis are torn on the knees but held together by a few, small white threads. His face looks as if it has never been under a shade tree. The lines and wrinkles on his weathered

4

face tell me he's had a rough life. As I approach his motorcycle, he asks, "Hey, man. You have a light?"

"Yeah, sure." I hand him my lighter and as I do he says, "Can you get me some cocaine?"

"I can get it but I don't have a way to get it. I don't have a vehicle," I respond – knowing there's no way this guy is an undercover cop.

"I'll give you a ride. Hop on."

The powerful acceleration of the motorcycle jerks me backward. The wind fills my ears with empty air sound. We fly down the road with one thing in mind. One purpose, one reason. Our determination pays off as we approach an area well known for its high volume of illegal activity. My ears are still ringing as he kills the motorcycle engine. For a brief moment, I recall the boy on the bus. The thoughts are washed out by the voice of my new biker friend.

"Hurry up, I don't have all day," he gruffly reminds me.

"I'll be quick man, no worries." My heart starts beating fast as I realize I am about to get heroin and cocaine.

Before I met this guy I had no money and no way to get any. Once he gets his cocaine and I get my heroin, we will probably go our separate ways. It doesn't matter though. We do whatever it takes to get our fix.

With the dope safely secured in my tightly closed fist, we drive to a local grocery store. Their bathrooms serve as a safe haven for shooting up. When you are homeless it is hard to have privacy. Public bathrooms provide that privacy.

We pull into the grocery store and park the bike next to the building. I am nervous as I approach the entrance. The automatic doors open swiftly to the motions of shoppers and children. A gust of air hits me as I enter the store. My focus is on the back of the store where I see a blue plastic sign pointing the way. My fast-paced walk gradually turns to a jog. I can hear my friend keeping pace but I don't acknowledge him.

Since I reach the bathroom first, I go into the stall that is against the wall. I like these stalls the best because if someone comes in while I am using, I don't run the risk of having people on both sides of me. My new friend goes into the stall next to me. I see his hand lower under the stall wall. I hand him his cocaine, a spoon and a needle. I start to get my heroin ready, but he interrupts me saying, "Hey man, let me try some of that stuff."

I know he hasn't used heroin in a while and I'm a little worried to give him some. He doesn't seem like the type of person to reason with though, so I hand him my leftovers under the metal door.

I return to my own priorities. I draw back the heroin and fill the needle. A couple shakes of my wrist and the air rises to the top of the syringe. I push the air through the needle and spin the needle around with my fingers. I look down and gently place the needle's sharp point against the vein protruding from my left arm. One quick tap with my index finger and the needle tears a hole. I pull back on the plunger to see a deep red color mix with the liquid heroin. PUSH. The warm mixture enters my veins with vengeance. Within seconds I feel the world's troubles subside into total bliss.

As I wipe the blood from my battered arm, I open the stall door. I look up and see my friend leaning towards the mirror with both hands on the sink. Sweat runs down his temple and off his forehead. He looks as if he is staring through his own reflection.

"Hey, are you okay?" I ask. He takes a slow deep breath and says, "Yeah." He lets go of the sink with both hands and his body drops to the hard tile like a bag of wet sand. Images of the boy on the bus flash back and start to haunt me.

When I was in the second grade my teacher asked the class what we wanted to be when we grew up. I tried to look ahead at where I would be in 20 years: a lawyer, a doctor, a fireman? With the imagination of an eight-year-old boy, I had no idea that my decisions and choices in the upcoming years would shatter all of those dreams. My loyalty to my profession I would choose would prove relentless and devastating. I would become a heroin addict.

I have fought many long drawn out battles only to be defeated time and time again. My addiction was very subtle in the beginning and as time went on, it became the aggressive dictator of my life. It has taken me to places I could have never imagined. Deep, dark places which seemingly felt I was in an unorthodox universe, far away from the rest of society. My days were numbered and I was brought to the brink of death on several occasions.

This did not happen overnight. It was a slow and painful process. When I decided I wanted out, it was too late. My addiction had already started running its course. It had woven its threads through every cell and synapse of my being. The foundation for my addiction was built on my decisions early on. It would continue to build upon itself like a towering skyscraper and I would be set underneath to carry its massive weight each and every day. Once the foundation is set, you can never entirely demolish it. Even after years of being clean, addiction particles surface frequently requiring daily mental exertion to choose to avoid the icy grip of drugs. If I regress and allow myself to feel its cold fingers even just briefly, it clenches around my body and soul like a metal trap with unrelenting jagged teeth tearing into me, grasping me, and refusing to release me.

Could this entire scenario have been avoided? Is my purpose in life to serve as a warning to others? Would the outcome of my life be different had I made better choices? What if I had dealt with my feelings and emotions instead of looking to drugs to console me and artificially remove the pain? How much agony could be erased if I merely said, "No thanks?" Was it really so easy to avoid or was this an unstoppable beast meant for me to temper?

1

UNCONDITIONAL LOVE

DALLAS

NOVEMBER 5, 2003

As my wife and I stare into each other's eyes, tears of sadness begin to fall. Despite our pleas and prayers and the medical efforts of many doctors, we both know now that nothing more can be done to save our youngest child, Dustin.

Once the happy host of an otherwise healthy and normal 17-year old body, our son's 10-year addiction to heroin and many other mind-altering drugs has now, at age 27, left him catering to nothing more than a rickety shell of skin and bones. More importantly, beneath this condemned and crumbling structure lays an empty mind where quick wit and brightness had played second only to his honesty and truthfulness. Spurred on by his need for more and more drugs, so went these qualities and the son we once knew.

Dustin lay dying curled into the fetal position, his head now resting in his mother's lap, I watch helplessly as the two merge together in the center portion of our kitchen floor. Unable to find a heartbeat, tears run down my wife's face as she watches over the trembling body of her unresponsive son.

"Come on Dustin...wake up and breath," my wife pleads as she shakes his lifeless body.

Watching from a distance, I ask myself, "Is this the end? Has Dustin finally lost his 10-year addiction battle to heroin? Is the heartache and pain now over for his brother and sister, who have watched their younger sibling fall into this deep dark hole of no return?"

As parents of a drug addict, we had been through this frightening scene many times before. Near-death experiences are but a common occurrence, the mainstay to a host whose body and lifestyle resembles that of a rollercoaster.

Miraculously perhaps, our son did not die that night, but instead would, once again, submit himself and the rest of his family to yet another round of drug withdrawals.

LATE SPRING 2005

Having spent the past six months roaming the streets of Salt Lake City, Utah our son was again asking to come home. Lord only knows what horrible events had taken place, but there was one thing I knew for sure: it had to be serious.

While most people would applaud an addict's willingness to come clean, I on the other hand, viewed this homecoming as nothing more than a repeat for disaster. It wasn't that I did not want our son back. His homecoming was overshadowed with my fear of the repercussions of housing a drug addict.

If allowed back in our home, I hated what Dustin would do to this family, and even more so, the pain he would put his mother through once again.

But Dustin used all of his street-smart conniving ways to convince my wife that he should be allowed once again in our home – something we had sworn would not happen again. It just always proved to be too hard emotionally, mentally, and physically. It is a situation no parent ever wants to be presented with: either let his life destroy ours, or turn our back on him.

"Please mom, please dad, it will be different this time," Dustin pleaded. " I won't go back to drugs. Please let me stay. Don't kick me out on the streets again."

From a less jaded point of view, Dustin's get-clean pledge might easily be misconstrued as the promising path to a bright and happy drug-free future. Unfortunately, as a family, we had all been here before. Although each of us would hold hope in our hearts that Dustin might have the strength to make it to a drug-free life this time, we all knew the odds were against him. After all, once an addict, always an addict. We had seen this played out too many times in his past to hope for anything different.

My wife's decision to let our son stay was a mistake and I knew it. Although I praise this woman for her unconditional love, a failure on Dustin's part to come clean might very well destroy what remaining relationship my wife and I had in tact.

Everyone has heard that a parent's love for his or her children is unconditional. That so-called "unconditional" love does vary though for each person from day-to-day. On any given day, or really at any given minute, one individual's level of concern, patience, love, and understanding might truly reach what we'd all consider an unconditional high point. When someone reaches this particular level, he or she would do anything and stop at nothing to help the recipient of such love. Unfortunately, you and your partner may not find that same level of love and understanding at the exact minute, hour, or even on the same day. This leaves the two of you bickering and squabbling as to what extent you are willing to help and love.

My wife's decision that day to allow Dustin to return home is a perfect example of when two people find themselves at opposite ends of that unconditional love spectrum.

Our son had become a professional salesman and his ability to manipulate those around him was alarming. Ten years of repeated lies, broken promises, and a loss of some $20,000 tends to wear out a person's unconditional trust and optimism. While my wife had somehow found the strength and willingness to forego another round of pure hell, I, on the other hand, refused to buy in. I wanted to know why now, at this specific juncture, had Dustin suddenly found the courage and fortitude to put himself through two weeks of painful withdrawals needed to become "clean" and then choose to stay clean despite a lifetime of continued temptation.

This was not the first time our son had attempted to turn his life around. But, as a now more experienced parent following the vicious circle of addiction, I had noticed what seemed to be a direct correlation between the timing of each of his so-called attempts to come clean and the situational instability that follows an addict living on the streets. Basically, I knew Dustin had done something very bad if he was so desperate for us to take him back in as he appeared. Whatever it was, it had our son on the run. He was ready to come home. He was willing to try and get clean. And my wife believed him. Now it was just a matter of deciding if I did – or could – too.

As he attempted to gain my support for our home as his safe haven, a partial confession emerged.

"Dad, I'm scared! I think I may have had something to do with a man dying," Dustin told me as I listened in disgust. "There was this big burly looking biker that stopped on the corner of the street where I was standing. I guess by just looking at me, he knew I might know where to find him some drugs." Dustin explained. "He told me that if I could take him to my dealer that he would buy enough heroin and cocaine for both of us, so, that's what I did." Not seeing the connection for why my son might feel like he had killed this person, I asked him to continue.

Dustin explained how the startling events with the surly biker had unfolded in the grocery store bathroom. "I don't know if he died," Dustin finished, his voice strained with fright and tears, his head lowered in shame and defeat. He barely mustered out his next thought, "All I know is that I'm tired of this kind of life and I want to try and get clean."

I wanted to believe my son was truly ready for change. I wanted to buy in, especially after this horrific experience he had just witnessed. But my common sense was holding me back. I can't count how many times I had heard him utter those words: "I'm tired of my life and I want to get clean." I had no evidence this time would be any different than the previous times.

Dustin had become quite the salesman over the past several years. After all, drugs are not cheap. If you're planning to support your addiction based solely on commission, you better have a good sales pitch. And Dustin had become a professional druggie.

A decade earlier, we, his family, were his naive classroom of clients, who at the time knew nothing of his sprouting addiction. He continued practicing his craft of lies on us until his addiction was full blown. This proved a successful apprenticeship for him, as we still had no idea of anything about his drug lifestyle.

2

JOINT ACCOUNTS

DUSTIN

JUNE 2000

All our family members are starting to arrive. The day seems picture perfect. The sun is unblemished against the blue sky. My parents' backyard has been transformed into a serene backdrop of manicured gardens and picturesque garlands to host our wedding. The grass resembles a precisely maintained fairway at a luxurious golf resort. A fountain trickles down jagged rocks where it pools in a smaller bowl then overflows to turn a water wheel completing the scene of peaceful bliss. The water is crystal blue and flowers border the entire pond. A cedar wooden bridge stretches over the curved waterway like an enchanted scene from a fairytale.

She'll be standing under an arched trellis that is covered in blossoming vines. We decided to do the more traditional wedding where I am not allowed to see my soon-to-be bride until she comes walking down the aisle.

I am excited but feeling a bit nervous. I'm not sure why. After all, this is her special day. I can't believe how many people are here. The backyard is bursting with people talking amongst themselves, new acquaintances making awkward small talk with and family members and long-time friends reminiscing of old times. Small children scatter around the crowd playing with their new friends. It all seems too perfect.

Only 10 minutes until the wedding starts and I have a few last-minute adjustments to make before we start. "Hey Kenny, you have the rings, right?" I nervously triple-check with my brother on the all-important items.

"Rings, check!" he says. "Who tied that tie?"

"What's wrong with it?" I shout back.

"Come here, I'll fix it," he says. He adjusts my tie into a crisp, flawless knot.

"Do you think I'm making the right decision?" I ask.

"Do you feel like you are?" He asks right back.

"Yeah, it feels right."

"Well, there is your answer," he grins.

I pull my lips inward and nod my head as we walk to our designated positions. I am overjoyed as the music begins. I feel more and more fidgety as each member of the procession nears me. Then, amidst the quiet commotion, everyone's heads turn as if programmed to move together all fixed on the same breathtaking view.

"There she is!" I think quietly to myself. She is so beautiful. This moment is surreal. I see nothing around me. She is all I see. I focus on her getting closer to me. Her train is still floating across the bridge as she steps off onto the grass. This is it. It's time. It is the end of one life and the beginning of a new one.

"Do you, Dustin John, take Sara to be you lawfully wedded wife?"

"I do!"

I am standing in our line greeting family and friends. Clusters of excited people bunch around us, all eager to congratulate us and wish us well. A close family member walks up to me and opens my suit coat. He slips a joint into my inside pocket and says, "Have a good time on your honeymoon."

I am taken aback by this bold congratulatory offer, but it is definitely not my or my now new wife's first encounter with marijuana. Fleeting memories quickly rush over me of the drugs we had experimented with together: acid, mushrooms, painkillers, and marijuana. It was all out of curiosity and wonder. My wife used meth before she met me but she hasn't used it since. I now only use on the weekends or special occasions and I figure that most people would agree that getting married is a special occasion. My wife and I will be flying to California tomorrow morning for our honeymoon.

14

Playing back this situation today, I can honestly say that at the time, I saw nothing wrong with accepting that joint, or smoking it for that matter. I had the attitude that smoking weed or dabbling in drugs every once in a while was not a big deal – as long as it did not get in the way of the important things in life. I had a good job, I was paying my bills, I would show up when I said I would. All the things that life asks of us, I was still doing. So to me, that justified recreational drug use as something I deserved or was entitled to. My attitude was: I work hard so I deserve it.

My plan at that point after my wedding was to honeymoon in California with my wife, have a great time, smoke some weed, and come home a happy, newly married couple. All these things happened. However, there is one thing that I never took into consideration.

I walk into the warehouse and it is in full swing just as it was before I went on my honeymoon. Because I have to wear a hardhat, long-sleeved shirt, cotton gloves, safety glasses, earplugs, steel-toed boots with metatarsal covers and long pants, it can get ridiculously hot in here. On top of that, I operate two huge ovens that cook aluminum to give it diverse solidity. When the ovens doors open, it reaches over 120 degrees. Even with the extreme heat, I still love my job. I have advanced quickly and I even received a good raise. I also get to operate a remote controlled crane that can lift five thousand pounds of aluminum.

"Dustin how was your honeymoon?" My boss yells out over the noise as he approaches me.

"It was great!" I holler back.

"Let's go for a walk," he says seriously.

Fear instantly grips my entire body as I turn to follow him. I have a sinking feeling I know what this is about. I just know it. Then, the dreaded words spill out of my boss' mouth.

"It's your turn. Your name was picked out of the hat," he says casually with a little curiosity in his voice. If only he knew the terror those words shot into my veins.

"Okay," I tell him, as if exuding calmness changes everything. "Let's go do it." My thoughts are crashing around me in a frenzied panic. *Playing along is not going to help the outcome*, I think. *I have to tell him.*

"Hey Kent, look I am going to come up positive for marijuana," it spills out, and I know I can't take it back. If only I could take it all back, everything.

He stops walking and shakes his head in disgust. "Why? What are you thinking?" he questions.

"I don't know. It was stupid I know. I just can't lose this job, please!" I plead.

"There is nothing I can do. It's too late." He says. "Go through the two doors into the nurse's station and I will be in there in a minute," He finishes with a hint of sadness in his voice.

Pushing through the door I am met by the nurse. "Hello. My name is Dustin. I was chosen for a random drug screen."

"Okay Dustin, have a seat and I will be with you shortly," she says with a welcoming smile. *How many times does she see this scenario?*

My thoughts are racing as I manipulate a story to tell the nurse. What should I say? What should I tell my wife? What will I do? How will I pay my bills? What will I tell my family? I am so upset with myself right now. What have I done? Was smoking weed more important than my job? Why is this happening to me? I need to create a false story to tell my family. They can't know I have been smoking weed! I know what I can do. My mind races to concoct a story about taking mini-thins to keep up with the long hours at work. Mini-thins show up on a drug screen as methamphetamines so I can say I tested positive for meth. This has to work. It just has to.

"Okay Dustin," the nurse interrupts my racing thoughts. "Come on in here." She hands me a urine cup. "You know what to do. I need it filled at least to here," she says pointing to the mark on the side of the cup.

"Okay," I say with false confidence. I fill the cup to the mark knowing the outcome is going to render me unemployed.

For some reason, I was hoping there would be a flaw in the test that day. I was holding on to a glimmer of hope that did not exist. At this point in my life, I had no idea that the choices I was making were the reason for my troubles. I did not see that by smoking marijuana, I could lose my job. When I would ponder that notion I would always think, "That won't happen to me." I learned firsthand that it can and did happen to me. For many years my thoughts and beliefs have been very contorted. I was such a good "salesman" – as my Dad referred to me – In time; I had even sold my soul. Because of this, my family and I would suffer countless devastating blows against an unstoppable opponent. Just when I thought the fight was over I would realize that it was only beginning.

2

A Good Son Gone Bad

DALLAS

Prior to delving into Dustin's drug-test unemployment dive, I'd like to share a little about my son in his early days as a child.

As the last of four children to be born, Dustin came into this world no differently than his two brothers and one sister before him – a pink and wrinkly seven-pounder screaming for attention.

By age one, the wrinkles had disappeared and by age two, we had ourselves a little lifeguard with beautiful olive-colored skin and pure white hair.

Over the next several years, things seemed to travel down a normal path. Our daughter had discovered the mirror, eyeliner, lipstick and was now brushing her own hair, while the boys ... Well, the boys were just being boys. Dustin's older brother had learned to throw a curve ball and while the neighbors were busy replacing windows, our newly acquired lifeguard had gained a real appetite for gummy worms and bothering his sister. Dustin was just a normal kid.

Although there were some hiccups getting Dustin through his final years of high school, with a little hard work and a couple of boots to the butt from me, he graduated. Not long after, our son would happen by a great little gal, a beautiful young lady that Dustin would quickly fall in love with. My wife and I wondered where our blonde little lifeguard had gone and how this slim but sturdy, mousy haired young man with my blue eyes and defined jaw had replaced him. Nothing made us realize more that Dustin had indeed become a man when he announced to my wife and I that he and his newfound love, Sara, were going to tie the knot.

Getting the news that our youngest son was now prepared to take on such a new responsibility left my wife and I with mixed feelings. On the one hand, we were both excited to see that our youngest child had finally reached adulthood. But, by this same token, we both agreed that in many ways, Dustin lacked the maturity and responsibility of being able to fully support a family. After all, keeping your newly acquired partner happy and provided for is not always an easy thing to do. I was especially concerned as Dustin's work history had been spotty at best. On a brighter note, he had recently acquired a good paying job with a solid local company. Better yet, Dustin had already received a nice raise, which indicated to me that I shouldn't be worried and that he was working hard.

Despite having these concerns, my wife and I moved forward with positive thoughts, a smile and several moving boxes to show our support.

As I reflect back to that day, it would be impossible for me to choose who was the happiest member of my family. My wife and I couldn't have been prouder of Dustin and our other children. From the look in Dustin's blue eyes at his wedding, we were sure his future could only include success, love, and happiness for him and his bride.

At the time of Dustin's wedding, neither my wife nor myself had any hint that Dustin had been dabbling in drugs. We weren't the fondest of a few of Dustin's associates in his high school career, but it didn't seem that they were dangerous. Equally as important to this scenario was our blindness to the availability of such drugs. We were clueless that such materials existed so close to our doorstep. As Dustin recalled during his wedding reception, a close family member walked up to him and tucked a joint into his jacket pocket then wished him the best on his honeymoon. We were oblivious to any such interaction or even the existence of such a readily available supply! I am to this day appalled that it was a family member nonetheless – another recreational user – who saw no harm in furthering this gateway of addiction for our son.

According to Dustin, although a tough thing to pinpoint, this dangerous and unforgiving way of life may very well rear its ugly head at a time when he and many other boys and girls find themselves transforming into men and women, wives and husbands, and soon-to-be-mothers and fathers.

In the process of compiling this book my son admits that his fight for survival may have very well begun on the day he said "I Do." Dustin now admits that his drug usage at this particular time in his life was rare and usually only practiced during what he deems as special occasions. It seems he dabbled in experimental drugs during his latter years in high school thanks to friends and girlfriends and his desire to fit in. He admits that at the time, he thought it was harmless enough and that since many of his peers were using, it posed no real harm. It was more of a fun, carefree pastime that his friends engaged in, and in order to fit in, Dustin participated with little hesitation.

Because of his exposure to these drugs at this age, we have to ask ourselves as a society what we are doing to help our youth understand the destructive nature of these drugs. Although there have been several national campaigns from D.A.R.E. (Drug Abuse Resistance Education) to basic public service announcements geared at talking to your children about under age drinking, the fact of the matter remains more and more people are becoming addicted to substances and often times succumb to these vices as a means of coping with traumatic life events. I feel that many have soft introductions: experimentation in high school and college, that turn into full blown addictions later in life when they come up against real world difficulties.

It is one thing to warn of the repercussions of addictive substance use, it is another to establish open lines of communication with today's youth and ensure they are equipped with the resources in life to deal with the emotional turmoil they will face. And what about the teens being introduced to these substances by family members – some by their own parents? Do they think this is a way of bonding, a rite of passage into adulthood? This mentality is far more common than we may be willing to acknowledge. While these parents or other relatives view this as a harmless pastime, my family has seen the outcome first hand and its destructive ability.

We have to wake up as a society and opt to take some responsibility for vulnerable groups of people. I'm talking about us as adults taking a better survey of our communities. Our neighbors, our babysitter, even the kids who play ball at the end of the street. We can choose to become involved in the community through religious groups, volunteer groups, or even as community organizers to establish open communication lines with these teens. All teens have role models around them. They have people they look up to, aspire to become, and model their life after. If they see their parents as unsuccessful, many of them feel they are doomed to the same unsuccessful fate. You don't have to be financially successful to still be successful in life, but young people don't always understand that. Real happiness can be achieved in a variety of ways, and if we share that with these rising men and women, and show them what it really means to be successful adults, they will rise to the occasion. They will model their life after what they feel they are capable of.

If you are reading this book as a loved one of an addict, I assure you there will never be an easy solution to fixing a long-standing problem. I can tell you that the biggest thing I've learned from our experience is prevention. Prevention is as much a part of our story as anything. Arming ourselves with the knowledge and capability to care and prevent our children, our loved ones, even other youth in our community from tampering with mind-altering substances can save countless lives and change the course of the world. Those seem like some pretty big ambitions, but I know it starts with just one person. If each one of us decides to reach out and be more aware, there is no stopping the difference that can be made in our individual communities and as a result in our nation. Just deciding to read this book and open your mind up to what is really out there is a fantastic first step. Hopefully the pages that follow will help you learn how you can best help those addicted individuals in your life, and can also make you more aware of how to prevent these scenarios from occurring in your own family. What I would give to have read a book like this in the early days of Dustin's addiction.

Not knowing then what I know now, I still question to this day whether the joy and smile on his face on his wedding day was true happiness or simply a chemical-induced shadow of things to come. Regardless, it would prove to be a short-lived smile.

3

ON THE ROCKS

DUSTIN

SEPTEMBER 2001

Almost 15 months have passed since the drug test debacle. My life has continued to snowball in an unruly direction. The last few months have been the foulest between Sara and me. It is amazing how quickly a marriage can turn with the stresses of real life weighing in. I haven't had much luck finding a decent full-time job. The under-the-table oddball jobs I have been able to scrape up have only lasted a few weeks at best and none of them have paid nearly enough. No matter what I try, I can't seem to catch the lucky break I am in desperate need of to support my new wife. The financial strain is pounding a heavy wedge between Sara and me. Our relationship is being stretched like a rubber band ready to snap with the tiniest tug.

"Will you help me hang these pictures on the wall?" Sara asks.

"Yeah sure," I agree. "How was work?"

"It was fine. You know, it's been a week since you lost your last job. Do you think you will find some more work any time soon?" she questions.

"Well, I have filled out a few applications for jobs around town and tomorrow I plan to continue the hunt," I say while squaring the picture frame against the wall.

"You're not going to hang that picture like *that* are you? That looks stupid. Move it over some!"

"Why are you being so rude?" I exclaim, confused where all this hostility has come from and why I am the object of it.

"I'm not! I am just saying that you need to move the picture over!"

I move the picture in a huff.

"You had me move it three inches! How come it looked stupid where I wanted it and now that it is three inches to the left it looks good?"

"You're being an idiot," she mumbles.

"You know what? I am being an idiot! I am sick of you treating me like this all the time! I have tried to just put up with your comments and let you talk down to me and I can't handle it anymore! I think it is obvious that this is not going to work. We need to just go our separate ways before we waste any more of our time."

"If we are just going to throw this all away there is something I need to tell you," she whispers.

"What?" I ask impatiently.

"I slept with another man," Sara confesses.

Rage instantly rips through me. "You what? Who is he? What are you saying?"

"Just calm down," she responds far too matter-of-factly.

"You're telling me that you had sex with another man and you want me to calm down? You are a married woman! You are my wife! I will not calm down! Get out! Get your stuff and leave! We are done. Don't talk to me. Don't say anything. Just get your things and leave!" What am I supposed to say? How can I respond to that? Fury engulfs me. My fists clench with rage, harder, harder. She has to leave. Now.

She stammers a protest, "But..."

"I don't want to hear it just leave!"

"Fine!" Tears streak down her face as she slams the front door vehemently and trudges off into the dusk.

So many blows hit me so close together: losing my job, losing my wife, losing all feelings of accomplishment and success. It all takes a devastating toll on my self-worth. In the blink of an eye, my world was flipped upside down. It was still late summer so I wasn't so concerned with kicking my wife out of our home. I knew she could go back to her father's house if she had nowhere else to go.

I left the house for a couple days so Sara could move her stuff out without having to cross paths with her. But then I had to come back home to it all – all the emptiness that is – and the harsh reality that only emptiness can fill you with. Once I returned, all I could do was look around my empty house and feel just as empty. Empty walls. Empty space. Where there used to be clothes strewn across the bedroom floor or dishes on the counter, there was nothing. I felt like I had nothing left, just a wreck of a home and a wreck of painful emotions. I felt like my life had lost its purpose. It had been so simple and full of reason before. I woke up each day with a purpose. Sara's news had left me alone and hollowed out by the woman that I had once cherished. I had started building my life around another person and let everything else fall into place. It caved in on me as I allowed that one person to destroy me with her choices and I could not cope with the pain that followed.

The hollowness overwhelmed me that day and into the night. I finally heard a dull thudding sound seeming to reach me in slow motion. Startled I looked around, broken from my trance of sorrow and self-pity to realize it was just someone knocking at the front door. It turned out to be an old friend from high school named Dave. That night, Dave and a few other friends brought some things over to help me cope and get on with life. Unfortunately, they were the worst form of medication. Dave kept asking me if I was okay with everything, and I would tell him I was. Lies were already coming easier.

"I hope one of you brought some good stuff," I said recklessly.

"What kind of good stuff?" A friend asked.

At this point I didn't care. I knew I just need something to numb myself.

"Anything, cocaine, weed, pills, I really don't care what it is, just give me something. I need to forget about reality for a while."

"Let's go in the other room," he said with a crooked smile.

My unfaithful wife and the ensuing divorce aggravated my addiction to the point of no return. After the divorce, I was forced into bankruptcy at the age of 22. I had accrued a large amount of debt during our relationship including two brand new cars, home furnishings, wedding rings, a stack of credit cards, and other miscellaneous expenses. It was not until years after that I pinpointed these events as the fulcrum propelling me into such a drastic life change. I accept that I had already planted the seeds of addiction years before from substance experimentation, typically out of boredom and to solidify friendships, but this was something bigger.

Because I had tampered with drugs prior to this, I knew that mind-altering substances could give me temporary relief from the intense emotions I was experiencing. That night I used cocaine and painkillers to numb the anguish I felt from my ex-wife's infidelities. Instead of going through a month of pain and grief, I chose to go through years of punishment. And I wouldn't go it alone. I would drag anyone in my path through my capsizing wake; including my closest loved ones.

At that time in my addiction I don't think my parents had any idea of the seriousness of what was going on beneath my calm exterior. I have always been a professional at concealing my problems. If I was bothered by something, most would not know it. And if they did, I could convince them otherwise. My only problem was I had pushed down and hidden from so many of life's concerns that I could no longer act as if nothing was wrong. Being inexperienced in the field of emotions I would choose what I thought was the easy road to rebuilding my life: drugs. I could not have been more wrong.

I finally moved out of my home. It was not a good place for me because I was alone so often. My brother gave me the option to move into his house. He and his wife thought it was best if I surrounded myself with family while I was going through divorce and bankruptcy. I decided it was in my best interest to make the move. Not only that, but the drugs were starting to get out of control. Friends were coming over at all hours of the night and I was not showing any signs of slowing down on the amount of pills and cocaine I was putting into my body.

My brother asked me to move in with him at just the right time because I was beginning to believe I had lost control of myself. And that is a feeling even worse than emptiness.

The pace at my brother's house is much slower and manageable. I enjoy the peace I feel living here. Despite my new surroundings, I cannot seem to escape an overwhelming depression that seems to trump the majority of each day. With this depression comes deep sadness and fatigue. Consumed in a world of my own emotional pain, I lack direction, motivation, and any resemblance of self-worth. With my once active mind turning to mush day-in-and-day-out, my mind puts itself to work. Fatigue plus sadness seems to naturally equal pain. My emotional pains are projected and transformed into physical ailments. This gives me something else to focus on. Another source of the pain that seems more tangible. In retrospect, I have to wonder, if I was so depressed and always fatigued, just how superficial were the physical pains I experienced during this time in my life?

For a long time I truly believed my body was experiencing acute pain in certain areas, especially in my neck and my back. Was my mind subconsciously paving an honest path for my conscious to get blasted on painkillers? It seems like this is a common scenario with prescription drug abuse and addiction. In fact, according to the National Institute on Drug Abuse (NIH), a 2010 National Survey on Drug Use and Health estimated that 2.4 million Americans used prescription drugs non-medically for the first time within the past year. That averages to 6,600 initiates per day. Nearly half of young people who currently inject heroin surveyed in three recent studies by the NIH cite opioid prescription drug abuse prior to heroin use.

Surely these are individuals similar to me. Bored, depressed, or experiencing extreme emotional trauma seeking an escape from whatever current situation they find themselves in. I have had many thought analyses on this topic. I do believe at that time, I did have some real body pain. I also believe that I was able to intensify the pain in my own mind, which altered my perception of it, and it really did make my aches and pains hurt more physically. This amplification was the superficial part of my pain. I didn't realize I was going through this convoluted process at the time, but it seems quite obvious based on my ensuing experience with my brother.

"Hey Dustin, come upstairs for a minute," Kenny hollers to me.

"Alright, give me a second," I shout back. While I'm walking up the stairs, I think to myself, *I hope he doesn't want me to do the dishes!*

I enter the kitchen and sure enough Kenny is standing by the sink.

"I'll wash, you dry?" he says with a goofy grin.

I size up the pile of dishes in the sink and grab a dishtowel. With his family so willing to help me through my tough times, I know I need to oblige with a smile.

The kitchen window overlooks Kenny's backyard. But it is not the tidy yard my eyes are drawn to. As I peer across the sill, I notice a small orange bottle in the windowsill. Nonchalantly, I scan the label hoping the bottle contains some potent magic beans. The label reads *OxyContin.* Trying to suppress my instant change of mood and keep my eyeballs from popping out into the sink full of water, I continue to dry a Tupperware lid. OxyContin is my favorite prescription drug and my mind begins salivating just being within reach of it. The only thing in my way is my brother. Time to play.

"Whose are these?" I question as innocently as I can while picking up the bottle.

"They're mine," Kenny says taking the bottle out of my hand. "My doctor prescribed them to me for my messed up back. Over the past few months the pain in my back has gotten so bad, I can't stand up straight for very long. I go in for spinal imaging again next Saturday."

"Wow. That sounds scary," I say with concern.

"Naw bro. No need to worry. I'll be fine. Plus these pills take away most of the pain."

"Can I try one? My neck and back have really been bothering me this whole last month. I took a couple Ibuprofen a couple hours ago but it hasn't helped at all."

"You know that's a bad idea, not to mention it's illegal," Kenny scolds.

"Please? Just one dude! I just want this pain to go away," I plead.

"Fine, just one. But don't ask again," He says dropping a small pink pill into my outstretched hand.

I finish the dishes with renewed fervor. An adrenaline rush sneaks through me as I hold the unanticipated treat and take it to my room to crush it up. Oxys have a more potent effect when crushed up into a fine powder and sniffed. I inhale the OxyContin and within a minute I am carefree and completely numb from head to toe. I feel bulletproof. My energy level is extremely high and I feel I can conquer the world. This is just what I need to ease my depression that always stirs up my perpetual pain and hopelessness.

Over the next three months I continued to take OxyContin every day. I wasn't getting them from my brother Kenny though. It only took me a week to find an alternate connection for OxyContin. I knew that if I asked my brother again, I would be scoured. That was the last thing I wanted.

Neither one of us knew the consequences involved with taking these pills in the beginning. I was never told or taught about physical addiction: in school or elsewhere. It wasn't until I went without for a couple days that I knew I had gotten myself into big trouble yet again. At first I thought I was sick with the flu or something. Once I figured out that sniffing another pill would instantly take away my symptoms, I knew I was physically addicted. That scared me to my core. Because of my rather lengthy learning curve, it would take me more than a decade to figure out how to stay clean. It was the longest, most miserable time in my life. My brother on the other hand, stopped taking the pills long before addiction could take hold of him. There were periods of time where I would get so frustrated that I no longer had control of myself. I would act out in ways that were self-defeating and completely irrational.

I'm driving up the winding two-lane road that leads to Payson Canyon. On board I have an OxyContin 20 that I bought earlier. I finally reach a pull-off on the narrow road in the heart of the canyon. I reach out for a CD case and a credit card to doctor the pill into a fine powder. I roll a crisp 20-dollar bill into a perfect, tight tube and sniff the line of the immobilizing painkiller. I wipe off the CD case to get rid of any evidence and check my nose in the rearview mirror for any leftover residue. With an uncontrolled amount of anger boiling inside of me I pull back out on to the road. Within twenty seconds, I feel my heart rate decrease to a slow and soft pattern of beats. But then I do something I could never imagine I would have the strength to do. My anger boils over. With a powerful snort, something else inside my head that is tired of the husk of a life I am living somehow manages to shoot the powder back out. All the calculated conniving I have done to contrive this moment of escape is ruined because some speck buried deep in the shadows of my soul suddenly refuses to accept what I have become. I am a mess of confusion, pain, anger, and loneliness driving down the dangerous road. Anger continues to fill me. I am angry with myself for wasting the powder. I am angry with myself for needing the powder. I am angry at the world for driving me here. I am angry with myself for driving me here.

3

Honeymoon Hangover

Dallas

Summer 2000

It wasn't long before Dustin and his new wife, Sara, were back home from their honeymoon. I can still remember the excitement I felt for them and I was jumping at the chance to ask how their trip went. I just hoped our young newlyweds hadn't yet experienced that first major fight.

As a parent, I realize that once your child has turned into an adult it's not a good thing to stick your nose into places where it doesn't belong. This can especially be true when not realizing the phone number you've just dialed now belongs to that of a new household. Despite my curiosity, I decided it might be best to let my son and his wife get settled in and back to work for a few days prior to me calling. I hung up before they could answer.

I hated waiting. For some reason I had this bad feeling in the pit of my stomach. It kept prompting me to call, but I didn't want to irritate my new daughter-in-law, so I didn't. Unfortunately, by the end of the second day I had still not received the anticipated phone call. The excitement I had felt for the past two days turned into frustration then anger. I was constantly thinking, "Why hasn't Dustin called? Surely they've both got to know that we'd like to hear how their trip went!" At this point, my stomach was telling me that something bad had happened and it was now time for me to initiate the call.

"Hello Dustin. This is dad," I said with a touch of frustration and concern in my voice. "I just wanted to call and ask about your trip. Did you have fun? How did everything go? Is everything okay? Why haven't you called?"

After a brief pause, Dustin replied. "Things aren't going that well right now. I've lost my job."

Hearing Dustin's news left me speechless. It felt as though someone had just ripped my heart right out of my body. How was my son supposed to be the man he now needed to be if he couldn't even keep his job a week into their marriage?

"What happened?" I asked in shocked disbelief.

Again, a long pause. "Remember some time ago when I mentioned that our company has a zero tolerance policy when it comes to drugs? Well, on my first day back to work, which was two days ago, my name was randomly drawn from the hat to take a urine test. I failed. I came up positive for methamphetamines."

Dustin's news was devastating. I felt the blood drain from my face thankful my unexpressive goatee hid most of my emotions. I didn't want to believe what I'd just heard. Praying for a miracle, I suddenly found myself reflecting back on one of my wife's trademark accusations: "I'm tired of you not being able to hear me – you don't seem to have trouble hearing anyone else." Surely I had just misheard him the same way I seemed capable of missing my wife's remarks on occasion.

In a daze, I had to verify whether there was due cause for the minefield that was going off in my head. I slowly repeated myself to Dustin. "What happened?" Then I began the deluge of fear-packed follow-up questions. "So what is your company going to do?"

"Like I said, the company has zero tolerance for drugs. The company has fired me," Dustin replied far too nonchalantly for my liking.

Hearing this again – for real this time, not as just some faint, surreal echo – left me furious. Not only would the results of this test leave my son and his bride in a financial bind, but also the repercussions of such results would surely follow him wherever he would go.

The test just had to be wrong, I reasoned. The mere thought that anyone working with my son could accuse Dustin of being a "Druggie" left me popping at the seams. As a parent, I was prepared to march down to the company's front office and punch the individual responsible for firing my son. There was just no way that my son – that cute little olive-skinned lifeguard – had been using drugs.

Being convinced that there was no chance our son was guilty didn't change the fact that I still had to face the grim task of telling Dustin's mother. This was not going to be easy by any means! How was I going to tell my wife that her son had been fired? More importantly, how was I to tell her that his termination was due to him supposedly testing positive for the use of methamphetamines?

As I had expected, my wife did not take the first part of the news very well. And if I thought that was bad, the second part: that her cute little lifeguard was now a 22-year-old potential druggie, was unbearable.

Prior to delving into her response, allow me to properly introduce my wife.

While the woman I married some 30 plus years ago can be as gentle and loving as the next, the faintest sign of attack on her family can and will turn this loving soul into the one you and I have come to know as "Godzilla." Having said that, please keep in mind that while my wife is an uncommonly fair individual, if you are found guilty of making false accusations towards her or any member of our family, you will pay dearly.

At this point, my wife and I raced over to my son's nearby home. We didn't want to validate his scenario as being a minutely accurate possibility by discussing how we would respond if he did confirm his employer's allegations. We desperately wanted to be there in person to hear him alleviate our concern and tell us the entire situation and drug test were simply ludicrous and that he had not been using drugs. We were his first advocates – completely trusting in our son and not questioning his good-natured self of being capable of the atrocities this employer had accused him of. We were willing to defend him against any offense – even more willing than he was.

Finally, just moments before parking outside Dustin's home, I uttered the condemning words. "What are we going to do if it's true?"

My wife thought about it for a moment before responding – still internally denying her little boy could ever be in the wrong. "We both know our son. There is no way that he is doing something like this without us knowing it. It just isn't possible!"

We walked up to Dustin's front door where he greeted us and invited us inside. A quick glance at Dustin's face let the two of us know that this conversation was not going to move forward without some prompting from us. An unsettling feeling came over me as my wife and we made our way towards the couch in their modest living room. The stale air dripped with tension as no one made eye contact.

My wife couldn't stand it any longer. "So, tell us what happened. How could this drug test turn out positive? It just doesn't make any sense."

Before discussing Dustin's fabricated explanation, I want to point out something very valuable that I have learned from this retrospectively consequential moment in Dustin's life. As much as we would like to believe that we truly know someone – whether it is a son, daughter, parent or friend – we must always keep an open mind to the possibilities that we may not in fact know this individual as well as we first thought. It doesn't mean we have to look for the bad in everyone or never trust others, but it is essential to be guided by logical conclusions and separate our emotions to prevent them from fogging up our good judgment. I now know that a family can save themselves a great deal of internal damage, physical and mental anguish, and much more by simply allowing themselves to acknowledge the unbelievable as a possibility. In order to do this you must be capable of taking all factors into account and separating logic and emotion. Although I do not have a psychology degree, my 10 years of personal experience in this arena should be worth something when I say that acknowledging the unbelievable as a possibility can and will be very painful. While it would be virtually impossible for me to convey our reactions and our responses to each and every event from which we have suffered through, to prevent, better repair, or cope with drug situations of any sort, you must keep an open mind while recognizing that things do not always appear the way they look.

My wife and I did not want to believe our son was capable of lying or using drugs. In our willingness to believe our son's story it allowed the two of us to avoid the pain and suffering that otherwise would have been the result. What I did not realize at the time was that some up front pain and suffering experienced immediately would have lessened the toll in the long run – on all counts – and possibly have altered an innumerable quantity of outcomes, each affecting the same amount of lives. In essence, we chose not to acknowledge the unbelievable as a possibility and therefore had no need to make our own logical conclusions withdrawn from emotion.

"No, I'm not on drugs. You know me better than that. I would never lie to you about something like this," Dustin beguiled us to soothe any suspicion regarding the outcome of the company drug test. "I think I know why the test came out positive," he continued spinning his web of illusion and deceit. "You know those little Mini Thins that they sell at some of the service stations? Well, I've been getting me a drink and some of the Mini Thins every morning on my way to work. "I think that it's the stuff in the Mini Thins that has thrown off the results of the drug test," Dustin said confidently.

Something about Dustin's explanation didn't settle well with me. I wanted to believe him, but my gut was saying otherwise. There was just something about the look on his face and the tone in his voice. Nevertheless, what could be done now? The company had already made its decision and with zero tolerance for drug use, our son was without a job.

Although my son's explanation had left a nasty taste in my mouth, Dustin's mother felt much differently. After all, when your own flesh and blood looks you square in the eye – and with those puppy-dog eyes – makes the statement: "I'm not doing drugs," it is easy to cast aside any notion that he or she could possibly be lying. This led her to solidly believe the company's test was wrong and that Dustin should therefore get his job back.

All hell was about to break lose. As previously mentioned, Dustin's mother is not a person you want to deal with when a family member has been wrongly accused.

"Let's go," was Dustin's mom's response to her son's answer. "You and me are going down to your company's front office. We're going to tell them about the 'Mini Thins' and you and I are going to get your job back."

Watching quietly from the sidelines, I listened to the words now reverberating around us. Much like the leadership and determination found within the voice of a military commander, my wife was now determined more than ever to see that justice was served – and in her son's favor. Dustin had stated that he was not guilty and that was good enough for her. I, on the other hand, noticed that Dustin's response and body language indicated that his mother had just put him between a rock and a hard spot. It was very obvious to me that Dustin knew something that we didn't. I could see that my son was hoping my wife would just simply drop the issue. I didn't like what I was seeing. Although, at that time I had no real evidence or desire to disprove his 'Mini Thin' explanation, my gut feeling was telling me that our youngest son had not only lied, but could possibly have a serious drug problem.

How could my son be caught up in this kind of thing? Drugs and drug addiction just doesn't happen in a small town like Payson, Utah. With less than 20,000 residents, and 90% of those affiliated with a religion on a regular basis, drugs just couldn't exist – or do they?

The truth of the matter is that you can find drugs. Whether it is doctor-prescribed, over-the-counter, or illegal drugs -– Cocaine, Meth, Heroin, etc. – drugs and the mind-altering abuse that accompanies them can be found in each and every town on this planet, no matter their size, or genetic or cultural makeup.

As much as I would like to tell you that my wife's efforts did in fact result in Dustin getting his job back – they didn't.

Dustin had in fact lied. We now know that the success of our son's story was dependent on my wife and I not knowing whether "Mini Thins" and "Methamphetamines" had any commonalities in their chemical makeup. In the very process of putting this book together, Dustin also admits he was betting that his sad, remorseful puppy-dog eyes would win our trust and get both him and us through this drug-test and job-loss incident.

As mentioned earlier, Dustin was becoming a skilled salesman and his earnings at his hypothetical betting table were growing. I must admit that Dustin's plan would have worked if not for the urine test. The results of this test – which was indeed done correctly – did not lie. Dustin had been caught. He knew it, his company knew it, and now we knew it.

As a parent, this instance would prove to be only the first of many unhappy days to come. We now had validation that our son was not only a habitual liar, but was officially among those individuals who use drugs. I can't speak for my partner, but as for myself, my mind was racing. I had many things going through my head, but if there were one question that stuck out more prominently than others, it was: "How serious is this?"

I wanted to know if my son was a casual user of marijuana or if my wife and I were dealing with a young man hooked on something even more dangerous, something such as heroin, meth, or even cocaine. Things we had heard whispers of from far away places, "bad" places, but things we believed could never infiltrate our town, our home, our family, our son.

I had to make a choice. I knew Dustin had done drugs to some degree. If I believed what Dustin wanted me to believe that "smoking weed or dabbling in drugs every once in a while was not a big deal – as long as it did not get in the way of the important things in life," then perhaps our problem wasn't as large as initially projected. But then again, reason tried to creep in and present the facts. My wife and I had just caught our son lying about the results of his company test and backpedaling more lies to cover up any misgivings we insinuated. I felt I had to trust my gut this time and go with the worst-case scenario. Neither my wife nor I want to view our son as someone with a serious drug problem, but I felt that with each passing day, and with subtle evidence mounting against him, we would just have to assume the worst.

Having barely made the required deposits for their utilities, and with pictures not yet hung on their walls, my son's marriage was already in trouble. The fact that my son had lost perhaps the best job he had ever had was starting to take its toll. Unable to keep up with their monthly bills, each and every conversation between the two newlyweds was tinged with a foreboding hatred brewing. And then to worsen matters, it wasn't long before my son suddenly found himself looking up the definition of infidelity. Hearing these reports, my wife and I were on high alert. How was our son going to respond? Was he strong enough to get through this with the help and support of his family or was there a chance he'd drown his pain and suffering with drugs?

Several days had passed since our last conversation with Dustin. A sense of great urgency had replaced the blood in my veins. My wife and I couldn't help but wonder where Dustin had disappeared to.

With all that had happened in such a short amount of time, I had a constant unpleasant feeling. Although I had only been made aware of one proven instance that Dustin had been using drugs to this point, I for some reason, felt he had not been honest with us for quite some time. Running the past few months through my mind, I recalled several situations that just didn't make sense to me. Places and things he had said he was doing. Many of them just didn't seem to add up now. I hated that I was just now stopping long enough to fully process and dissect the pieces to this complicated puzzle that I was just barely realizing did not fit together.

I hated where this thought process was taking me. It turned my stomach and infuriated me at the same time. I thought it best if I didn't upset my wife with these same thoughts and uneasy feelings. But I had come to a stark conclusion: Dustin was using drugs not only for fun and pleasure, but also to assist him in times of pain and discomfort. Tortured with this inevitable truth and the repercussions that were surely attached to such a conclusion, I found myself deeply distressed regarding my son's future.

This was a huge storm. A class five tornado churning with enormous chunks of turmoil and heart-stopping debris, ready to demolish all within its path – starting with Dustin. Having realized this, I feared the worst. I found myself consumed in deep thought day-by-day and night-by-night. It was a scary place that had consumed thousands of heartbroken souls. An eternal black hole where bad spirits shouted evil things. Allowing myself to stay much longer in such a putrid place frightened me to death. Despite my fears and the horror that loomed ahead, I somehow knew I had to stay. There was no question. This place that had consumed my thoughts was what they call "hell." And somewhere near was my son, Dustin.

Over the next several weeks, my wife and I watched helplessly as our son's future continued to crumble. Having lost his beautiful wife, a nice home, and a promising career had left onlookers of Dustin's life like myself worried and afraid.

Dustin had been disappearing with increasing frequency. Although I knew that Dustin had made arrangements to move in with his brother, the fact that he was making himself quite scarce concerned me. On the rare occasions that I did get to speak with him, or at least the vapid exterior that was left of him, his responses to the few questions I was allowed to ask just didn't make sense. The young man standing in front of me wasn't the son I once knew. A dull, glazed over look engulfed his eyes. Hollowness echoed within his words. Although it was in fact the outer shell of what I once viewed to be my son, the body now before me presented no presiding owner within.

4

ASLEEP AT THE WHEEL

DUSTIN

NOVEMBER 2002

Blowing the crushed OxyContin back out of my nose that day was out of frustration and fear. It only proved a temporary ray of hope that I would overcome this battle. I would have had better luck putting a Band-Aid on a severed limb. I didn't know how to stop the tsunami of unending destruction that targeted me. As my drug use increased, the string of lies, deceit, and dishonesty followed. My family was beginning to reach the end of their rope with me. As for myself, I had decided that this was my life. I was living as a drug addict and I'd resigned myself to die as one. Despite my situation, there was a bright spot in my life: Deena.

Over the last several months Deena and I had developed what I would consider a very good relationship. As time went on and our relationship progressed, we found ourselves dabbling with various drugs. One thing led to another and we soon realized we had both developed the same problem: a heroin addiction. The bright spot that I had considered a good relationship slowly turned into a scorching pit in the depths of hell. Although I cared about her and needed her in my life, it would only further strain my ties with my family. Although my parents had allowed me to stay with them several times, my addiction would trump any and all virtue I could find inside myself. Having Deena in my life somehow made me feel like life was worth living even though I was homeless and running from my problems. Over the past year, I had moved out of my brother's home and moved back into my parents. That only lasted a few months. My parents got sick of all the drugs and paraphernalia littering my room. They repeatedly reminded me of their "zero-tolerance" policy, but I continued bringing the drugs in.

Having reached my squatting area, a place only a stray cat would consider home, I sat and pondered the possibilities of getting my life back together. After an hour or so, I realized I had to do something. I needed to find a way to turn my life around. With all the anger and humiliation I felt building up inside me, I decided I needed to start somewhere. I needed a job.

Over the next few days, with the help of several friends and my father, I was able to get a job at a local printing company. I wasn't sure how I was going to hold down a job knowing how demanding my drug habits were. Luckily, I had friends who were willing to give me a ride to work. When they weren't available, I rode the bus. After managing to keep my job for two weeks, a miracle considering the 110 additional miles I travelled almost daily to satisfy my growing addiction, I realized I wouldn't continually have time to ride local transit and be to work on time. I needed a car. I had only one viable option. I turned to my parents to help me get a vehicle. Being homeless made holding a job difficult. It was all I could do to get to work without looking like I was living as a caved Neanderthal in the back woods of a dense forest.

My parents agreed to co-sign on a car with me because of my "efforts" to get clean and hold down employment. I was able to continue fooling them for the next few weeks. It made it much easier to both get my daily fix and get to work with my own vehicle. But with my body demanding more and more drugs, my brief glimpse of stability was about to be uprooted from under me. The next experience lodged me into depths of insanity I shutter to reflect on. I reached a place in my life where my soul seemed lost in a devastating turn of events.

I am awoken by Deena's medium-length auburn hair brushing my cheek as she kneels close to my scruffy face. She's shaking my shoulder trying to get me to wake up. "Wake up Dustin!" she commands.

"I'm awake," I say picking myself up out of my weathered sleeping bag among the sagebrush-scattered meadow.

"Okay let's get going. I didn't get much sleep last night so do you want to drive?" she asks.

"Sure," I grumble. I grab for my paraphernalia and trudge to the car. The fog is thick this morning. I don't mind. I know I'm meeting up with my dealer. When we reach the halfway point on our trip separating our county from my dealer's county, my eyes grow heavy. I look over at Deena, sleeping in the passenger seat. I watch as my eyelids slowly descend over my watery eyes. I drift off to sleep. As my driver's side tires veer over the rumble strips, the steering wheel trembles and I am shaken up in panic.

"Are you falling asleep?" Deena says half asleep. "Let me drive." She demands.

"I'm fine. Really, I'm awake now. I'll crack my window."

"Are you sure?"

"Yes I'm fine."

"Okay," she relents. She turns back over and I watch as her eyes slowly close. I turn my head back to the road. Within 30 seconds, I feel the onslaught of tiredness drift over my body again. Without a fight, I lose all consciousness.

If I would have known that traffic was at a dead stop a quarter mile up the freeway, I may have fought harder to stay awake. If I would have known that I was about to drive 70 mph into a wall of parked cars, I may have fought harder to stay awake. If I would have realized that Deena didn't have her seatbelt on, I may have fought harder to stay awake.

I am violently awakened by the sounds of death. I hear Deena's curdling scream, one comparable to someone who sees their own death, right before they live it. The impact was so violent that my ears start to ring in slow motion. Like a night terror, the world seems to be spinning off its axis. The sound of shattering glass and plastic overpower the ringing vibrations deep inside my core. The screech of folding metal in baritone succession triggers an explosion. I am struck in the face with the violent force of the exploding airbag. I feel no pain as the car bounces off other vehicles like a drifting pinball. Wondering when this slow motion nightmare will come to a stop, I brace for the worst. The last impact is so powerful, my legs slam together like a sledge hammer. My kneecaps feel like they have disconnected from the tendons. The car fills with the toxic smoke left behind from the spent airbag. It is nauseating and I start to run out of oxygen. It is the smell of death. I can't open my door because it's pinned up against another car. I look over to see if Deena is alive. She moves but she is in terrible pain. She holds her wrist.

"Are you okay?" I stammer.

"My hand! It hurts!" she cries.

"We need to get out of the car. If you can walk, try to get out. I have to crawl out your side." I say with slight panic.

She opens her door and gets out. I use my upper body to hoist me over the center console and make my way to the open door. The oxygen from outside breaks through the dense smoke that fills the car. I inhale a huge breath of air as I exit the car. As I stand, my legs buckle underneath me like the limbs of a young tree. I fall to the hot asphalt in pain. *They are broken,* I think to myself. Fear grips my body. A department of transportation worker in a reflective vest runs up to us.

"Are you guys okay? What happened?" he asks.

"I fell asleep at the wheel," I cry. "Her hand might be broken. I smashed my legs together and am having a hard time standing."

"You guys relax. We have paramedics on the way." I didn't want to go to the hospital. I was alive and all I cared about, ironically enough, was that I was being delayed from my next fix. Fearing I won't make it to my destination, I try to stand again. Pulling myself up off the car bumper I maneuver slowly and manage to half stand, half lean. The pain is so intense that I almost fall to the ground again. I force myself to continue standing though and after 3 or 4 minutes, the pain begins to subside. I scan over the wreckage and ponder what just happened. I suddenly realize that I need to make sure there is no paraphernalia scattered in the car. The cops would soon be on the scene and I know I have to hurry. I open the passenger door of the car and there is baking soda scattered all over the carpet. The box is lying on the floorboard. I hear the howl of the sirens moving in closer. I grab the box of baking soda and shove it under the dash. I run my hand over the white powder to make the soda sink deeper into the carpet fibers. (To smoke cocaine, you have to mix it with baking soda.) I breathe a sigh of relief. A patrol car is first on the scene followed by the ambulance. The sirens are deafening. There is only one lane open for cars to squeeze past the major pile up. They are moving slowly as they stare at the wreckage. As the police car pulls to the embankment, I feel a bead of sweat run down my temple. Doing my best to hide my guilt, I speak with the overzealous officer. I tell him what happened and assure him that we don't need medical assistance. Somehow, we escape any kind of punishment or heavy questioning. Once I know we aren't going to jail, I feel a huge load being lifted off my shoulders. I begin to calm down and my pulse starts to slow. Now I am only worried about how we can meet with my dealer without a car. I am still in a state of shock from the accident but I can feel the adrenalin being replaced with heroin withdrawal. I decide to ask the officer if he will give us a ride to the exit we need to get to. He declines my proposal saying he is not allowed to.

"You can ask the tow truck driver if he will take you though," he offers.

"Thank you," I say joyfully thinking we can still get our fix after all.

As Deena and I get into the tow truck, we are completely silent. I feel an unspoken message between us. We know we have just dodged a bullet.

As we approach freeway speed, I notice the tow truck driver reaching under his seat. He pulls out a pistol. Fear seizes my body. I am frozen in apprehension. With a blank stare, he points the pistol at Deena's temple and calks the hammer.

"You thought you would get away with this?" he yells. "Think again." He pulls the trigger. I feel the warm blood splatter on my face. My ears are ringing from the gun shot blast. Deena's body falls in a slouching position and her lifeless hand lands upright in my lap. As the blood drips down her arm, my entire body goes cold and I am paralyzed in terror.

"Please! No!" I protest.

"Now it's your turn!" He points the barrel at my face. I close my eyes as tight as I can. I take one last breath. He pulls the trigger.

I wake up to feel my saturated clothes sticking to my tense body. I am shivering and scared. My body is in extreme pain. I feel my face to see what kind of damage the gunshot made. It was only cold and wet. No hole, no blood. I look around me to see where I am. I look to my left and see the old warehouse in the desolate meadow. I feel a sharp burning sensation in my arm. I look down at my arm to see a syringe still in my vein. I start to recall the events of last night. I remember what had happened now. The tow truck driver was a nightmare. I am relieved and mad at the same time. It would be easier if I had died. The recent turn of events with the car wreck and my insatiable thirst to please my addiction have made my life unbearable. I will never get my old life back. This is what I am. I am a homeless drug addict, sitting in a field with a heroin needle sticking out of my arm. With no way out,

I must accept what I have become. I realize that my nightmare was only what I wish would have happened.

I wished the driver had shot me in the face. It would have been much less painful than the reality of what I had done. The car had been paid off the month before I totaled it. My insurance had just lapsed. I was responsible for the damage of four other vehicles. Miraculously, no one had been injured. Knowing the responsibilities that had become mine to bear, I didn't have the devices to cope with the aftermath. After they loaded my car on the wrecker, the tow truck driver dropped us off at my frequent meeting spot and Deena and I got our heroin fix. Deena and I just slept on the streets of Salt Lake aimlessly wandering from shelter to shelter. Did we have a plan? Did we care what happened next? I don't recall exactly. It was a jumble of emotions interspersed with my need to satiate my drug cravings, Deena just tagged along looking for her next fix too. We felt like parasites thriving on the fringe of society desperate for only one thing.

After three days of this, we both realized something had to change or we would die. We were equally worn out, tired, hungry and out of options. We decided to make the 60-mile way back towards our families. It took us an entire day, but we made it. I can only imagine how we looked to passersby. Disheveled, dirty, psychotic – I don't know. We must have been quite the spectacle hitchhiking down the city roads. After an all-day trek, we finally made it back.

My next mistake was showing up at Deena's home with her. Her father was outside their ranch, welding horseshoes together in an old barn. When we arrived, I could see his fists clenching together as he began walking in our direction. His cowboy hat was worn low on his brows and it was too dark to see the fire in his blackened eyes. It was a long dirt road driveway into their farm so I knew running away from this large man would probably cause a horseshoe to be driven into the back of my skull. With all the courage I could muster, I chose to wait it out. The closer he got to me, the larger he became. His fists now looked like two 12-pound sledgehammers, easily wider than my face. This man was one mean cowboy. He was built like a brick wall and was wearing a flannel shirt and a 6-shooter. His handlebar moustache made him look even more intimidating if that were even possible. With my head hung low, I watched as puffs of dirt billowed from his cowboy boots with each hefty step he laid down.

Then he stopped directly in front of me. I felt my guts turning inside out. With his bushy furrowed brows and small slits barely showing his eyes, my heartbeat began to pound in my eardrums. With a gnarled wad of Copenhagen protruding from his cheek, a brown stream of tobacco juice shot from his lip and splatted directly on my shoes. I was okay with that. I didn't have much choice given the situation. After all, it was much less painful than being hit with one of his sledgehammers.

"What in the hell do you think you are doing with my daughter?" he demanded. "I will pound you into the ground like a fence-post!" He spat another juicy wad of dip at my feet.

Believing he was very capable of such things, I did absolutely nothing. Knowing I had a part in his daughter's heroin addiction and the one responsible for the crash, I was only hoping to survive this night with only a tobacco shower.

"Get the hell off my property and I don't ever want to see you with my daughter again!"

That was enough for me. I turned around and walked down the lengthy dirt driveway and disappeared into the surrounding pastures. I was far from any main city lights, but the old street lamps lining the back road lit my path. I didn't have a specific destination. I only knew I wanted to be as far away Deena's father as I could get. So I walked. I walked away from Deena's and I would never return.

4

HEROIN PILE-UP

DALLAS

It was difficult, to say the least, to accept that I had a family member – my own son even – addicted to drugs. This fact was putting a major wedge between all of our family relationships. Often, a simple conversation between my wife and I would turn into a full-blown war. Added to this were the opinions of our two other children and before we knew it, none of us would talk to the other for days. Dustin's drug problem was beginning to tear our family apart at the seams.

Despite our differences and concerns, both my wife and I each tried in our own way to help Dustin. I guess every member of my family felt that as long as Dustin showed an ounce of effort or desire to turn his life around, we as a family, should stand by his side. Dustin was actually able to somehow secure a job at a printing shop. Although this opportunity gave each of us hope that Dustin could somehow get back on his feet, it also served as another expenditure on our part. Having lost his Dodge truck several months ago, our son now needed a mode of transportation to make a reliable showing for work.

On the surface, my wife and I were quick to show our excitement and support but much like a duck paddling its way through thick mud, underneath, our smiles were somewhat artificial as we were hesitant to finance a vehicle for someone we no longer knew. Although, it would appear Dustin was at least trying to be self sufficient, my wife and I knew that before co-signing with Dustin on a car we must also consider the facts:

1. Between Dustin's stay at our oldest son's home to the present, Dustin had been arrested and convicted for possession of drug paraphernalia and

theft on two separate occasions.

2. In each of Dustin's convictions, the judge sentenced him to serve anywhere from 30 to 60 days in the County Jail.

Obviously, these facts did not rest well with either my wife or myself. So, the question I now put before you, as a reader is - do we sign?

If I were a betting man, I'd dare say that around 99.9 percent of you are calling this question a no brainer! Those same readers are also thinking that only a moron would co-sign with an individual who has just been released from jail with a drug-riddled history in tow. Well, you are right. And, that's the way my wife and I signed the papers: Mr. & Mrs. Moron.

I know what many of you are thinking right about now. You're thinking these parents are about as smart as a box of rocks and I ought to throw this book in the garbage. Well, maybe we are stupid morons. And, just maybe we deserve the 10 years of pain and suffering that we went through. But, on the other hand, I guarantee that you will not know for sure until you are put into such a position.

As my wife and I reflect back on each of our decisions we still remain in total awe as to how far each of us did in fact go due to the love we had and still have for our son. For all of you readers who are saying that's "BULL," stop and think about it. Have you not at some time in your life made the statement or even thought: "I would take your place, if it meant that you would be saved?" Or "I would kill anyone who tries to harm you." My point is that a great number of us are willing to do almost anything in order to help save or protect a loved one.

Unfortunately, Dustin's inability to block out the pain of such a tragic start to his adult life would again come back to haunt him. And, yes for those of you who look at my wife and I as an idiotic couple, you just might have some legitimacy to your claim. I say this because in our efforts to help Dustin get back on his feet, (co-signing on a vehicle as to help our son get to and from work) we only enabled him to do more wrong. In retrospect, instead of using his new set of wheels to get to his new job - he would eventually use the car for the sole purpose of retrieving his drugs and perpetuating a failed future.

In our defense, Dustin did manage to maintain his job for almost four years. During this time, we hoped the evidence of Dustin's consistent paychecks translated to him being over his little bout with drugs. After more than three years maintaining his position though, his addiction started to become bigger than he was once again. My wife and I started receiving phone calls from our son's workplace. Dustin's boss wanted to know where our son was at and why Dustin had stopped showing up for work. This was not a good sign and because both my wife and I knew that he must have reverted to his old ways, we would have no choice but to send Dustin back to the streets.

In retrospect, not only would our mistake of helping Dustin purchase a car contribute to our son's continual use of drugs, but also more importantly, it would nearly cost him his life.

Our son needed a "fix" and he needed it in the worst way. Unfortunately, Dustin - since being kicked back out on the street and now sleeping in the back seat of his car - had not gotten a good night's rest in several weeks. Despite his concerns, Dustin along with his newly acquired girlfriend - were again racing their way north to Salt Lake in hopes of finding Dustin's heroin dealer.

Now you've got to remember that an addict will do just about anything to get his or her fix. An addict's motivation to gratify a drug craving empowers him to do or become almost anything. So you can only imagine how simple it must have been for our son to drive an hour north even with both eyes closed! Unfortunately, in reading Dustin's last chapter, you will again understand the theory or statement that "for every action there is an equal an opposite reaction."

As evidenced from my son's recounting of his accident en route to his dealer, an addict's priorities are far from the norm. Learning what happened that day from Dustin's point of view, I find my son's thought process completely appalling. Let's think about this for a minute. My son, the heroin addict, has just crashed into several lanes of parked cars. He did not just crash into them, he plowed into them going around 70 mph. There were real people in those cars: your mother or mine, a father, a sister, perhaps a newborn infant hardly large enough for a car seat all suddenly crushed by this out-of-control, sleepy-eyed heroin addict making a mad dash to meet up with his dealer. Even with his girlfriend by his side in intense pain with a broken hand, the addict's priorities and bottom line concern for anyone else is periphery – almost nonexistent even – compared to their drug lust. Now this next part is what is really appalling to me. All of this tragedy now rests in plain sight for my son to see and all he can think about at that particular moment is - "How can we meet with my dealer without a car?"

Although our son admits that many events over the past 10 years are sometimes a bit foggy in his memory, he does remember most of what happened on that day he and his girlfriend crashed on the freeway.

"There are several things that I remember about the crash that morning," Dustin said to me as he and I tried to reconstruct one of several past events in his life. "The thing that jumps out at me the most right now is how close I came to killing a lot of people because of my need for heroin." Dustin adds, "Although it is easy for me to say that now, in retrospect - at the time of the accident - all I could think about was how I was going to get my fix now that I didn't have a vehicle!"

5

CHECKMATE

DUSTIN

JANUARY 2004

Trying to clean up the recent wreckage in my life had proved too much for my inebriated mind and I chose to run rather than face the consequences of the horrible crash and then losing my relationship with Deena. My freedom proved to be short lived. I used more and more heroin each passing day. I was at the point where I knew it was only a matter of time before I would be thrown in jail. Within a month, my warrants were really piling up. One was for lack of compliance and not bothering to show up to court hearings for the crash. It wasn't long before I was caught by officers and hauled off to jail. I spent 30 days in Utah County Jail and was released upon completion of the Judges orders: paying the $5,000 in automotive repairs and court fees. I knew it was only a matter of time before I was back here trying to convince the judge for "one more chance."

After standing in front of the same judges time and time again, the sentences grew substantially with each repeat offence. The furrow in the judge's eyebrow would get deeper and more pronounced each time he saw my face. I would think I would get off with a smaller sentence because a judge sees thousands of people per year and there is no way he remembered me. Wrong! He knew exactly who I was. He knew my story and he remembered everything that he told me the last time I was in his courtroom. I am not sure how they remember every little detail but they do. The judges knew I was stuck. I couldn't get out of revolving door that was destroying me. I spent another 30 days in jail.

Now that I had a month of sobriety under my belt, I was hoping my parents would allow me to move in once again. Throwing me to the streets fresh out of jail would definitely lead me right back to the only thing I knew: drugs. That was my plea. At the time I felt it was a legitimate argument. I didn't know I was lying to everyone including myself. I was truly convinced that I was speaking from truth and knowledge of my past mistakes.

This was not the case. I had warped my mind over time and manipulated everything and everyone so often that my lies weaved tightly into my reality. Somehow, my parents agreed to let me move back in with them. I was able to pull together about three months of sobriety before returning to my old ways.

What confuses me most to this day is even at the time I didn't really want to start in those old habits again. I couldn't figure out why I kept going back to a lifestyle that had already stripped me of any integrity and trust I had started to rebuild. It was a lifestyle that repeatedly left me miserable, remorseful, depressed and undignified. Yet, I would run into a few old acquaintances and one thing lead to another – and it didn't take much time.

Then I was searching for ways to come up with money that my newly sobered mind would allow without crossing any freshly made moral boundaries that I started to obtain. It is, after all, a progressive disease and I have never been one to butcher the cow before slicing his throat.

I would always hurt the ones closest to me first. As a last resort, I would steal from my suppliers. It is still painful when I think about my priority order of whom to offend first. My dealers were always the last resort because they were the ones closest to my craving. Strangers were at the top of the list, then acquaintances and family. To this day, I believe this is because I knew if I were to bite the hand that fed by stealing from my heroin dealer, I would not have any way to get heroin. It is hurtful for me to say those words, but I believe that is the reasons for what I did next.

Finding a minimum of $30 every 8 hours proved to be a difficult task. This of course, was just enough money to keep my withdrawals at bay. I had learned some money making strategies, all of which were illegal. Prioritizing by least amount of jail time, I started to conjecture a plan of action. I had found a few construction sites that would prove easy money and a small chance of being apprehended. A couple of my close friends and I would scout out these sites for anything of value: sheets of wood, tools, welding leads, and power equipment. A lot of times these places were gold mines. My casual swagger seemed to give me qualified rights to be on the site and remove whatever I wanted. They say dogs smell fear, well I knew people smelled suspicion. Being unattached to my thoughts and feelings, there was no chance I looked suspicious. After several free for alls at the local sites, I was again out of money schemes. I had to dig deep to find other ways. Within a few short minutes of digging, I came up with another option.

My parents were out of town for the week. I thought that if I could pawn some of my father's tools and have them back where I found them before they arrived home, I could get my fixes without them ever knowing. Who was I kidding? This never worked as well as I planned in my head. All I wanted was immediate satisfaction and relief from the heavy withdrawal pain setting in.

Now sober, I easily forget the intensity of pain I endure from opiate withdrawals. Considering I was willing to say and do such things to my own flesh and blood, my withdrawals must have been excruciating.

I planned to take one or two tools and have them back in a couple of days. Turns out, I depleted my parents belonging down to almost nil. I pawned electrical tools, hand tools, videos, CDs, cameras, camcorders, and other items that could yield some quick cash. I was in over my head and I didn't stop there. I went on to find my parent's stack of checks hidden in their computer room. I knew that if I took checks from the center of the book, it would give me enough time to not think about what I had done along with the pains associated with having a size 10 boot removed from my butt. I took about 7 checks to the local Quick-Mart and was writing them for about fifty dollars over the purchase price of my usual 32-once Pepsi and a pack of

Marlboro Smooth's. My dad knew the storeowner so I knew I was busted before I pulled to the drive-up window. Going through heroin withdrawal was much more painful than a major butt-kicking by my father, only because when the beating happened, I made sure I was on heroin to block out any physical and emotional pain that was there. I knew I was in for a world of hurt but I drowned it out with another blast of heroin. Numb, again at last.

My parents came home from vacation sooner than I realized. I was hoping that I would have some time before they noticed their tool cabin was now more of an abandoned shed. With only a few lonesome extension cords and drill bits, I tried my best to spread out the old remains in hopes that it would look like $2,500 worth of equipment. I was hoping for more than a miracle – like my dad would never go to his shed again. Unless my father had gone completely senile on his trip, I knew I was in big trouble. You just don't mess with a man's tools! I knew the outcome and the consequences before they even happened, but my drive for heroin was too powerful. I accepted it and chose those results as long as it meant I got my heroin. I was its slave and I was very obedient to its vicious demands. Being trapped in the cycle of heroin addiction, my brain now wanted me dead, but would settle for me being high. It got what it wanted and I continually succumbed to its unyielding grip.

I remember clearly the day my dad found out about the checks I had stolen. I had never seen so much rage and anger in my father's eyes. I remember thinking that he might not ever stop punching me. It was a scary moment for me and I remember it very vividly, despite the heroin I had on board. My shirt was ripped completely off my thin frame. All I could see were fists coming at me and the rage in his eyes. I was a grown man, but never once did I feel like defending myself. I knew I had brought this on myself and I knew I had it coming. After the incident, my father calmed down and made me an offer I will never forget. With my shirt ripped into pieces and my skin a deep red color, my father stood next to me and said, "You can rip my shirt now if you want to."

I declined his amiable offer. Though my father lost any small strand of respect he may have had for me that day, I gained a new level of respect for him. At that moment, even though he pummeled me good, I realized my father's love for me was immeasurable. Through my drug-induced haze, I experienced what it felt like to be a worthless son and brother. If only a miracle could have sobered me that day so all the hurt and despair could have stopped after my brilliant idea to steal from my parents.

Unfortunately, my addiction would continue for many years. It was too powerful and I could not stop it. I knew that stealing from my family was out of the question so I had to come up with another way to supply my lethal habit. Stealing from my parents only shamed me to a new low. Frustration filled me as I realized I had also AGAIN relapsed. I lost every ounce of self-respect I may have had left for myself. I gave up on sobriety as I walked away from their home that evening. This fueled the fire that was boiling deep within me. I decided if I couldn't defeat my demon, the only other option was to feed it.

5

SAFE HAVENS

DALLAS

JANUARY 2004

O ur son's situation continued to decline and as his need for drugs increased, so did his crime habits – crimes that would also prove costly and painful to those closest to him.

After several short stints in the County Jail, Dustin would again plead for us to let him come back home. Although we did not take too kindly to the idea of housing a jailbird, on the good side, being locked up enabled our son to get clean. As a parent, we felt our son was entitled to one more shot.

As parents, we knew that there was hardly any chance at all that Dustin would stay clean. But by this same token, being in jail allowed - or forced - our son to not only go through the first stages of withdrawal, but being behind bars also gave him a head start. Dustin had not only made it through withdrawals or what we had come to know as the first stage of the rehabilitation process, but his body had now been free and clear of any heroin for at least three weeks. During the process of an addict's recovery, every minute, hour, and day that that person's body remains free of drugs can possibly mean the difference between his or her failure or success. So three weeks seemed like a major accomplishment to us in our son's messed up life.

Despite the fact that Dustin's body had been free and clear of heroin for nearly a month, the family meeting as to whether or not we wanted to go through this pain-staking process of letting him so fully back in our lives again did not end without dispute.

This ongoing circus of events had proved taxing in many ways. The emotional ups-and-downs we had slogged through were beginning to surface in physical appearance. For example, my appetite dwindled each time I took to worrying about Dustin's whereabouts. At work I became prone to sipping my Dr. Pepper and worrying with an undetectable slug of chew tucked in my cheek. This was my version of twiddling my thumbs or pacing the floor I suppose. This replacement of food resulted in my own gauntness, although I looked robust compared to the skeleton Dustin would become on each of his disappearances. Although my color-blindness rendered my acuity to precise tint null and often void, my hair was beginning to look more and more pale to me. My wife interpreted this change for all those with full-color vision as a charcoal-brown turning to a silvering gray. To use the word "suffering" to describe our situation and its definition "the act of pain and/or hardship" seems a bit ironic - especially under these circumstances. Unfortunately "pain" was truly the only commonality being shared among the members of our once strong and healthy family.

Several months had passed and while we each knew how quickly things could change, our son seemed to have it all together once again. Not only had he found himself another job, but also more importantly, he had been drug free for nearly 60 days. Now this might not seem like a lot to you, but for an individual who had - and who will always have – a drug addiction coursing through their veins, this was a major milestone.

Yes, Dustin was doing well and it was beginning to show. His frail body and sunken cheekbones began to take on a more healthy appearance. In addition to Dustin's physical appearance, he had just brought home another paycheck, which indicated that his head and thought process were staying on task.

Although Dustin's road to recovery appeared to be heading in the right direction when viewed from the exterior, little things were once again starting to concern me. With each passing day, my son was beginning to spend more and more time with several of his old friends. I was familiar with a couple of these individuals and had never felt good about any of them. Two of these so-called friends of Dustin's in particular were a total waste of skin and everyone knew it. When these two smelly turds weren't busy tugging on Dustin's arm, I feel justified in assuming they were most likely standing in some fire pit roasting their tiny viennas with the Devil.

Knowing that Dustin's pals would undoubtedly influence our son in a bad way, I pleaded with him to avoid spending time with them. For a short time, it appeared as though our son was respectful of my wishes. But this only lasted so long. Despite his efforts, Dustin was once again lured to give way to his demon.

As a family, we have an understanding with Dustin that once his drug demon surfaces in our surroundings, he loses all privilege to the presence of our home and us immediately. This is especially hard given the number of times Dustin has fallen off the wagon. Often, at the time of his fall, he may not even have a decent pair of shoes on, a coat, or even a sleeping bag to keep him warm at night. There has only been a handful of situations that we have allowed him to stay, but only under very strict guidelines. Having said this, our attempt to be lenient most often becomes void within weeks or even days, which would unfortunately leave him once again walking the streets.

Finding the money to support a habit such as this was turning into a full-time job. It wasn't easy to find the money, but Dustin transformed the ingenuity, creativity, and quick wit that he used to be praised for into his principal tools used to support his own demise.

Utilizing the cover of darkness, Dustin soon added a new certificate to his wall of accomplishments: professional thief. Construction sites, according to Dustin, were a great place to start because an individual could often find expensive tools such as air compressors, jack hammers, table saws, electric drills, and much more. Unfortunately, when our son's inability to find and sell items outside our home ran dry, that cute little blonde lifeguard I still tried to picture him as, often wasted no time in stealing from his own flesh and blood.

Little did I know it, but the value of my family estate was dropping fast. My wife and I used to own more than 100 music CDs, over 100 DVD movies; two

Xbox consols, $20,000 worth of camera and video equipment, several large and small game hunting rifles, two skill saws, and a grinder. Those are just a few of the items that have been involuntarily donated to finance Dustin's addiction.

From this long list of long lost possessions, we learn that an individual hooked on drugs can and will do whatever it takes to finance his or her habit. By this point in time, there is no line that cannot nor will not be crossed. Dustin managed to pawn at least two-dozen items belonging to my wife and myself – not once, but twice. Again, this was just one more situation in which we had allowed our son back into our home, before being forced to send him back to the streets.

Our visits to the pawnshop were not only getting expensive, but left me feeling embarrassed and ashamed. *How could my kid do this to us, his own parents? What had I done wrong in raising this child? Somewhere along the way I have failed.* These thoughts and questions pummeled me nonstop throughout the day and made it difficult to sleep at night. My own self-worth waned, and my anger towards Dustin was at an all-time high. I just couldn't figure out where I had gone wrong, and how I had been responsible in any way for what Dustin had become.

The very thought of what our son was putting us through had begun to create a mountain of unforgivable hatred. At times, the very sight of Dustin's face left me wanting to wrap my hands around his worthless little neck. I was getting very tired of him lying to me and the rest of our family. Anything and everything that came out of his mouth would later prove to be a lie. Our boy, no, this "thing" now living in our home had turned into an alien. A transformation was taking place in our son and I couldn't stand it. As previously mentioned, our son was once an individual of quick wit, humor, and great kindness. Unfortunately, the frail stick figure posing before us now consisted of lies, evilness, and suspicious behavior.

Although it would be easy to direct the hate we were feeling toward our son, my wife and I knew that it was not our son who was lying and stealing from the family, but rather the drug: the new owner of Dustin's mind, body, and soul.

As I pondered my son's actions and his new way of life, a feeling of fear and sadness began to consume me. There was a thought that suddenly consumed my mind one day: *For if after I die, God has scheduled me for hell, I need not worry anymore. I am already there.*

"I swear dad, I have no idea what has happened to your skill saw," Dustin said as he assisted me in building a small footstool.

"How about my new electric drill? I need the drill to screw the footstool together," I accused.

"Nope, haven't seen the skill saw or the drill," Dustin calmly rebuttaled.

"I've already got them out of the pawn shop once. I want you to look me square in the eye and tell me you don't know where either of those tools are," I replied.

"Like I said, I'm telling you the truth dad. I honestly don't know anything about either one of your tools, I promise," Dustin finished.

But, those tools had to be somewhere. As much as I wanted to believe Dustin, the evidence proved otherwise. If we were to face these concerns, issues, and situations again they would be handled differently. I just hope our mistakes improve your handling of similar ordeals.

You may have noticed an alarming pattern in this book thus far. In many chapters, there comes a point where our son is kicked or forced out of our home. Then, by the beginning of my next chapter, you notice that we have again welcomed him back into our home. Obviously, as parents, we instinctively want to protect our wayward children. We yearn to supply them with food and protection. As parents, we want to believe in our children. We want to think that when they tell us something looking us straight in the eyes, that it is in fact the truth. This same thought process is typically shown under different circumstances; such as if the addict you are trying to save is a parent or friend rather than a child.

As much as you want to help this individual, you cannot afford or allow them to stay within the four walls you and I call home. Giving this person a place of refuge is not going to wash away his or her addiction. It will simply give them a secure place – a safe haven really – from reality. They will use this refuge to only continue their wrongdoing. Even worse, by allowing the addict this safe haven, you have now invited the additional trash, troubles, and debris that come with housing a drug addict. This includes other friends and faces with the same habits, individuals who are only looking for their next hit, drug dealers, and, last but not least, some pretty nasty loan collectors. I can't begin to tell you how many times my wife and I have had strangers practically march right through our front door looking for our son. The loan collectors wanted their money: the cash loaned to our son so he could buy heroin. From our front porch, we have even witnessed drive-bys. This is where several scary looking individuals drive by our house real slow looking for someone. We always knew that someone was Dustin. But we wouldn't know until years later that the scary looking individuals were employed by one of his dealers.

If only we knew what we know now. It would have saved so much grief to take our own advice. But time and time again, we let Dustin come home. We continued harboring him and perpetuating the cycle of addiction.

I cannot stress how important it is to stick to your guns and not allow your own home to become an unsafe place for you and the rest of your family. There are many better alternatives to assist addicts in breaking addiction and the ensuing recovery. Many of those alternatives are decisions our family finally made after years of semi-self-inflicted turmoil. These choices have made so much difference in our lives, and especially in the life of Dustin. If only we had known sooner. Avoid as much turmoil as you can. Learn from our experiences with the demon that is addiction.

The other aspect that can cause grievous self-inflicted wounds when dealing with an addict is trusting the addict. When you trust an addict – even a recovering addict – to come back into your home, you put yourself and everyone in your home in a vulnerable position. Emotionally, mentally, and even perhaps physically, you will all become a victim. There are those that suffer repercussions from second-hand smoke. Well, we became second-hand druggies in a manner of speaking because of the legal ramifications we had to deal with due to Dustin's reckless behavior that had no boundary – not even our bank account was safe. And if not for my incidental "drinking habit" (aka Dr. Pepper) our second-hand drug symptoms could have caused us to lose our home.

"Hi there Mr. John, what will it be today ... Root Beer or Dr. Pepper?" my buddy asked through his convenience store's drive-through window.

"Dr. Pepper today, thanks," I replied.

"I'm glad you stopped by, I've been wanting to ask you something about your youngest son, Dustin," my friend replied.

With an open view to the store's soft-drink machine, I watched as the storeowner began to fill my cup. I had the awful feeling that his next statement wasn't going to be good. My thoughts raced, wary of his next comments, to the mixture of dark syrup and popping bubbles of carbonation reaching the halfway point of my refillable cup. As I pondered the contents of my cup at the halfway mark, I had to decide if I was going to view what he had to say as half empty or half full. Knowing that my son has been heading in the wrong direction made this call an easy one for me to make. In addition, I knew that what my friend was about to tell me would most likely punch a huge hole in the bottom of my cup leaving me with no drink and more importantly, no hope!

My pal spoke, breaking me out of my half-empty contemplation. "I know that in the past you and your wife have sent your youngest son over here to cash several small checks from your account, but recently ... this past week,

I've noticed he has asked me to cash three or four checks. A couple of them have been up around $40 to $50."

I was dumbfounded. The man continued. "It's not that I mind cashing these checks... I guess my main concern would be that you and your wife have in fact given him your permission to do so," he finished.

Taking a moment to process this information, I silently chewed on this development. When was the last time I had offered Dustin any financial help? I concluded I had handed him a $20 dollar check to cash around a week ago, but nothing other than that.

Hesitating to dig this hole any deeper, I proceeded to ask my friend when Dustin had last cashed a check there. The storeowner reported Dustin had cashed a $30 check there less than an hour previously.

The look of devastation that suddenly consumed my face must have explained quite a bit as my friend immediately apologized. Who knew how severe the damage was. Thanks to my soda stop though, I at least had a lead to investigate and maim before it became worse.

First I had to verify that my wife had not been aiding and abetting Dustin without my knowledge. Doubtful. Then I just needed to track down my son to deal with him. My instinct was telling me that Dustin was long gone with his ill-gotten gains and headed an hour north of our town looking for his supplier though.

Wanting to give my son the benefit of the doubt, I quickly made a call to my wife's work phone. "Did you by any chance give Dustin a $30 check to cash?" I asked.

Never in my life had I wanted to hear the word "Yes" so badly then at that particular moment. Unfortunately for all of us – there would be no miracle on this day.

"No, why do you ask?" my wife said in a hesitant voice. "Something's wrong isn't it? What has Dustin done this time?" my wife said with tears creeping into her voice as she started to wander into despair mode.

Not having all of the facts and with the subject being what it was, I didn't feel good about continuing this conversation over the phone. It was obvious that our talk was beginning to upset my wife and I wasn't too excited about laundering our problems with any large-eared co-worker that might be eavesdropping.

By the time my wife had pulled into our driveway, I had had only a small amount of time to assess the damages to our checkbook. Upon review, it appeared as though our son had tried to cover his tracks by cleverly pulling three or four blank checks from within the middle portion of the checkbook we were currently using. Not knowing to whom each check had been written, the amount, or the details of these missing checks, my wife called our bank. I, on the other hand, grabbed my cell phone to call Dustin.

Although our youngest had a special talent – up to this point – for surviving most life-threatening situations, life, as he knew it was about to come to an abrupt halt. The thought that my own son could, would, and did steal from his very own mother and father had me about as pissed off as I had ever been. What made matters even worse was that Dustin knew that at this particular time our finances were very tight. The more I seethed over the situation, the angrier I became. Lord only knows just how bad off we were going to be before all of this was tallied up. This little cuss, depending on what other checks he may have written, could very well have cost us our home!

It took a couple of attempts before I finally reached Dustin on his cell phone. When I did – I left no mistake that Dustin had just been served a subpoena by the Devil himself. Furious doesn't begin to describe the rage that coursed through me.

"Where are you at?" I demanded. "Mom and I want your scrawny little butt home now." I slammed the phone down and continued to seethe.

Meanwhile, my wife was still trying to find out just how much trouble Dustin had gotten us into with the bank.

"Yes, this is Mrs. John. I'd like to talk to someone about our checking account," my wife said with fire and furry in her voice. "It appears as though our youngest son might have stolen several checks from one of our checkbooks. We would like to see if you could look up some check numbers and tell us to whom they were written out. Also, I need to know the amounts of each check."

Dustin had cashed several checks on our account. One of which rang in at $400. The best part was, this particular check had been written out to the court system with the purpose of bailing a friend out of jail. Our wrath could hardly be contained as the damage continued. In addition to the $400 check, Dustin had cashed several checks totaling nearly $200 dollars, some of which, I knew had surely been used to purchase drugs.

After learning of the total damage our son had caused by digging into our checking account, I suddenly found myself bathing in a frenzied cesspool of hatred and rage. Although what I felt at that very moment would be virtually impossible to describe, let me just say that during this "hot tub" excursion, the Devil and I became very good friends. Thank God that Dustin wasn't in front of me right now.

Prior to this incident, Dustin had avoided a total cut-off from our family because of that unconditional love concept I explored earlier. Until now, at least one of us, either my wife or myself, were somehow able to capture a glimmer of that love just when the remaining family members were again ready to ostracize Dustin. But not this time! Dustin's luck had run out. The flicker of love we had left for him was temporarily extinct in the wake of his home-hitting atrocities.

"We take you in, give you a place to stay – and this is how you repay us?!" I began my verbal assault on Dustin after a wait of nearly two hours for him to show up at our home. "What are you thinking -- Never mind, don't answer that, I know. You weren't thinking. Tell me, how in the world did you think you were going get away with this? More importantly, how the heck do you propose that your mom and I survive this financial mess you've gotten us into?" I said as I poked my finger into his chest several times. "You're lucky I don't take your stupid little head off with a 2 by 4. Just so you know – you are no longer living here. Get your stuff packed and get the hell out of here!"

Hearing the entire conversation, my wife waited for our son to leave the room before approaching the next topic, however distant from our hearts at the moment.

"How's he going to go anywhere, and where do you expect him to stay? You do know that it is below freezing out there and it's nearly 11 p.m.?" my wife said with mounting fear.

"I really don't know where he is going to go. Nor do I care how he's going to get there. I don't even care if he freezes to death tonight," I replied as tears of hidden concern, pain, and anger rolled from my cheeks. "Can't you see?" I said to my wife. "He is playing us. He doesn't care about you and me. No more than he cares about the financial disaster he has just put us into."

Now I know that many of you are thinking: It sounds like Dustin has some pretty stupid parents. After all, how in the world could two educated adults – already suspicious of their son – not be aware that $900 had been taken from their checking account?

In response to that thought let me suggest that, in retrospect, you are correct. I will be the first to admit that we were some pretty stupid parents at that time. Knowing of our son's drug problem, we should have been monitoring our money much more closely in all aspects. In our defense, we really didn't understand or believe that Dustin would be capable of so blatantly stealing from his own parents. At that time, we, as a family were nothing more than a novice to the drug addiction lifestyle and the patterns it invokes.

Looking back on this episode, I tell you with full conviction that this situation can be prevented. If you are willing to acknowledge the unbelievable as a possibility, as mentioned earlier, and logically prepare to counter attack any possible means of damage before they present themselves, you can guard your finances and your belongings from financial ruin. Hindsight may be 20/20, but that is why we're sharing this story with you: so that our hindsight becomes your 20/20.

6

Receipt Deceit

Dustin

April 2004

I am wandering around a large store parking lot. Stopping here and there against a cement lamp pole, I am trying to figure out what my next action item is. As I watch the throngs of people pushing their overflowing carts to their vehicles, I start to notice the small white slips of paper they all seem to be carrying. I watch attentively to the fate of these papers. Some are crinkled, and then tossed half-heartedly in the general direction of the trashcan. Some are merely dropped amidst the chaos of loading groceries and children into the vehicle. Some are littered by negligent shoppers avoiding one more piece of trash floating around their car. *That's it!* I think to myself. *I can gather these receipts and use them to make a fortune!*

With lots of repetition and my unswerving attention to detail, receipt shopping became my most profitable scamming tool. I learned that retailers would give cash back if the purchaser paid for their items with either cash or a debit card. I quickly learned that if items were purchased with a gift card or with a credit card, there would be no cash back, only in-store credit. Eventually, I found a way to manipulate even in-store credit to cold hard cash as well through a variety of transactions, but for now I want to discuss what I would do with my new-found gold mine: cash back receipts.

After filling my pockets with receipts, I would go through them to determine which ones were most profitable as well as if they were do-able return items. I started off with small items until I mastered the skill. The larger the item, the more skill it took. I would also have to discard any fear of being caught. First, I would look to see how the item was purchased. The ones that were paid for with either cash or debit, I would deal with first. Second, I would figure out what each item was. Most receipts have shortened abbreviations for the product name. I studied them and over time I was able to figure out almost any item. Some receipts only have the UPC number. These were more difficult to work with but eventually I got fast enough that I could locate items in a store by the UPC number. This probably seems a daunting task to the normal person. At first, it was for me too. But everything gets easier with practice. And I was willing to sacrifice anything and ready to go to whatever lengths I needed to scour up cash for drugs. Third, I would find the receipt with items that were high priced and not too difficult in size. Once I found a smaller item that was worth $20 to $100 and was paid for in cash or debit, I would then enter the store to search for the item. Matching the UPC on the item with the receipt was very important. If you try to return a similar item that is not the right one, you might as well put the handcuffs on yourself. This would raise a huge red flag and would be a simple mistake I wasn't willing to make. After I was sure I had the right item, I would grab it off the shelf and put it in the bag that I placed in my pocket before entering the store. Carrying the stolen item to the customer returns area was simple. With so many people going so many different directions, it was impossible for me to be singled out. I would wait in line for as long as it took and then approach the customer service desk.

"Hello there," I am as friendly as possible. "I just need to return this."

"That's okay. Is something wrong with it?" replies the worker.

"No ma'am, I just don't need it anymore," I say with playful confidence.

"Okay, It looks like I owe you $38.87."

Cha-ching! With the item in a bag and having a receipt, who would question the legitimacy of my transaction? No one.

Over time I became less fearful and more confident in my fraudulent transactions. I started out returning key chains and small hardware but developed enough skill to return leaf blowers, vacuums, and even baby strollers.

Receipts that were only good for in-store credit (purchased with credit or check), I learned how to turn into cash as well. There were a few more steps in this process so it wasn't my first choice in scamming for money. I would do everything the same way, however, the customer service worker would give me a "gift" card with in-store credit on it. I would then take the card and walk around the store until I found a good candidate to complete the process. I would ask certain customers (usually younger) if they were paying in cash for their purchases. This was always the difficult part of the process. Most people are skeptical when you start asking questions and poking around in their business. I found an easy way to get past this. I would offer them a deal they couldn't refuse.

"Can I buy your items for you with my gift card and you pay me in cash? I have $80 on this gift card and you only need to pay me $55. You will get $25 of free stuff."

Time and time again I would walk out of the store with cash in my hands.

I would also use receipts as fake decoys. I could walk into a home and garden store and push a brand new lawn mower out the front door. As long as I had a receipt in my hand I could act as if I just purchased it. The receipt was never for a lawn mower either. It was just a receipt I had found in the parking lot. The security alarm went off a few times as I exited the main entrance but I just kept walking confidently onward into the parking lot. Never once was I stopped.

Receipt shopping supported my heroin and cocaine addiction for years. It was the simplest way to supply my drug habit. Because I became so deft at receipt shopping, I earned the nickname "The Receipt Bandit." I learned I was given this alias in a strange way. I was talking to group of homeless squatters that I occasionally dealt with. While working some deals with them one day, they asked me how I supported my habit. I told them I was receipt shopping. They just looked at me until one guy blurted, "So you're the Receipt Bandit? No way!?" After some clarification, I realized I was given this nickname by other thieves and drug users who frequented the same areas of town as me.

Everyone in the 25-mile radius knew my nickname except for me. Now I felt like I was some kind of crazy folklore or urban myth that had come to life. One guy warned me that many retail store employees at several locations were well aware of "The Bandit." I had noticed the security in the stores had increased over time but I didn't think one man could be the cause of all that. I started noticing "shoppers" following me through the stores at times and feeling like I was under surveillance. Had I known of my nickname during earlier shoplifting sprees, I may have tried a little harder to dodge those eerie shadows. Discovering my own legend and new name around town didn't slow my felonious behavior. It actually made me feel like I had a reputation to uphold. So I did just that.

I knew this kind of dishonesty was something that normal people would be ashamed of, even if they only had a shred of a conscience left, they would be morally nagged for at least a little while about their crimes. My conscience was officially dead at this point. Because of my new life I had created, I felt no remorse. Shoplifting gave me a sense of false pride. I loved to push my limits and see just how much I could get away with – and I did. I got away with plenty. I continued to uphold my reputation as one of the best shoplifters around. There was nothing too big or too impossible for me to get out of a store. Riding lawn mowers, mountain bikes, barbecue grills. No amount of security would stop me from doing what I did best, or so I thought.

My body is heavily afflicted and showing signs of my negligence. I have lost 30 pounds, which says a lot given my naturally small build. My eye sockets are sunken in and dark. My cheekbones are protruding out. My facial features mirror that of a naked human skull. My collarbones look like two crooked rods. The blisters on my feet have made my skin raw and bloody. I don't remember the last time I took a shower or brushed my teeth. I was able to change my socks last week when I was at Kohl's. I put on a new pair of socks and shoes and walked out of the store. I do this often. I can't go into a store without stealing something, even if I don't need it. I continue to thrive off of my receipt shopping methods.

Being homeless and miles away from my dealer, I know I have to find a way to get to Salt Lake. I've already done my receipt shopping the evening before so now all I need is a way to get 60 miles north of here. It is no easy task. As I am walking back to my "camp," I notice a car for sale in a parking lot of a local pet store. The car quickly slips my mind as I remember I still have some heroin. I rush back to my campsite.

"Should I save my last shot of heroin for the morning?" I ask myself quietly. Without hesitation, I continue to prepare the drug into a liquid. My mind fills with empty promise as I anticipate another numbing shot of heroin. With needle in vein, I push the plunger. Effortless tingling fills my entire body. My eyes get heavy. My breathing becomes shallow and I lay comfortably on the cloud beneath my withered body. As sprinkles of fresh rain begin to dance on my face, euphoric bliss sends me to a deep and comfortable sleep.

6

No Truth, No Trust

Dallas

It has been my experience that an addict can never be trusted. Unfortunately, I have gained this knowledge from years of doing the opposite: trusting an addict. This statement is not only sad, but also hard to grasp because the individual you once knew and are now trying to help is no longer with us. By that I mean once a person becomes truly addicted, that person undergoes mental, emotional, and physical changes and does so very quickly. As the habit progresses, the individual you once knew suddenly at some point in this process, disappears. What you are left with is a drug-infested figurine. A shell of a body no longer owned or operated by that loved one you once knew.

At first the individual will turn to legal ways to finance his or her habit. This includes maintaining a job, even taking out loans with the intent to repay them. As the addiction grows, so does the bill. The more drug being consumed, the more money needed. When an addict's legal sources fail or prove unsustainable, he or she begins looking for any other resources. Often, the best resources are the people closest to them. An addict has the ability to detach all personal emotions for someone they once termed near and dear in order to manipulate them into supporting their addiction – knowingly or unknowingly. Addicts will do their best to convince you that they need your financial help for something important: a house payment, a car payment, or even groceries. They may convince you that they haven't eaten in days. Based on what I have seen in my own crisis, many drug addicts transform into magnificent salesmen. Manipulating people, playing on their emotions, even lying straight to your face. This will work for a while, but once friends and family catch on to why the addict needs money, the cash flow quickly runs dry.

While in the process of writing this book, my son admits that in the early stages of his heroin addiction money was not that big of an issue. According to Dustin, once you learn some of the "tricks of the trade" an individual whose body and mind requires one to two balloons of heroin each day can participate in one of several money making ideas, processes, or schemes to successfully finance the addiction. Perhaps the scheme most of us might recognize is the "Will Work For Food" idea.

Broadening my knowledge as to how this "Will Work For Food" idea functions, my son admits that many homeless individuals can become very wealthy by essentially playing the right card at the right time. As part of getting to know people, a person's facial response and their body language allows this "practicing homeless" salesman the opportunity to play one of several cards. By cards, I mean by getting to know human response and habit (including the knowledge of how to read an individual's body language) sets the stage for one of several untruthful stories. If you fall into the "extremely gullible" category, before the conversation with the addict is over, you may find yourself forking out $10, $20, $30 or more and thinking it is going to a very deserving cause. You will find yourself walking away from this unfortunate person applauding your benevolence at having the opportunity to truly make a difference in that person's life.

As Dustin and I continued to talk about the various schemes and scams that are commonly practiced among addicts, I found myself in total awe and bewilderment. Did you know that an individual who is on the streets could earn anywhere from a few bucks to several hundred dollars per day just by watching for crinkled up receipts that you and I just happened to leave laying in our shopping carts while picking up a few groceries at one of our nearby retail stores?

It appalled me to learn of Dustin experience as the "Receipt Bandit." It occurred to me that every time I left my receipt in the bottom of my shopping cart, or even just threw it away in a public trash can, it's the same as giving a drug addict the money to go purchase his or her next fix.

The addict stands on the outskirts of a retail store's parking lot. Keeping a watchful eye on individuals exiting the store, the homeless addict closes the distance. Unaware, that you are being watched, you begin to load the numerous bags of groceries and other products into your trunk or back seat of your vehicle. Moving the cart aside so as to not hit it when you pull out of the parking lot, a tiny white paper lies crumbled up in the bottom corner of your cart. Having already registered the amount into your checkbook you now view this little white piece of paper as nothing more than an annoyance. Something that when you get home you will simply have to discard anyway. Rather than make the effort to retrieve it, you leave it. It makes little sense to do otherwise. Little do you know, but because of your laziness to pick the receipt up out of the cart, our camouflaged addict with his or her stealth-like training swoops in and nabs their little gold nugget.

The second stage of this cunning little game consists of the addict returning into the store where he or she refills the cart with the very same items, which were on your shopping list as detailed by the handy dandy receipt. Once the addict has completed this process, he or she makes their way to the customer service desk where they insist on getting their money back on some or all of the items.

Now, as I revisit that homeless individual who consistently stands on the curb with his or her "Will Work For Food" sign, I don't want to be unfair or misleading. Not all who live on the street intend to take your contribution for the sole purpose of financing a drug addiction. Many panhandlers are people who have families, are out of work, and truly need assistance.

Even with that charitable disclaimer, you need to be aware that naivety is an addict's target. You must be aware that the dishonest motive exists and it is not the rarity. According to Dustin's accounts, it exists in greater abundance than naïve, charitable, everyday people realize.

7

THE JOY RIDER COLLIDER

DUSTIN

MAY 2004

I wake up to the gray-gold morning sunlight peering over the towering, snow-kissed mountains. The dew from the ground seeps through my ragged Levis sending goose bumps all over my body. I reach down and pull up my bunched up, blood stained sock around my left ankle hoping to help fight some of the chills. My feet are covered in blisters and dried blood from yesterday's journey. My back is aching and stiff from the uneven meadow that is home to an abandoned warehouse – and me. I brush the ants and other small bugs from my damp sleeping bag and cover my possessions with a warped piece of cardboard. I feel the onset of withdrawal entering my body and question why I didn't save any heroin for this morning. Like an accelerating virus, the withdrawals weave their way through my frail body. Being 60 miles from my dealer and not having transportation, I know I have to think of a plan. But it doesn't take me long when heroin is my goal. I will find a car. I can't go to a dealership because they will want a copy of my driver's license. Mine has been suspended because of 2 DUIs and failing to obey a variety of court orders. I will have to find a car for sale by owner. *If I sound interested in the car, they will be more than willing to let me test drive it.* I think with promise. *This plan will work. It has to.*

"The car!" I shout excitedly into the empty warehouse as I recall the moments before reaching my squatting ground last night. "The car I seen yesterday. It will work perfectly!"

I wind through the scattered sagebrush surrounding the warehouse and rush on my blistered feet into town. Adrenaline masks any pain I should be feeling only allowing me to focus on the anticipation of my plan working and heroin being pumped through my veins once again. I must execute my plan flawlessly. I cannot afford to mess up or else it will delay the gratification that only heroin provides me. I must play my part perfectly. Lying comes easy. Anything that expedites the process of heroin intake has become my dominant instinct.

I approach the small-town pet shop. I see the FOR SALE sign from two blocks away with my heightened senses. Even my pulse races in eager anticipation as I approach the car. *This is it,* I think. Approaching the store entrance, I clear my throat and take one deep breath. The lady at the counter looks up to the sound of cowbells clanking against the glass door.

"How can I help you?" she cheerfully asks.

With all the confidence I can muster, I speak to the woman like a seasoned salesman. "I was looking at that car for sale out front. Is that yours?" I ask genuinely.

"Yes it is," she eagerly replies.

"Well I am interested in purchasing a car. What kind of gas mileage does it get?" *Just a few more questions to sell my interest. Make sure the questions are good questions that someone buying a car would really ask.*

"About 31 miles per gallon," she says with a smile.

"Perfect!" I lie. "I want to take it for a test drive if you don't mind."

"Oh, of course!" she says.

"And if you don't mind, our family mechanic told me not to buy a car unless he looks at it first. I wouldn't want to get on his bad side!" I say with a smile. *So gullible.*

"Absolutely!"

"Okay, his shop is just 20 minutes north of here, so I hope that having the car for an hour or two won't put you in a bind," I explain. *Everyone is so trusting.*

"No no! Not at all," she responds looking for her keys to hand over.

"Well, after he checks out the car and assuming there are no major problems, I will bring you payment. You take cash, right?" I throw in to complete the sale.

"Preferably," she says, a little amazed with her own luck of not even having to negotiate the price. With a smile on her face, she places the keys in my hand. As I turn to walk out, I smile at how convincing my words became. It was evil and for some reason, it felt good. I could feel Satan smiling at my latest achievement.

After meeting up with my dealer in Salt Lake in my borrowed car, I realize that I need to hurry home before the owner of the car gets worried. I pull into a parking stall at a local grocery store and doctor my heroin into liquid form. I draw it into my syringe and look around to make sure there aren't any curious passersby taking an interest in my activities. With the coast clear, I stick the needle into my protruding vein and slowly watch as the warm liquid enters my body. My eyes slowly close. My breathing begins to thin as my body takes on the pleasurable relief of synthetic courage, artificial peace. No longer in pain, I put the car in drive and head for the interstate. I notice my eyes are heavy as the sun drops below the horizon. I am feeling somewhat relieved now that I am headed back to the anxious car owner. I'm exhausted and can't wait to get back to my camp and enjoy the bliss of a heroin-induced coma. I set the cruise control at 70 mph as I come up alongside a diesel. I unroll the driver side window as I light a cigarette. I look over to see the large diesel tires spinning and howling against the pavement. The steady hum of the tires is the last thing I remember.

I awake in a panic like I have never experienced before. I can feel my heart bursting in my head. The sound of a semi ripping through car metal and plastic is unnerving. I notice the car is bouncing off the side of the diesel with every impact. Going 70 mph, the car's front tire finally gives way to the constant slamming of the 10-ton rig. When I finally catch my bearings, I am able to barely steer the car off to the shoulder. I watch as the truck driver continues down the interstate, completely oblivious to my brush with death. As the car comes to a stop, I notice the driver's side mirror hanging on by one small electrical wire. I get out of the car to inspect the damage. The entire driver's side of the car has been dented in like a tin can. The car still operates once I change the shredded tire. Luckily, there is a spare in the trunk. With my syringe and other paraphernalia on the passenger seat, I know I have to change the tire quickly. The evening is growing colder and darker each minute. I know this little mistake is going to cost me in more ways than one. By the time I return the car to the pet store, it is obvious the storeowner has locked up and gone home for the night. I don't bother to call or notify her. I am too afraid of what the outcome would be. I just park the car where I found it with hopes that she won't notice the car is in shambles. Leaving the keys in the ignition, I close the door and walk off into the night.

The thoughts of what I have just done crush me like an incoming ocean wave slamming against a merciless stone cliff. Stumbling through the streets, it all becomes too much to bear. Excruciating fear grips my body with each step. *What have I done? How much more unmanageable can my life get than this?* I need to escape the pain of what I have become, the pain of what is in store for me. I know of one way to do that, a way to forget about everything. *There is no way out!* My thoughts resound in my head, crushing any shred of hope. *I have failed as a person. My life is over!* I sob bitterly, scared, empty. I reach my squatting area and sit with my head hanging down between my raised knees in shame. I feel the cold air chill my body through the tear in my dirty jacket. I empty my last two balloons of heroin into the dirty spoon and mix it with what water I have left in a plastic bottle. I cook the mixture in the spoon with my lighter. As I draw up the liquid, I know I am doing way too much, but at this point I don't care. I stick the dull needle into my battered arm once again. As I feel the drug enter my body, I tip over sideways losing all control. My eyes become heavy. My body is so comfortable. My brain shuts down. My thoughts are finally peaceful. I lay here motionless as the last faint breath escapes my mouth.

The overpowering blast of heroin should have killed me last night. Fortunately, it did not. I am feeling the repercussions of such a large dose this morning as I maneuver into a standing position. The ache is deep and relentless. I overslept in the gnat-infested field and the sun has been beating against my face for hours. Knowing I needed to get up and figure out how to get some more heroin, I make my way out of the field. Being drained, dehydrated and weak, I begin to realize I don't have the energy to find a way back to my dealer.

Walking towards the road I stopped short of the curb and just stood there. Not knowing what to do or where to go I decide to sit down on the curb with my arms crossed over my knees. My head falls into my lap and I begin to cry. Knowing I injected a shot of heroin last night that should have taken my life made me afraid of myself and what I was capable of. I wasn't trying to kill myself. But I wasn't not trying to kill myself. *It is time to make a change. A change for the better*, I command myself. I am only three blocks away from the hospital. In the shape I'm in right now, I don't think I can walk one step further. *I am going to do it! I have no other options. I have to check myself into the hospital.* I have decided.

I did check myself into the hospital that day. It was a last ditch effort to save me from myself. The hospital has a brief inpatient treatment program that aids addicts who are trying to get sober. They also house patients who are mentally ill so I was mixed in with patients with a variety of ailments. I was stationed in the wing of the hospital called The Pavilion. This was my third time in The Pavilion. My family had brought me the last two times during brief stints of living with them in an effort to help me get more serious about my desire to get clean.

One procedure offered in The Pavilion is called Rapid Detox. Rapid Detox is a procedure used widely in America to help drug addicts and alcoholics break the addiction cycle without having to consciously experience the torturous pains inflicted by withdrawals. An anesthesiologist puts the patient to sleep using heavy relaxants and other medications, depending on which doctor you have. Once the patient falls into a deep sleep, the doctor injects the patient with Narcan (for opioid dependent patients). Narcan is an opiate blocker that causes the opioid receptors in the brain to release the opiates that have connected to the receptors. The Narcan covers these receptors not allowing anything else to attach to them. This causes the patient to experience violent withdrawals while they are sleeping. It is a 3 to 5 day time warp for them. All the worst withdrawal symptoms take their toll while the patient is unconscious.

When I went through this procedure the first time, I woke up feeling terrible. I continued to feel awful for two weeks. I made it through the withdrawal phase successfully. Unfortunately, I relapsed 90 days into my sobriety. The most difficult part in divulging this experience is that my Grandparents were the ones who paid for the procedure. It is not covered by insurance and it cost upwards of $5,000. Knowing how much time, money, and efforts were lost on my failed attempts at sobriety is a painful reminder of the power of my addiction. Despite all the help and support I had been given by my entire family, I was not able to stay sober.

Because I had been in the Pavilion two previous times, I knew how it worked before I walked in. Knowing my family would shun the idea of me going back, I didn't bother to tell them. I knew I was on my own this time. After all, I was homeless and my family had put some distance between themselves and my addiction. My mom was working at the hospital at that time, so it was only hours before she knew I had been admitted. The hospital's policy was to not give narcotics to patients coming off of opiates. They gave me some non-narcotic medicine that took some of the edge off of my withdrawal pain, but it was still a daunting task to get through the withdrawal period.

I knew I couldn't be kept there under my own will. I could leave at any time if I wanted. In retrospect, I now see that my choice to leave The Pavilion after the third day was not going to end well for me. Back then, in my own mind, I truly thought I was ready. I couldn't have been more wrong. Heroin stays in the body for three to five days so it hadn't even gotten out of my system entirely yet. My decision to leave The Pavilion prematurely was a decision that led me to one of the worst places I ever experienced as an addict.

I have been out of the Pavilion for a week. As long as I stay on the medication the doctors gave me I don't feel the need to use other drugs. All I have done is walk the streets trying to figure out how to begin a new life; some way to build some sort of sturdy foundation under me. I am easily overwhelmed thinking about all the things I have done to destroy my life. I don't know where to begin in repairing it all. If you are homeless heroin addict, lying in a wet field, with nothing but a withered blanket and a backpack full of semi-useless items, what do you do? It's easy to say: "Go get a job," but how do you get to work without a vehicle? Who would hire someone who has no way to get to work, shower or get a good night's sleep? Running these thoughts through my head, I start to become more and more irritated and less hopeful for my future. I allow the negative to take over. I only see dead end after dead end. The pessimism builds on itself and within 10 minutes I come to a conclusion. I know exactly what I am going to do. Determined and unstoppable, I stand up from my sagebrush field at the base of the mountains and I walk towards the bus stop.

Three hours later, I lock the bathroom door behind me as the butterflies in my stomach dance in anticipation. Escape from my failures is only seconds away as I draw the last of the mixture from my spoon. The thought of being stranded in Salt Lake at a gas station is not the least bit bothersome. The disappointment of relapse fades as I thrust the plunger inwards. Within seconds, the intense burning sensation floods my body and instantly I rise up, floating on a perfect billowy white cloud. A knock at the bathroom door drops the cloud from underneath my body. Throwing my drug kit into my backpack, I flush the toilet to make my bathroom visit more realistic. "Almost done!" I yell out wiping up any blood droplets or residue left behind. Double-checking the area, I proceed out of the gas station bathroom.

7

LIES AND MORE LIES

DALLAS

MAY 2004

"Hello, have I reached the right phone number? I'm looking to speak with Dustin's father or mother," my wife heard as she answered the phone.

The woman on the other end of the phone went on to detail how Dustin had stopped by her pet shop earlier in the day. According to this woman, she and her husband had put one of their vehicles up for sale. It became apparent after listening to the woman that Dustin had given her the impression that he was interested in purchasing their car. The lady continued telling my wife that Dustin had asked to take the car for a test drive, but had not since returned with the vehicle in question. According to the woman, Dustin had been gone for more than five hours.

After explaining to the woman that we had recently discovered our son was using drugs, my wife advised the woman to contact the police immediately and report the vehicle as stolen.

As one might imagine, upon hearing this grand auto theft news, my wife and I were very upset. I was not only ready to wring Dustin's neck, but do some major house cleaning.

It took days before our son finally showed his face. When he did, he acted as though nothing had ever happened. His irresponsible arrogance infuriated me even more.

"Where in the world have you been for the past week?" I demanded. "Have you got something to tell your mother and I?"

After a long pause, Dustin hesitantly replied, "What do you mean? I've just been hanging out with some of my friends for a few days. You act like I've done something wrong."

At this point I was livid, but I wanted to be fair. After all, if I was going to hang my son from the nearest tree, I had to be absolutely sure he had been given sufficient opportunity to correct his story.

"I want you to come over here and sit down on this chair in front of me," I commanded as I prepared to ask him one more time where he had been for the last week. "I want you to look me square in the eyes and tell me that you have not done anything seriously wrong,"

Again a short pause. Dustin pulled his head up and looked me square in the eyes and said, "I don't know why you and mom feel that I've done something bad? I love you guys and I wouldn't lie to you if I had been out doing something wrong."

He sounded so convincing looking at us without a seeming care in the world. I had now given my son at least two opportunities to confide in us the trouble he was now in. Despite giving him more than one chance to come clean, Dustin chose to deny any wrong doing rather than just telling us the truth.

I know that my statement about hanging my son from the nearest tree sounds a bit harsh, but after listening to Dustin deny any wrong doing for the second straight time, these words had left me very angry and totally out of control. The yelling commenced.

"What kind of kid have I raised? How can one of my children look me straight in the face with those puppy dog eyes and a swagger of sincerity in his voice and lie straight to my face?"

Contemplating my next move, my hands began to sweat. I could feel my temperature mounting and spreading its way through my entire body. My cheeks flushed and I could sense a transformation. Was steam coming out of my ears yet? Was I as big, green, and muscly as the Incredible Hulk yet? For the first time in a long time, I actually felt like I wanted to kill someone. But how could I? After all, this individual was my youngest son... Or, was he?

We kicked Dustin out that very moment and we watched our youngest son once again walk out our door and down the street with only a thin t-shirt and worn jeans. I was both physically and mentally drained and I was really starting to hate Dustin for what he was doing to my family. I didn't know what was bothering me more: whether it was the drug use itself, or Dustin's lies about his whereabouts and claims of not using when it was obvious he was.

Several years had passed and neither my wife not I had felt any progress had been made with Dustin's commitment to lead a normal, drug-free life. Our efforts to save our son were going nowhere. We were going in one big circle and feeling emotionally, mentally, and physically drained because of it. Not only was Dustin's support group growing bruised from riding this broken wheel of repeated lies and halfhearted attempts, we too were in desperate need of our own kind of detox. Basically, we all needed to take if not a few days off, perhaps at least a "lunch break" from our ongoing efforts to save Dustin.

Though the wounds and scars of this battle will never completely heal, my family and I will always remain steadfast in our efforts to endure to the end with all of Dustin's repeated slip-ups. It is because of our collective strengths that I have been able to move forward so many times instead of just giving up and washing my hands completely of Dustin's choices. Since dealing with the repercussions of Dustin's "test drive," I finally found myself moving forward with life once again. I could only hope that my son was also finding that same energy and desire to choose life over death in his daily battles wherever he was.

So, once again we were starting at square one with Dustin. The problem still remained: how are we going to get our son off these deadly drugs? There was no solution in sight and we were becoming exasperated. We were hitting dead end after dead end. Trusting him was getting us nowhere, and indeed only penalizing our stupidity. Tough love of kicking him out didn't seem to have any impact on him either – it just aggravated our worries as we obsessed over not knowing where he was and if he was dead or alive. Both my wife and I found ourselves asking each other the same question: "What do you think he is capable of doing?" Little did we know, but our out of control son was about to show us just how far a drug addict is willing to go to get his fix.

8

RELOCATION DEVIATION

DUSTIN

AUGUST 2005

The anger and disappointment inside me begins to boil over. Countless relapses have taken their toll on my body as well as my emotions. My latest relapse has pushed my emotional state to a new place I have never experienced. Confusion, shock, disbelief, fear, disappointment, and anger are all fighting each other for the top spot in my newly emptied soul. Within the blink of an eye, I am loaded with drugs once again.

It happened without a second thought of what I was doing to my life, without a second thought about what it would do to my family's life. *What is wrong with me?* I think. *Why can't I stay sober?* Thinking through every possible solution to get sober and STAY SOBER is not going so well. I am running out of ideas. The only thing I haven't done is relocate. *That's it! I need to move away! Far away! Far away from here. I need to physically remove myself from my surroundings.* Everywhere I go I see places I have done drugs. My blood has been spilled from needle stick shoot-ups in every gas station bathroom within a 50-mile radius. Everywhere I go I see someone that I have done drugs with. I can't even look at a spoon or a Q-tip without thinking about shooting up. Even tin foil triggers me to use drugs. I must get away from everything!

But where can I go? I have no vehicle. I have no money. I have no home. All I have is a women's 10-speed bicycle that my sister let me borrow to get around town and my old worn out backpack. Maybe I can ride the Greyhound bus somewhere. Somewhere warmer! Somewhere with less memories of my past! *What about Southern Utah?* I think. I can go there! I will take the Greyhound to St. George! St. George is almost 250 miles from here. Just enough distance to put my past behind me. I will start a new life there. I will get a job printing at St. George's local newspaper. I will reinstate my suspended Driver's License and I will get a vehicle. I will rebuild my life! This is an opportunity for me to start all over. I can do it this time. I have to do this. I am not ready to give up and die just yet.

I pedal the rickety 10-speed over to my parents' house to tell them about my latest and greatest plan to move to St. George. I don't want to move so far away without at least letting my parents know I am going. I get the feeling they don't think I am really going to go through with it. Either that or they don't want to tell me that it is not a very practical idea. There is nothing anyone can say to change my mind. For this to work, I need to ride my sister's pedal bike to the Greyhound Station today. It's about 25 miles away but if I leave around noon, I will make it in time for the 5 pm departure. I worry if I don't get on that bus tonight, I will be high by tomorrow. It takes a little over five hours to get to St. George by Greyhound. That should be plenty of time for me to figure out what to do when I get there.

The bike ride to Provo is tougher than I expected. It's not easy to do physical activities when you have only been sober a few days. Luckily, I have some pills left over that were given to me by the hospital. They are non-narcotic but they help keep my blood pressure from spiking and keep my muscle cramping at bay. I take some anxiety medicine that helps me relax a little as well. Unfortunately, these pills only take the edge off. I think my adrenaline is the main source of painkiller right now. Thinking about starting a new life far away from everything I know is helping me stay positive and keeping my mind off needing another hit of heroin. I feel invigorated with my spur-of-the-moment plan! It is definitely exciting. I ignore all the things that may go wrong. If things do go south for me, I will cross that bridge then. After all, things can't get worse for me than they already have. None of that matters right now. I am determined to make something of my life and this is a way for me to start rebuilding. I have only been using for a couple weeks since my last 90-day sobriety streak so within a few days I should be feeling a lot better.

It feels good to be sitting at the bus stop and not pedaling that bike anymore. I was able to round up $38 on my bike ride here by asking passersby for spare change. Looking up at a sign illuminated with red LED lights, I see the ticket prices. In a right to left scrolling motion, I read:

```
Cedar City OW-$40/RT-$65 St. George OW-$56/RT-$100 Las Vegas
                     OW-$85/RT-$150
```

My enthusiasm plummets. I don't even have enough money to begin my journey. I know I have to get back on the bike and find at least $18 before the bus leaves in two hours. Before I am able to stand back up again, I notice a familiar vehicle in my peripheral. As it pulls near, I sigh in relief.

My mom and dad have come to say goodbye and wish me well. I debate for a moment between needing to come up with the rest of my ticket price and saying goodbye. Each minute could make a difference between me getting that extra money, aka staying sober, or not. I decide to quickly say my farewells and tell them I love them, I owe them that much. I begin walking towards their un-parked vehicle.

"So you're really going to do it, huh?" my dad questions while putting the truck in park.

"Yeah," I say looking at my mom's swollen red eyes. Knowing she has been crying makes me sad. I feel a heavy lump in my throat as I continue to speak. "I need to get away from this place Dad. Everywhere I go and everything I see triggers me to use drugs and I can't do it anymore. I need to start over somewhere unfamiliar to me. I need to meet new people; people that don't use drugs. Ya know?" I say with sad hopefulness.

"Well we hope you do make it out there on your own. It's not going to be easy. Mom and I want to give you a little bit of money to help you out. Here's forty dollars. That's all we have so make it last." He hands me the folded bills then requests a farewell hug for both him and my mom.

"Thanks. I love you," I muster as tears roll down my cheeks. I'm sure I have cost them quite a bit and their departing gesture of love sends a fluster of emotions through me.

"Do good okay my son," My mom says tearing up.

"I will do my best mom," I really hope I can live up to this. What is my best?

The weight of sadness swells through my body as I lose their taillights amidst the turns and traffic. I have no idea what is in my future, but watching pieces of my past slowly fade is painful. Not knowing when I will see my family again begins to supersede all other thoughts. I haven't seen much of my family in the last few years due to my drug use, but for some reason, leaving the area my family and I have come to know so well begins to pull at my heart in a way I never imagined. Is this homesickness before I've even left?

I have to shake off the sadness and think about something else. I brush away my wet cheeks with my holey, stained sleeve, and walk up to the ticket counter.

"One-way ticket to St. George," I mumble through the hole in the Plexiglas enclosure. I hand over my now complete fare and grasp the perforated ticket through a slit in the glass. I walk back to the bench where I left the bike.

I am the first one to load onto the bus. I want to find a good seat and the bus seats are much softer than the metal bench I have been sitting on for the past two hours. I find a single seat against a window toward the back. All the other isles have two seats but this one is connected to a storage compartment like the ones you see on airplanes. I enjoy the thought of not having to sit next to an obnoxious chatterbox. I want some peace and quiet, some time to ponder what is in store for me when I reach my new home. With my back-pack and 10-speed in the storage compartment of the Greyhound's belly, I begin to sink into my seat. The engine in the 15-ton rig comes to life as my body vibrates against the seat back and the drone in my ears causes me to hold a long drawn-out yawn. A slight change of pressure fills the cabin as the driver closes the front entrance door. I look out the tinted window of the bus and watch as the bus pulls away from the station. *This is it. No turning back now.*

I wake up with the sudden jolt of the massive rig coming to a stop. Wiping my eyes with the palm of my hand, I squint trying to focus through the bright illumination of the cargo lights placed throughout the bus. Looking out the window, I notice a familiar gas station. Knowing now that we are far from St. George still, I settle back into my seat. As I do, a group of new riders board the bus: three women and a man. They continue walking down the aisle until they reach the back of the bus. Two of the ladies sit in the adjacent row next to me and the man and other woman sit directly in front of them. I can tell they are all friends. They have been talking amongst each other from the moment they boarded the bus. They seem to be a fun and friendly bunch. They are all about my age or at least within a few years. Still, I don't feel like socializing with strangers. What would I have to say? Hi, I'm homeless and running from heroin? As they laugh and talk over the top of each other, the only thing I can think is, *Please don't talk to me or ask me anything.*

"Hey where you from?" one girl shouts in my direction. I know she's aiming the question at me. I look out the window in oblivion. Had the woman not been so persistent, I could've gotten away with my snub tactic but she wouldn't let up until I surrendered an answer. She asked me again so I decide to respond in hopes of getting her off my back.

"I grew up here in Utah. What about you guys?" I mutter.

"We're all from Texas. We're takin' a trip to California to meet up with my husband. We all have a 6-hour wait in Las Vegas though," her southern drawl is cute combined with the flawless white smile she flashes.

"That sounds like a fun layover. I haven't been to Vegas for a while. I think you guys will have a good time there. Have you been to Vegas before?" I question trying to be sociable.

"Well, Doug has... wait, I don't even know your name?"

"Dustin. My name is Dustin," I smile.

"My name is Michelle, this here next to me is Valerie and in front there is Doug and his friend Susan," she says pointing to the seat in front of her.

"Good to meet all of you," I say with slowly mounting enthusiasm.

"Nice to meet you too," Michelle says with the three others.

Our conversation continues for another hour. We discuss trivial things like what we do for fun and places we have been. The group of us get along surprisingly well. At the end of the conversation, Michelle and her entourage invite me to go with them all the way to Las Vegas. Due to lack of funds on my part, I am quite hesitant to risk the abrupt change of plans. However, Michelle's persistent personality doesn't brush off easily. With a handful of Michelle's tenacity and some financial help from my new friends, I am now on a one-way trip to Sin City. Las Vegas, Nevada. Just the place for a recovering heroin addict.

After the long bus ride through the vacant Nevada Desert, it is refreshing to see the bright lights of Las Vegas. The sun gave up hours ago and Vegas is in full swing. I begin to visualize the music and ambiance of a slot machine packed casino. The flashing lights blanketing the city mesmerize me. As we pull into the Greyhound Station, I have already gotten out of my seat and scooted toward the front of the bus. The moment I step foot off this bus, my new life will begin. I am thrilled.

"I'll meet you guys at the front of the building," I shout over the commotion of exiting travelers.

Stepping off the bus is such a relief. Even though I am surrounded by the fast pace flare and excitement of the Las Vegas Strip, I notice a sense of calmness about me that I haven't felt in a long time. The urge to use drugs has dissipated. I don't know how long this sensation will last, but it is nice not thinking I need to get high constantly. Even the physical pains associated with heroin withdrawal have subsided. It is probably a combination of excitement, adrenaline, and coming off of only a two-week binge instead of a six-month one. Maybe this adventure is just what I need right now. Maybe this will turn out to be a great experience after all. The station attendant allows me to store my bike in one of their empty offices until I come pick it up. I hope it will be safe there while my new acquaintances and I tour the Strip.

6 HOURS LATER

All of us go to a tattoo parlor on the Strip. Michelle and Derrick both get small tattoos. We've all had several cocktails touring the Boulevard so I hope they won't regret their tattoos tomorrow morning. I love all the beautiful sites and shows up and down the Strip, but it is coming to an abrupt end. Michelle and her friends board their next bus to California. I just met them hours ago, yet I feel sad that they are gone already. What do I do now? Where should I go? I have never been in Las Vegas alone – alone, with no money, no transportation except for an old bicycle, and nowhere to go. Las Vegas is a fun destination when you have a purpose or a reason to be there. My reason for being here just left. Why did I not think about what I would do when they were gone? I can't call home. I just got here 6 hours ago. I decide to find a pawnshop and sell a pair of sterling silver earrings I had in my backpack. Maybe that will produce enough to get me a ticket up to St. George.

Going back inside the bus station, I ask the attendant behind the desk where the nearest pawn shop is. Luckily it is Vegas and there is no shortage of pawn shops. I start walking down the street in the direction the attendant pointed me.

As I walk, I begin to really take note of my surroundings for the first time, analyzing them from a practical angle instead of the happy-go-lucky, this-is-all-so-exciting angle I rushed off the Greyhound with. I notice the kind of area I am walking through. The dingy sidewalks are lined with dim, graffitied streetlights. Shreds of discarded neon flyers scatter the sidewalk. I almost hit a homeless man swinging the bus station door open. He is sitting slouched against the outside wall. A weak, withering breeze sweeps shreds of discarded neon flyers past him and down the desert sidewalk. It is unnerving. The last thing I need right now is to be surrounded by a neighborhood of dope dealers, prostitutes, and homeless people.

I quicken my walk to the pawnshop. It soon comes into view with its cheap neon signs advertising CASH FOR GOLD. The clerk at the pawnshop senses my urgency in my demeanor. I explain that I need enough to get me back to St. George and he helps me out. He gives me a high quote of $40 for the earrings. Since they're only worth about $60, I know I've made a good deal with the pawnshop. I am grateful for his high offer and can't help but feel blessed a little. Making my way back down the dark and littered street towards the bus station, I see the same homeless man. He is still sitting on the left side of the door. As I get closer, he looks up in my direction. He has been staring at me since I began approaching the building. With no eye contact or acknowledgment, I reach for the door.

"You lookin'?" whispers a gruff voice.

"What?"

"Are you looking for anything?" the man repeats.

"You mean drugs?"

"Crack! I can get some crack. You want a rock?" he offers with a toothless grin.

I can't escape my demon no matter where I am – even on the verge of entering the Greyhound station and carrying on with my plan. Time slows and my world seems to spin around me as I consider the proposition. *Just a little won't hurt. Life isn't really that bad. Look how much fun you've had living on the edge moment-by-moment already. I'll figure out my next move after this little break.* The thoughts pound through my head rapid fire.

Like a marionette attached entirely to strings, I reach helplessly into my backpack beginning to shake with anticipation. I fish around until I find the pocket I have stuffed the $40 in. It all feels surreal. I mindlessly pull out the wadded cash and hand it to the decrepit homeless man. He gives me some crack cocaine in return. I have made it 7 hours into my new life drug free. That streak comes to an abrupt end.

The last five hours have been hell. Being alone and broke in Vegas is terrible, but being alone and broke in Vegas while coming off crack cocaine is worse. Surely everyone who passes by me knows I am coming off crack. I am extremely uncomfortable and jittery. My back feels like I have been swinging an 18-pound sledgehammer all day. Having no safe haven to stay at, I just have to hang out here wandering around the bus station or curled up in some nook. No plan. No food. No money. No life. While wallowing in my own self-pity and contemplating suicide as a viable next option, I suck down a stale, bent cigarette.

A clean, well-dressed lady approaches me by the front doors.

"Do you have a light?" she asks politely stirring me from my trance.

"Yeah, sure," I respond reaching into my pants pocket and fishing out my lighter.

"You look down. Is everything okay sweetie? Where are you headed?" She asks with concern in her voice. I am unaccustomed to this type of person taking an interest in me. Usually it is only tattered thugs, like the homeless man, who seek me out, ready to take advantage of my never-ending vices.

"I was supposed to be going to St. George but I screwed that up. It's kind of a long story ma'am," I explain shamefully lowering my head to avoid eye contact with her.

"I have time," she smiles. Her sincerity causes me to look up, curiosity filling my mind trying to figure out why she is taking such an interest in me. Her gaze is pure and innocent. I feel some sort of connection with this woman that I have never felt before. Not in a sexual way but more a spiritual connection. Looking into her eyes I can feel her love and goodwill for mortal beings whatever station they are in life. Her demeanor is more real – more genuine than anything I have ever felt. Whatever "God" is, I feel him looking down on me through this woman. I feel like I have known her for years. Her soothing nature and relaxed gentleness calm me down considerably. I can't figure out exactly what it is, but something about her captivates me. She is an angel. My angel, sent to save me from myself since I couldn't even handle that job. She is here to guide me back onto a path I need to take. She derails my thought of my last-ditch option: suicide.

Still in a bit of a daze, half from the cocaine, half from wonder at her kindness, I engage in conversation with the woman telling her everything.

"I'm from Utah. I wanted to get to St. George to get sober and get away from all my old memories. I met some friends on the bus that wanted me to come here to Vegas with them. Once they left, I spent the last of my money on drugs. Now I am stuck here in Vegas." Everything gushes out. I don't know if this is the therapy I need or if I have just officially gone crazy.

"You wait right here!" the woman says and I watch her walk into the bus station. Within a couple minutes the lady comes back outside and approaches me.

"Here's your ticket to St. George. And you're going to need some money when you get there," she says handing me $100 and the ticket. "Now, you get your butt on that bus, okay." What has compelled her to do this? I can't fathom her compassion for a total stranger whose life is obviously screwed up beyond comprehension.

"Are you serious? Why? Why are you doing this for me?" I stammer. "I can't thank you enough!"

"You don't need to. Just get to St. George."

"I will! I promise!" I want to make her proud of me for some reason. I've already disappointed so many people in my life I don't want to add her to the list.

The woman smiles one last time and walks back into the bus station. I am only about fifteen seconds behind her, but when I open the lobby door, I find emptiness. Not a soul in sight except the ticket worker behind the counter. She was gone.

With renewed vigor, I decide to get on with my sober life. Get over my minor setback and start fresh once again. The woman has given me hope. First, I need to find something to eat – having a full stomach will make staying sober easier. It will help me focus on my priorities and give me strength to stave off my withdrawals and pending drug cravings.

I cross the street and order a cheeseburger from a rundown fast food stand. I haven't eaten all day. The food tastes delicious and I devour it while thoughts of the woman keep circling in my head. I wonder who she was and why she helped me so generously. She never even told me her name. Shame and guilt creep over me for even accepting her money. I know who I am and I knew it is a lost cause for anyone to help me. I hear the woman's voice speaking inside my head. *No you're not a lost cause! You can turn your life around! You have it somewhere inside of you!* Rage builds within me. I feel my skin flush as anger floods my body. *I will get on that bus and I will turn my life around! I didn't come all the way here to give up so easily!* Finishing the last bite of cheeseburger, I dispose of the wrapper and walk out of the restaurant. The latest turn of events has rendered me with a large dose of ambition and as I'm walking to the bus stop, I notice a half-smile forming on my face. *I can do this!*

St. George · Day 1

It's amazing how different I feel today. Yesterday I was standing at death's doorstep and today I feel determined to succeed. I am staying at a nice motel near the center of town. Once I arrived here, I called my parents and asked if they could help me get a motel room for a couple days so I could have a place to clean up and sleep. Luckily, my parents didn't ask how I was able to afford my stay up to this point. Not being questioned eased my anxiety and tension during the call. They understood that I couldn't go to a job interview smelling like sweaty socks so they kindly charged two nights stay for me on their credit card. I am grateful they were so willing to help me out yet again. I don't know what I would do if it wasn't for their help.

Now that I've secured lodging in a respectable manner to get myself taken care of, my next order of business is to call the local newspaper and see if they are hiring any printing press operators. I really need that job. Getting a position at the newspaper would be just the break I need. It is already late, so I will call in the morning.

With my spare time in the evening, I head to the hotel's pool. I meet two guys and their mom also enjoying the pool. The two guys are twin brothers named Jed and Judd. They are three years younger than me. It is imperative that I avoid any association with anything or anyone drug-related so I begin my assessment of the twins. Being in the "drug game" for as long as I have, I am a pretty accurate judge when it comes to knowing if a person is on drugs and what drugs they may be on. My first impression of the twins is that neither of them are active users of any drug, nor do I have any reason to suspect they ever have used. As I continue our conversation, I come to find out that Jed and Judd do both indeed have their heads on straight.

The only way I can tell the twins apart is their hairstyle. They say they live in the outskirts of St. George about 30 miles from here but their father is in the hospital with a bad illness. They don't want to be too far away if something bad were to happen to him. Hearing that causes me to think about how far away I am from my own family. It is random times like this when my selfish lifestyle smacks me in the side of the head and makes me recognize just what I had become. A profound and painful realization of all the guilt and sorrow I have created in my life, and induced on my loved ones burns through me like a nuclear bomb as it detonates. Knowing I am the common denominator of all the agony, I know I can't entertain these miserable thought too long without throwing myself into a severe depression. I end my conversation shortly after with the twins and say goodnight. Time to get some rest. I have a busy day tomorrow.

DAY 6

I can't believe it! I thought I would be out of lucky breaks by now for sure, but it just so happens that the newspaper is in need of a pressman. One of their employees just quit a week ago and they had just barely placed an ad for the job opening. Everything keeps lining up for me even more though. The press boss, Ed, used to work at the same newspaper I did back in my hometown so we both worked with a lot of the same people. I think that solidified his decision to hire me. I can't believe it! What luck! Maybe there is a God and maybe he is looking down on me and wanting me to succeed after all?

Ed is a great guy and helps me out tremendously with the bits and pieces I've chosen to disclose to him about my situation. I explained that I don't have a vehicle or a Driver's License and next week he offers to help me get back on my feet. I paint my situation to sound like I am just moving here to relocate for a change of scenery and completely downplay my real situation. Better to avoid that mess. Ed invites me over to his home to eat dinner with him and his wife this weekend. I can't believe how things have turned around for me already. I came to St. George on a whim with no real plan in place and a week later I have a full-time job and a place to stay. Speaking of places to stay, my employer offers to cover my expenses living in a hotel for a few weeks until I can get into a more stable living situation. It's not as nice as the last hotel but my employer in only interested in the cheaper weekly rate.

Although I am in no place to complain about the living accommodations my employer has chosen, I'm not so sure about some of the tenants staying here. I know I have no room to talk, but I seem like a clean-cut schoolboy compared to some of the company I've seen around here Yesterday, a co-worker of mine was joking about all the drug activity that takes place at the hotel I'm staying in. He referred to it as the "Spun-Time Inn." You see, if a person has been using meth, they would be considered "spun" or "spun out." He was implying that the hotel I am staying at is a meth hotspot. Obviously, I just laughed at his joke. If only he as well as my employer knew my reasons for being uncomfortable in that environment. More things to hide, more things to have to ignore in order for me to stay clean. I can't reveal anything of my past to my new co-worker friend this early in the game. The stakes are too high. With the new knowledge he provides about my current housing situation, it leaves me standing on shaky ground. I don't want to come off as ungrateful by requesting a hotel change from my boss, but I just don't feel safe at the Fun Time Inn. Especially because I know I am my own worst enemy.

I am in no position to complain. Being the new guy at work, requesting a change could cause me to be labeled as the needy guy who complains all the time. That could be hazardous to my employment. What could I even say anyway? "Hey I was wondering if I could move to a different motel because I heard there were people using drugs there?" In return, they would probably state the obvious: "Hey Dustin, did you know people use drugs in every hotel on earth?" How could I respond to that? The only way out of this is to tell them my past and I just can't do that. I can't incriminate myself like that. My co-workers will shun me and treat me like the scum I am if they knew the real me and what I was capable of. They will look for a reason to fire me. I have seen it all too many times in the workplace. I don't want that to happen to me, but on the other hand, I don't want to be living under the same roof as active drug addicts either. I guess I will do everything I can to ignore the other tenants at the hotel and stay as far away from them as possible. I just don't see another viable option.

DAY 12

Ed is a man of his word. He and his wife have me over for dinner tonight. They are such a nice couple and they both treat me very well. His wife's cooking is wonderful and it is a relaxing environment compared to what I am usually around. I don't remember the last time I have eaten a home cooked meal. I know I never have with two people that only two weeks prior were complete strangers to me.

The next day, Ed drives me to the DMV and pays for my Driver's License to be reinstated. Afterwards, he takes me to a mechanic shop that is owned by a friend of his. There are two vehicles parked in the lot in the front of the building. One is a tiny economy car that probably gets 300 mpg and the other is a full sized Ford Bronco that gets about 6 mpg. Ed asks me which one I prefer. Both vehicles are older models. They are equally dinged up as well as equally operational. Of course I choose the gas hog that rides like an M-1 tank. It isn't my "addict-mind" or my small penis that chose the much larger, less economical vehicle but rather because I am an American guy. Ed talks with his mechanic friend and works out a deal to purchase the gas-guzzler for $1,500. In return, I agree to pay Ed monthly payments of $100 until I pay it off. After we leave the shop, Ed takes me to get the truck licensed and insured. He pays for that too noting that I don't owe him anything. I am now legally driving a 1989 full sized Ford Bronco. I don't know what makes total strangers feel like helping me out. I guess there might just be more good people out there than selfish screwballs like me.

Now that my withdrawals are really tapering off, I am starting to feel like myself again. Luckily for me, I only had a few rough days where I felt pretty sick. I was able to get through them and didn't have much issue with sleeping which was nice. Usually when I come off heroin or other opiates I can't sleep for almost two weeks. This time I had woken up a few days in a cold sweat but other than that, it had been fairly mild. I keep thinking how glad I am that I left Utah County when I did or I would still be getting high. Maybe I would be dead.

DAY 17

On my day off, I decide to drive out to visit Judd and Jed. While I am there, I attempt to cut my own hair. It has been a while since I have had a haircut so

I decide I should try to trim it back some so I don't look like such a dingy wild man. I need a a more clean-cut look about me for my new life. It's off to a great start and I want my appearance to match. Jed and Judd can't stop laughing as they watch me try to cut it myself while looking in the mirror. By the time I finish, it doesn't look all that bad. Jed has a CR-250 dirt bike. He is rebuilding it and it is currently in pieces in his bedroom for some reason. I have never seen someone rebuild a dirt bike in a bedroom. That cracks me up for a good 20 minutes. It feels so good to interact with people and live my life without any thought or hint of drugs. It feels good to find joy and humor in real life.

Everything about Judd and Jed's place is awesome. Their home is more of a cabin. It sits on 20 acres of rolling hills comprised of sagebrush, old volcanoes, and deep red rock cliffs. Dirt trails thread across their land, crisscrossing and zigzagging in every direction. I am in awe at the beauty of this area. I had no idea St. George sat in a volcanic field. This is the first time I have stood next to a cinder cone. It is amazing. That's another perk to being sober. Not only am I finding fulfillment in normal relationships with others, but I notice and appreciate the beauty all around me. When I am using, I see nothing but a black tunnel that only has one entrance. The further I go into the tunnel, the darker everything around me becomes. Now there is light. So much beautiful light.

Since things are starting to look up for me and I have been staying sober, my mom and dad decide to make a trip down to visit me and bring me a few necessities. Even though I am working, I have only received one paycheck that only has two days worth of pay on it so I am getting financially behind even with all the help from people. I made a phone call a few days ago to update them on how wonderful things were going for me. By the end of the conversation, they realized I didn't have much of anything. No food or snacks, no toothbrush, toothpaste, or hairbrush, none of the basic things that you need for everyday living. I had lived without those things for so long, I had grown accustomed to not having those kinds of supplies on hand. Anything of value I had acquired was sitting in one of a handful of pawnshops near my hometown. Knowing I can't survive on bars of hotel soap and travel-sized bottles of cheap shampoo, my parents offer to bring me some basic supplies. It is a 3-1/2 hour drive for them, but I am grateful they are willing to come. I am excited to have the opportunity to see them, and even more so, to prove to them that I am not wasting the love, energy, patience, and resources they have invested in me. I can't wait for them to see all that I have accomplished while I've been here. Getting and maintaining a job, finding a car, getting my license reinstated. My accomplishments just make me feel good about myself once again. There is nothing more self-gratifying than achieving that which you've set out to do.

When my parents arrive, they unload several boxes from my dad's pick-up truck. The boxes are full of things to make my life more relaxing and enjoyable – starting with a whole bunch of yummy snacks and foods. They've also brought me a portable boom box to listen to CDs, shampoo, conditioner, soap, some dishes and plastic utensils, a carton of Marlboros, new socks and briefs, a couple new T-shirts and my old CD case from high school that has sat in their basement for years. After carrying all the boxes into my hotel room and going through all the miscellaneous items, my parents and I just sit in my room and have a nice conversation. They only stay a few hours but the time I spend with them gives me a nice boost to continue my quest. After they leave, I listen to Under the Sun by 3 Doors Down. In that moment I am completely happy. True and unpolluted serenity has entered my life once again.

DAY 24

I have been doing meth now for two days and feel like complete crap. So much has changed in the last week since my parents visited. I was smoking a cigarette outside my hotel room after work when a guy came out of the room adjacent to mine. We started talking and by the end of our conversation I was in his room smoking meth with him and his girlfriend. I don't know why I stayed. The state of the cramped hotel room was not alluring – if anything, it was alarming. There are three to four people who stay in the room. The man who pays for the room never comes outside. I had never seen him until the guy who first started talking to me brought me inside. The meth host man just lies on a mattress that has been pulled off the bed and placed in a corner at the back of the room. He is shirtless, overweight, and smelly just lying there in his own filth like Jabba the Hut. I don't plan on going back to that room again. I felt odd and out of place.

I have no explanation for why I caved – especially so easily. I didn't feel drug cravings or any other weaknesses. I wasn't sad or angry or upset. It just happened. I went along with it because I am an addict. That's what addicts do.

Addiction doesn't rest. Addiction doesn't sleep. Addiction doesn't die. When addiction is left stagnant it lifts weights and work out on a Bow-Flex. It bulks up doing crunches, curls and squats. Power lifting and building itself stronger and meaner than ever before. This time, it would prove to be just that.

On my third day of using meth, I want out. I am starting to see my life crumble as I become more lax and despondent at work. I keep having visual images of myself as a methed out Jabba the Hut. It is a disturbing visual. I decide the best thing I can do is wean myself off the hard meth with some heroin, my old friend. My next-door neighbor knows a heroin regular and within 6 hours I am introduced to Daniel. Daniel shoots up heroin and cocaine every day. He works for an air conditioning company here in St. George and he always finds time to make the 2 hour and 20 minute drive to Las Vegas to hook up with his dealer. We make arrangements for him to start taking me with him when he goes. It works out well because I work graveyards. He works during the day but because he is an installer, he drives a company vehicle and is out and about all day. That gives us enough time to make the trip to Las Vegas before I have to be to work. The sick irony in all of this is that I moved away from my hometown because I wanted to get away from drugs. On top of that, I had been making hour-long trips almost everyday to my dealer to pick up my heroin. That wasn't an easy task. Now that I am in St. George, I have to drive more than twice that far to get my fix.

The long car drive gives me plenty of time to think. I am baffled. I never realized the drug community was so omnipresent wherever you are. You can't move away from it no matter how far you run. I figured there would be plenty of drug action in Las Vegas with its transient, global pull and vices that are flaunted on every billboard and stage. I never imagined the small town in Southern Utah I thought would be my starting over point, my get-my-life-back-point, would be just as much of a pitfall as my hometown. Before I acquired my drug addiction, I had even taken a trip to St. George with a friend of mine. It was spring break weekend and not once did I suspect anyone in the entire city to be using drugs. I definitely never thought I would be back in the same town let alone a low-life hiding in the shadows of the town with my drugs. I am right in the thick of the drug commerce of St. George now. I can slowly feel the town closing in around me. I am starting to feel trapped here and I don't know what to do.

DAY 40

The felonious crowd I have been hanging around has dropped my morale even lower than before I arrived in this town. I called in sick to work on Friday because I was coming off heroin and I physically couldn't have worked. Not only was it a Friday, but it was payday. I knew I needed my check to afford more heroin, so I stopped by the warehouse to pick up my paycheck. Surely my boss would understand. Even if you're sick, you still need to buy things. My boss was upset that I had left him in a bind, so he claimed he was too busy to go into the office to grab my check. Of course, his response upset me. I was getting sicker by the minute and I needed more heroin. Knowing he was standing his ground, I call the main Human Resources Department and ask them to issue me another check due to the circumstances. Of course the HR department calls Ed and bring him up to speed on the situation. Ed is furious. He fires me on the spot and asks me to surrender the Bronco he helped me purchase within 24 hours. Now I have no job, no vehicle, and one less good friend.

To further complicate my life, I've missed my rendezvous with Daniel, so he travels to Vegas solo. I have $600 from my paycheck, no vehicle, and no heroin. I have to come up with a plan to get to Vegas.

I become ever so clever and resourceful when drugs are my motivation. I seize any and every opportunity and usually everything aligns for me somehow or another. I ride my bike to a nearby gas station and seen a woman pumping gas. As I approach her, I notice she has a young daughter sitting in the back seat. I decide to proposition the woman anyway.

"Excuse me. I had a huge favor to ask of you," I say softly.

"Um, okay. What is it?" she replies a little uncomfortably.

"Well, I need to get to Las Vegas to pick up my paycheck. The problem is I don't have any way to get there. If you gave me a ride, I will fill your tank and give you $50 cash." I can tell right away she needs the money and is considering the offer.

"Well, okay. Sure, I'll help you out with that," she says with an extended hand and we shake.

Obviously, there will be no check in Las Vegas awaiting my arrival. That is only a prop I use to sell my chicanery. Filling her gas tank and handing her the $50, I open the passenger door and we are on our way to Las Vegas.

When we get to Vegas, I have to really think on my toes to complete my lie and make it into a smooth transaction of picking up my supposed paycheck. I tell my driver I need to contact my "boss." I stop at a payphone and call my dealer. My dealer tells me where to meet him, so I direct my driver near the rendezvous point. Once we are within walking distance, I allow my driver to park and tell her I will just walk to meet my "boss." I guess since she has already been paid, she doesn't care and just wants to be done with it so she can get back. I hop out of the car and walk to the meeting point, conveniently out of view of my driver. I wait for my dealer, collect my heroin, hand over some cash, and head back to my driver. The hardest part is not to be able to shoot up immediately. I have to endure and almost 2 hour and 30 minute drive back. Since I've already paid my driver, she doesn't care to see my "paycheck" as proof of my story. I guess the proof is that I returned and didn't just disappear somewhere in Vegas.

Once I see how easy this is for me to pull off, I continue to ask strangers for rides to Las Vegas. Of course I can't afford to travel to Vegas daily now to obtain heroin since my job is no more, but every time I scrape enough money together, I make the trip.

My ride-hitching tactic comes to an abrupt halt when I use it on the wrong group of people. My last Vegas trip to score heroin is with some fellow drug addicts. Instead of picking up a "paycheck" like I tell everyone else, I am en route to secure some "meth" for them. I am really only going there for my heroin and nothing else. Once we arrive in Vegas, the lie becomes more complicated – especially since they are well versed in drug transactions themselves.

I make the call to my dealer from a pay phone. I follow my dealer's instructions and we drive to the rendezvous spot on the deserted outskirts of town. I retrieve my heroin and head back to the car. Once I return without their meth though, things go really bad for me. I come up with some half-hearted excuse, but they don't buy it. Why did I think my lie would work on them? They vow to get their revenge. Their threats pour in from all sides. The next 12 hours are the scariest 12 hours of my life.

The menacing crew traps me in the back seat of the crammed two-door coupe. I have no exit route. The surly man in the front passenger seat is easily 260 pounds. He isn't full of muscle but his shoulders are much wider than his seat and he doesn't have a neck. His shoulders blend in to his head. The man sitting next to me is also much larger than me. Both men wear bandanas but I doubt it has any gang affiliation. It is more just to make them look mean and tough.

I decide I can escape if I play my cards right. I am in no rush to see their threats fulfilled. I tell them I need to go to the bathroom, but they refuse to stop – they're not chancing my escape by letting me out of their sight for a minute. What a mess I have created! I have no way out and it is clear they are not going to show me any mercy. I am scared and intimidated by the three of them. The driver is about my size. All three of them have their ears gaged out; big enough for a thumb to fit through their lobes. I don't feel like I'm in a comfortable enough position to try and fight three guys from the back seat of a car and they definitely have the advantage over me. I figure my best option is to wait it out until we arrive back in St. George. I have no idea where they were taking me.

The gang leader of these men is waiting for our arrival. I recognize his car when we pull into a driveway. I have seen the car driving around town and I remember it distinctively. It had limo tinted windows so I have never been able to see who was driving the car but it was the only Jet black Mustang with a red pin stripe around town. It is dark by the time we arrive in St. George and we make so many turns that within minutes I am completely lost. I am starting to think that I am about to find out whom the mystery driver of the Mustang is.

We park in the driveway near the mustang and the two bigger men get out of the car. The bigger one yanks me roughly out of the back seat. I am a rag doll to his brawn. He clamps his hand on my arm and drags me around the stately home into the backyard. I am shoved through a back door and stumble into the kitchen of the home. It is a nice kitchen. Tidy, well-kept, high-end appliances gleam around us. It is eerily dark inside the home. It seems like dusk has seeped through to the interior of the home where lights should be accenting the hardwood floors and emphasizing the sleek, expensive furniture. A faint glow shines from a room somewhere beyond the kitchen highlighting family pictures hanging on walls, shelving lining the adjacent family room and other neatly placed knick-knacks. This home has far too much of a homemaker's touch to be solely occupied by street thugs.

Walking through the kitchen area, we stop in a large open room, most likely the living room. This room is tidy and nice as well.

"You stay right here!" commands one of the men as he throws me toward a couch by my arm. "Dax wants to see you," he adds as both men disappear down a dark hallway.

Sitting on the couch in fear, I begin to look around. I try to adjust my sight to see through the dimly lit room. Suddenly, a loud noise buzzes from somewhere below me. It sounds like the whiney whir of a chainsaw. The high-pitched rev sends shivers through my body and I instantly begin to perspire. Before I regain my composure, I hear someone walking towards me. Two shadowy silhouettes' appear at the hallway opening. I can't make out any facial features but I can see that they are both men about my size. Through the blackness I hear an audible voice that says, "Dax is going to kill you." I freeze. The thought of being dismembered by a chainsaw makes me nauseous. My knees shake and become weak. I look back at the two shadows standing in the hallway when both men let out a sickening chuckle. I wonder if these people are some kind of weird sadomasochists or serial killers. The sounds echoing from underneath me suddenly stop. I take in a deep breath and exhale slowly. I am relieved the chainsaw has shut off but now I feel unnerved not knowing if that means Dax is heading my way.

3 Hours Later

In a daze, I try to figure out how long I have been sitting in this room. It seems like an eternity. After the chainsaw sound stopped hours ago, I have not heard so much as a squeak or even a footstep. Did everyone leave? What is going on? I don't like the idea of getting up and looking around because I don't know if they are watching me somehow from another room. Not to mention I have counted at least 7 different guys milling around here. Maybe they are just waiting for the right time to kill me. All the stress and uncertainty of the situation, not to mention I haven't eaten or gotten any heroin in days, is draining my energy. I need to make a move. Walking as quietly as I can, I make my way back through the kitchen towards the back door. The knob won't turn. I spin the lock to the left and turn the handle. The door opens inaudibly. Leaving the door open, I walk around to the side of the house and slowly peek around the wall. The driveway is empty – completely empty. How did they leave without me hearing them? Maybe they didn't leave? Maybe they are still here and they want me to attempt an escape. Maybe they went to get more people? I'm not going to wait around to find out. With every ounce of energy I can muster, I sprint off toward freedom putting as much distance between the house and me as I can.

I don't stop running until I am completely spent. I don't know where I am running to and I don't care. I am just relieved to be out of that dreadful house. Worried I will see one of the men drive past me, I cut through alleyways and between sheds as I weave through the rural area. I can see a busy street in the distance. Where am I? Cutting through a grocery store parking lot, I begin to feel a sense of relief. I suddenly recognize where I am. After a quick rest inside the grocery store, I make it back to my hotel. I lock the deadbolt behind me and begin to doctor a blast of heroin. Finally. Within minutes I pass out in the bathroom on the cold linoleum floor.

THE NEXT DAY

Waking up sore and stiff from the cold, hard floor, I stretch attempting to rid my back of all the kinks it has developed from a night on the floor. Knowing I only have a few minutes before the onslaught of withdrawals rip through me, I mix up another shot of the potent powder. I have been surprised to see that the dealers I was introduced to in Vegas were Mexican. I thought that was strange. I wonder if they are in some way connected to the dealers in Utah. I guess it doesn't really matter. The only thing that matters now is I need to get out of Southern Utah before my luck runs out. Last night was not my idea of a good time. If I stay around this town much longer, I am sure to run into that same crowd again. I need to leave here. I need to get back home.

DAY 45

I am too ashamed and embarrassed to tell my family that I have screwed up once again. I don't think they can handle much more of this addiction of mine. I know it eats them up every single day knowing their youngest son is a heroin addict. Just weeks ago they came to visit and everything was going great. Now I have ruined it all. To make matters worse, someone stole my sister's bike. I had locked it up outside my hotel room against a rot iron staircase the other night. When I woke up the next morning, it was gone. If my family finds out I relapsed again, surely they will assume I sold it for drugs.

I call my dad and let him know I am ready to come home. I don't disclose the real reasons I want out of this place. I explain a complex, confusing story to cover my drug involvement and other troubles. Hopefully by now he hasn't put together the obvious equation of Dustin's long, complex excuse + pleading with family for anything = Dustin messed up really bad again and is lying. One thing I forget to take into account is that since my parents think I still have the bike, they make the 250-mile drive in my dad's gas guzzling pick-up truck to have enough room to haul the bike back. Otherwise, they would save themselves $200 worth of fuel and drive the smaller sedan. That's about the price of a new bike. The entire conversation is uncomfortable, but by the end of it, my parents are on their way to get me.

I need out of St. George so bad I don't even have time to score more heroin. It is a long ride home, especially coming off opiates. To prolong my misery, I won't even be able to procure heroin for quite a while once I get home since I haven't been in touch with my dealer in two months. I can't remember his phone number and even if I could, the number would probably be different, or worse, my dealer could have gotten busted. I am able to acquire an OxyContin from one of the tenants staying at the "Spun Time Inn" and that will help get me by until my parents come tomorrow morning. Knowing I will need more heroin or pain killers by midday tomorrow, I will have to figure out a way to travel the 60 miles north to my dealer's area after I get back home.

THE NEXT DAY

My mom and I go to the grocery store to pick up a few things. As we are unloading the cart, I see one of my old friends, Kyle. He spots me too and makes his way through the rows of cars to catch up with me. My mom is not happy that we are getting on so well. She tries to hurry me along, but Kyle and I are quick to make arrangements to meet later at a park. I used to ride almost every day with Kyle in his black Nissan up to Salt Lake City for months. Some days we would make the trip as many as three or four times depending on how much money we came across. My mom is seething on the drive home. She isn't stupid. She knows exactly what we are planning. She knows that Kyle has been my drug transportation in the past. Both she and my dad hate me hanging around my "druggy" friends.

The early evening is pleasantly warm. I have escaped my parents' home – perhaps only to not be allowed back in when I return. My need for more heroin wins out over having warmth, comfortable shelter, and food though. I'll have to take my chances. Kyle should be showing up any minute. The wait on the park bench seems like it is taking forever. I just want my heroin. I hope he hurries. I feel like crap and my nose won't stop running. Once we score our dope, I think I will have Kyle leave me in Salt Lake. At least that way I won't have to keep finding rides up there. I can find a nice spot to build a camp along the railroad tracks. I can't believe how fast my surroundings have changed. I can't believe I am searching for a place to go again. A place to rest. A place to sleep. I can't believe this is my life. What am I? Who am I? I feel so lost and alone. So empty inside.

"Come on! Let's go!" Kyle yells out as his truck screeches to a stop.

"It's about time!" I yell back and jog to his truck, barely shutting the door before he accelerates out of the parking lot.

8

STREET TALK

DALLAS & KRIS

This chapter contains an account from Dustin's mom Kris, as Dallas was ill at the time of publication.

On the street, a balloon of heroin can go for a dime. Translation: "A tenth of a gram of heroin, sold inside a small, deflated balloon weighing slightly more than a Cheerio, costs $10." Unlike a regular economy based on the principles of supply and demand, the drug economy and pricing is strictly based on what is most popular in a given area and what an addict is willing to pay for a fix at any given moment based on their desperation. In comparison, street value for a single 7.5 mg prescription Percocet is $7 to $10. Prescription drugs are usually crushed into a powder then sniffed up the nose, or liquefied and injected with a needle. The irony of this is that a drug user can locate a street drug such as heroin much easier than he or she can locate a prescription medication such as Lortab, Endocet, Percocet or some of the high-end prescription drugs like Oxycodone, Morphine, or Xanax.

Understanding the street value of these drugs directly correlates with their availability. Just like basic economics, the more available a product, typically the lower the price. So we see that our prescription drug monitoring system is working to some degree. If Oxycodone, Morphine, Lortab, Endocet, and Percocet were as available as heroin and meth, this dying world we now live in would perhaps already be dead.

Through Dustin's experiences, we learn more about the illegal drug economy. The potency, purity, and form a drug comes in vacillates depending on the area in which you purchase it. Dustin noted a major difference from his Utah heroin compared to his Las Vegas heroin. In Utah, Dustin could buy heroin in $10 increments, but it was less potent and rarely in powder form. His Vegas heroin was much more potent and sold in its pure, light-brown powder form costing him twice as much. Because it was so much more potent though, it increased his tolerance for the drug and left him lower than low when he came off his high. This left his drug-crippled mind and body needing more and more. We had no idea his decision to move to St. George would cost him so much in recovery.

AUGUST 2005

Dustin proposed yet another scheme to us to break free from his addictions. This time, he felt that relocation was the answer to all his woes. He explained that moving far enough away would distance him from the drug traffic and the familiar sights and sounds of his routines. Since he couldn't remove all the cues that triggered his cravings, he decided removing himself from the situation was the next best option. Indeed it seemed like one of his more logical plans to me.

Although I was eager to support Dustin, my husband looked at this latest plan with more practical skepticism. Dallas and I were beyond the point of recognizing Dustin's truths from his lies. We had lost the ability to distinguish which story – or part of a story – was him talking and which parts were the drugs talking. We decided it sounded too good to be true. Why would this plan be any different? Why would this idea prove more truth than lie?

Dustin had honed many practical skills in order to feed his addiction. The varieties of deception are unlimited to an addict and only become apparent to those affected by them once they realize how they have been duped once again. One particular deceptive ability came in the form of manipulation. Dustin developed quite the knack for playing off of different family members at any given time. He could get me alone and somehow through his words, tears, his pretend remorse, his false penitence, I would become his pawn.

Being thus turned, I would act on his behalf in defending him before my own husband even to the convincing of supporting Dustin in some manner. We all became means to an end for him. He could focus in on each of our soft spots for him and manipulate them like none other.

It was at this particular time of his addiction that Dustin once again tugged at my heartstrings until, as his mother, I succumbed. I felt pity and compassion as only a mother can, that my son – my baby, needed my help once again no matter the cost. Which is saying something because at that point, Dustin's drug repercussions had already cost us $20,000 and counting. At other times, Dustin would play his dad, knowing that Dallas would then soften me up and talk me into driving him to another drug run to get another fix because he couldn't stand to watch Dustin be heroin sick: hot and cold sweats, chills, nausea, total body aches, malaise, and stiffness.

Dustin was clean when he told us his latest plan to escape to Southern Utah. We could tell because he could actually look us in the eyes. He wasn't shaking. He didn't have the false air of infallibility about him that he often emitted when he was high. There are so many emotions on the spectrum of being high that it can be difficult to figure out which are related and which are not. There are the highs, the lows, the withdrawals, and the in-betweens. When your child or other loved one has learned to disguise it so well, it can be challenging to distinguish their own true temperament. "Normal" has suddenly become abnormal because you see them on drugs more often than not. We assume Dustin was typically clean when he chose to interact with us. Otherwise, he was hiding in some shadow somewhere avoiding us and reality.

With Dustin's assumed sobriety already in place, his sincere desire to obtain employment, stay sober, and reclaim his life, how could I as his mother not cheer him on? I was all for this plan. I felt like I could even breathe a sigh of relief once he was on his way if not only for the fact that this would keep him far enough away to be unable to pawn our possessions for his drug money.

Even though I was eager to support Dustin and celebrate his assumed success at finally breaking free from his addictions, part of me still worried he would fail. I wanted to protect him as I had when he was a young boy. A part of me wanted to keep him within reach so I could watch his every step. What I hoped would be his every success I soon realized was merely just his every failure. It was becoming painful to see my grown son failing so drastically each time he dragged himself out of the gutter. I wanted to be there to help drag him out each time.

My brother has been in law enforcement for many years. Knowing of our struggles with Dustin, he persistently told me to let the law handle Dustin. "This drug addiction is bigger than you and Dallas. By always being there for him, it just enables Dustin to continue his evil practice. If you don't let him go entirely, he will end up in an alley somewhere dead from an overdose, or killed by a dealer that he tried to double-cross in order to procure his daily drugs."

His reasoning seemed harsh to me. How could he know what we experienced? How could he know of our ups and downs and lower downs each time Dustin fell? How could he expect me as Dustin's mother to really just let him go? Dustin is my son – my youngest son even. When am I done being his mother? Don't I have to try to help with everything Dustin asks of me? If I don't, doesn't that make me a bad mother? "Tough love," my brother said to us over and over. Dallas and I were so confused. Our hearts would tell us one thing, and reality would tell us another. And so, we let him go. He would take the leap venturing off into the wide world far from home on the Greyhound bus at 5 pm that evening.

Dallas and I wanted to tell Dustin goodbye. We knew he only had his sister's bike for transportation and most likely no money, so we withdrew all we had left until payday: $40 from an ATM. Hopefully he could buy himself some food with the money until he got situated with the job he was hoping to acquire in St. George.

We pulled up to the bus station. Seeing his tiny frame from afar was enough to set me off crying as I thought of how helpless and alone he was. Dallas handed him the cash and said his goodbye. Then it was my turn. As I hugged him a little more tightly and longer than usual, I noticed he was just skin and bones. The drugs had taken a toll on his frame. This set my mind racing in a flurry of doubts. *What did this mother do wrong in raising this child? What could I have done differently to avoid this terrible monster taking hold of my own flesh and blood?* I felt an uneasiness wash over me about the whole thing, but was still hoping for the best. Dustin disappeared into the bus depot to purchase his one-way ticket. We watched and waited from the parking lot to see that he really did get on the bus. He was on his way to what we hoped and prayed was going to be a better life. *Please be drug free, please be sober.* Dustin said he would try. *I love you Dustin, but I hate what you are doing to yourself, and our family.* Both Dallas and I let out a sigh of relief as we drove away, not saying a word to each other the entire drive home.

It had only been a day when we heard from Dustin. He called to ask for our help in acquiring a motel where he could shower, wash his clothes and look presentable while he looked for a job. We didn't ask him how he had paid for his first night, we didn't want to know. This request sounded reasonable, so I called a decent motel in his area and spoke to the proprietor of the motel arranging for two days and two days only for Dustin to stay there. I instructed the gentleman that Dustin was not to use that card number, I told him emphatically to destroy the number and made it clear that the card number was not approved for any other usage. I believed this insistent instruction was necessary to protect ourselves from Dustin coming up with any other stories regarding any other payment. This may seem harsh, but we had been burned too many times before to not protect ourselves with specific, ardent instructions concerning financial matters.

Dustin called us a week later with great news. He had obtained a job at the local newspaper as a pressman as he had planned. He was good at this we knew because Dustin had worked alongside Dallas for many years at our own hometown newspaper. Dallas was proud of Dustin's work in the pressroom.

He had been very meticulous in his work. Dustin had proved himself in the industry wanting to be precise, color matching, and fulfilling any and all aspects of his job. The only area he would fall short in was attendance. Dustin called in "sick" frequently. It wasn't until much later we would learn it was real sickness: dope sickness that cost him his good job and seniority at the newspaper.

Things sounded like they were going well for Dustin in St. George though. Dustin's new boss had been extremely nice to him, helping him obtain his driver's license and a vehicle to get back and forth to work. Dustin was elated at his progress in such a short amount of time. Little did Dustin know, but his new boss, Ed, was Dallas' friend and was reporting to us what was going on in St. George. Ed was giving us frequent updates regarding Dustin's work progress. So when Ed called to let us know about Dustin's firing, we were heartbroken and livid once again. How had he managed to screw this up? When fate had smiled so kindly upon him, why did he mess it up once again? Why couldn't he leave the drugs alone even in such foreign territory? How was it possible that he had still been able to make drug connections so far from home?

After a month and a half, Dustin called to tell us a complicated story with several winding layers that ended up in a request to come back home. We asked Dustin several times if he still had his sisters' bike, to which he assured us he did. You can imagine our disappointment when we arrived to find Dustin's story had changed as he claimed someone just barely stolen the bike from right under him while he was waiting for us to pick him up. To say the least, we were upset. Not only did his lie cost us a couple hundred in extra gas money since we had to drive our truck down instead of our compact car, but we had no reason to believe the bike hadn't been pawned to pay for more drugs. Not much was said during the long ride home.

In our small hometown, it wasn't long before Dustin ran into one of his old drug buddies, which irked me to no end. They found each other in a grocery store parking lot and it seemed as though they were conniving up some plan for the rest of the day. As Dustin left our home that evening, I knew he was reconvening with his old friend and they would be up to no good. Dallas and I warned him about leaving our home. We would not allow him back under our roof this time. We thought that would be enough of an ultimatum. As Dustin walked out the door though, it was clear he wanted drugs over a warm home, food, and his family.

9

ROBBING MAFIA

DUSTIN

OCTOBER 2005

It is a cold night for this time of year. The chill of wind easily blows through my thin, worn out hoodie causing me to shiver. I've lit a small fire inside a rusted coffee can, but it is doing little good to warm my hands. The ground shakes and the loud rumbles from the nearby locomotive creeping down the endless track uncover a memory of an old friend of mine.

I met him a while back while I was up here in Salt Lake. He was standing outside of a local gas station. As I walked out of the station, he asked me for a ride to a pawnshop that was a few miles from where we were, and then to give him a ride home. During our drive to his house, he revealed to me that he was an intravenous drug user. As I ponder this man so much like me in so many ways, I decide to reconnect with him somehow. Hopefully, I can remember where he lives. I know he will have heroin. Maybe I will get lucky and he will give me a place to stay or even a place to hang out for a few days. My fingertips are frozen and starting to go numb. Sleeping in a house would be a whole lot better than this place. Maybe if I find him, he will let me crash at his place for a few nights. In the morning I will take the transit bus downtown and try to find his house.

I never would have supposed that my plan to introduce Max into my life would prove to be a new abyss in my life. It was a time when my already pitch black life witnessed the darkened terror of Satan's lost souls. It was a hell on earth. It would take me places and to levels in my life that only God knows how I am here to tell about it.

121

As the bus circles the train station, I realize how close I am to Max's house. My body pulses with the familiar rush of approaching heroin. It is like I have an internal heroin Geiger counter. The closer I get to my next hit, the more excited my brain becomes. I know this response is astonishing and appalling at the same time. I am not only addicted to heroin, I am addicted to this lifestyle. There is something about being homeless and trying to find heroin that is extremely addicting. There is so much thrill of uncertainty. So much pleasure in finding the only thing I truly seek. This drug has not only gotten hold of me physically and mentally, it has turned me into its slave.

As heroin's puppet, I board the commuter train and catch myself staring at a woman and her child. *How does this lady go about her day without using heroin?* The thought captivates me. I continue to spin it in circles. I have forgotten what life is like without heroin. It has long since evaporated from my memory. Life without heroin is unfathomable. I try to feel sorrow. I try to feel grief. It's not there. I am completely detached. My eyes look right through the woman, I feel nothing. Piece by piece, I feel the person inside me turn cold and black. My soul is dying; I don't even care.

The commuter train pulls me back to reality as it comes to a jerky stop. I stand to exit and try to catch my bearings. Exiting the train, I recall the bar across the street and begin to walk out of the parking lot and head east towards the main road. As I approach a baseball field, my surroundings look familiar and by memory I recall his apartment two houses down. I begin to doubt my decision to show up unannounced. What if he gets crazy and pulls a gun on me? I don't know what people are capable of and I don't know this guy well enough to just show up at his front step. I bury that fear with the hope of heroin and proceed to the side door. I look around me nervous of being watched as I knock on the makeshift screen door. The reverberation of the screen door sends chills through my body. I see a frail, evil looking lady peer through the curtain that covers the window in the door. She just stares at me. I give my friendliest smile but there is no change of expression on her worn face. She finally cracks open the door.

"Yes?" she grumbles.

"I know your son. I was just in town and thought I would stop by," I smile again willing her to trust me. It works because she gingerly opens the door.

"He's, he's in his room. It's back there," the woman stutters and points the direction down the dim entry.

As I walk toward the sounds of muffled television, I am taken aback by the syringes lying haphazardly on the kitchen table. There are makeshift crack pipes and bloody napkins strewn across the kitchen counter. I don't know why this blatant display of paraphernalia makes me feel so uncomfortable – me of all people – who hasn't shown a sign of a conscience for months.

The bathroom is at the back of the hallway. His door is to the right of the bathroom. As I turn the corner, I peek into the bathroom. Dried blood and used needles fill the sink. I stare in disbelief not entirely sure what to make of the scenario in front of me. I can't act frightened or uncomfortable or they would grow suspicious. I shrug off the repulsion that meets my eyes with every glance around the room. The door swings open from the weight of my knock. Max sits on the ground with his legs bent up in front of him. I quickly survey the room. He's leaning against the foot of his bed, trying to administer heroin into a vein. He has looped a tourniquet around his arm and with a syringe in his mouth he looks up at me.

"Hey man, what's up?" he says nonchalantly.

"Not too much. I was just in the neighborhood so I figured I'd stop by."

"Good to see you again. Hey you wouldn't want to go to 7-11 with me would you? I got to drop off a couple balloons of heroin to a buddy of mine."

"Sure, I'll go with you."

"Okay," he says.

I can sense his frustration as he tries to find a vein in his arm that has not yet collapsed. I have never seen track marks like his. His arms look like they had been beaten with a baseball bat. I can see a large open wound where an abscess has eaten his flesh. There is blood dripping down to his elbow as he pulls the needle out and tries another spot. He then grabs the syringe like a butcher knife and plunges it into his arm repeatedly yelling "You son of a bitch!" The needle buries itself deeper into his flesh with every stab. After piercing himself repeatedly, the needle gives way to bone and breaks off inside his arm. He throws the used syringe against the wall in annoyance. I stand, still in the doorway, speechless. I forgot to blink as I watch him mutilate his body. I am in complete shock. I have never seen anything like this before. What is left of my moral compass is triggered at this sight and starts swaying in misdirection. Suddenly, I remember myself when I was 7 years old. I was camping with my family and throwing a softball in an open meadow with my father. It feels like it was a lifetime ago. I chew on the unattainable carefree bliss and happiness I experienced with my family during those simple times of youth, knowing I can never feel that again. The memory quickly dissipates as I snap back to reality. Knowing I must continue with my plan, I brace myself for what's to come.

Four Days Later

I have been staying at Max's house for the past few days and today I asked him if I could move in with him. Being this close to the heroin has made my withdrawals much less frequent and painful. Another benefit: I haven't had to sleep under a shredded tarp or find an abandoned, secluded field to sleep in.

I'm not here all that much during the day. I spend a lot of time trying to acquire things for Max in exchange for drugs. I think that is the main reason Max agreed to let me live here for now. He wants random stuff, so I steal it for him. I am fine with that. As long as I have a roof over my head and I don't have to experience withdrawals, he can ask me to steal as much weird crap as he wants.

The time I am here, I focus on ignoring what goes on. I must numb myself to placate my heroin craving. If I allow the awful happenings to bother me, I might mess up my sweet addict setup. Max's mom and grandma both live here too. His mom's name is Betty and she also uses heroin. Betty was the lady who answered the door the day I arrived. She goes out during the day panhandling for money. She also has some clientele that will come over at different hours and pay her for sexual favors. I have already noticed the regulars. They knock on the side door and ask for her. Betty meets them and they go downstairs into the room where I sleep. The only thing in my small room is a dirty, stained mattress, an old sleeping bag, and miscellaneous drug paraphernalia scattered about. I don't sleep on the mattress. It makes me sick to think about what takes place on it so I just lay directly on the floor. Betty has a friend named Susan who comes over often. She shoots up heroin too. Susan is married and her husband doesn't know that she uses. She also turns tricks here to supply her addiction. Betty and Susan trade off with different men. I see these men walk in and I don't know if I'm more ashamed of them or myself. It's almost like we acknowledge each other without trying to pass judgment. Deep inside I am sickened.

As for the grandma, she lies on a bed in the front room all day. She has health issues that immobilize her. Mel is a sweet old lady. She seems to care about me because she keeps asking me if I am doing drugs with her daughter and grandson. I lie to her every time she asks. I don't know why I can't tell her the truth. It's not as if it matters. She's just an old lady who is stuck here – like me. Maybe I don't tell her because I am worried she will want me to leave. Or maybe deep down, I just don't want to disappoint her. Of all the people I know I've disappointed, I can't figure out why my head thinks it matters if she is disappointed in me too. Obviously Betty and Max don't care, but I have to hold on to the small hope that maybe I'm not at their level – yet.

I feel so bad for Mel. She needs help administering her insulin and she can't get up to use her portable toilet by herself. I heard her calling for Betty yesterday and after being frustrated that her daughter didn't answer her cry for help, she started screaming and yelling. Finally, Betty came in with a syringe in her hand. I watched as she told Mel she needed to give her some insulin. I could see the syringe. It was not insulin. The cylinder on the syringe was full of something dark brown: heroin. Betty stuck the needle into Mel's arm and pushed the plunger. Within 30 seconds, Mel passed out. "That should shut her up," Betty snickered. I felt the cold wind off her body as she walked past. I was horror struck by what I had just witnessed.

Since I am but a fly on the wall to these awful scenarios, I find myself shooting up more just to numb myself to it all. I don't want to have to accept what I am becoming, what I am. It's easier to just shoot up on cocaine, heroin, or both to deaden any sense of ethical right or wrong that registers in my mind. It is too late for me to escape. I have no way out, I am too far in. What is left of my soul is lost and broken beyond compare. Better to abandon any hope of change. Hope is a word I have deleted.

Two Months Later

Max and I sit at his kitchen table passing a crack pipe around with a guy named Jackal. As the early evening fades into darkness, we just sit and stare at each other, contemplating our morning plans. Although Max has a good setup with the Mexicans delivering our dope to his door, Max wants more. He wants to get enough heroin and cocaine so that he can sell it himself. He figures this will be the best way he can sustain the demon within him.

The problem with Max becoming a dealer is that he uses more dope than all of us combined. If he starts dealing, I know I can get my morning fix from him and I won't have to try and hustle money while I am in withdrawals. There is nothing worse than having to roam busy city streets while you are dope sick. I will be his right-hand man in his operation, so that means I will get first pick, after him, of the supply. Considering this pro, I decide to go along with his plan.

For Max to be a competitive dealer, we decide we need to rob a rival group of Mexican dealers to get a head start on business. I volunteer to be the one

who carries the gun. I was raised by a hunter and know how to handle guns.
Jackal will drive me to the rendezvous point. Jackal is a 55-year-old friend of
Max's who claims to have been in and out of prison most of his life. Judging
by the tattoos that blanket the majority of his body, I am inclined to believe
him. Max agreed to let Jackal move in with us if we pull off the robbery
successfully. The biggest perk of the successful swindle is that he and I will
both get a generous supply of drugs for free.

There is something about Jackal that doesn't sit well with me. As I inhale
from the same crack pipe as him, I try to figure out why he seems so weird. I
am not sure what it is, I just have a strange feeling about him. He creeps me
out. I'm not scared of him, he just seems capable of bad things – worse than
even I can delineate. When I get that kind of feeling about someone, I am
seldom wrong. The idea of having him live at Max's in the room adjacent to
mine makes me uneasy. Knowing we have to pull off a successful robbery
together in order to get the reward, I keep my ill feelings about him to myself
and just keep passing the pipe around.

The anticipation is eating through me but I do my best to hold my
composure. The crack has my heart beating so hard and loud I worry the
others can hear it. I have never pointed a gun at anyone and I am scared. It is
too late. We made a pact that our heist is happening in the morning no matter
what.

"So," Jackal breaks the silence. "Tomorrow morning we call up the
Mexicans and meet them on Twenty-first Street." He matter-of-factly reviews
our plan and hands me a 45-caliber pistol.

We agree in a stoned haze and break from the table to go about our
evening. I walk downstairs to my room and sit on the floor against the wall
with the gun in my lap. The cold steel of the chamber whirs smoothly as I
spin it. The barrel is only long enough for me to be accurate at a short
distance. The trigger squeezes effortlessly. So easy to kill. I contemplate life
but not in a way I have ever viewed it before. Typically, when I have thought
of taking my own life, it has been mixed with so much emotion: fear, sorrow,

regret. I try to force myself to feel those sentiments now, but I find they escape me. The only thing I feel for is the insatiable want for more heroin, cocaine, something. It is enough of a desire to make me suppress the other thoughts vying for consideration in my mind: *Why did I offer to do this? What if there is more than one Mexican in the car? What if Jackal leaves me hanging?* It's going to be dangerous. I might die. I might kill someone. *I don't care.* If I don't go through as the gunman, I won't get a share of the drugs and I desperately need them. The questions bombard me, swirling in and out of my mind, racing. I am so full of doubt and fear that I'm nauseous and weak. I decide that all these thoughts are making this too much for me to deal with. The rush of crack cocaine is unnerving and I need to calm down. I decide to do another shot of heroin. Within 3 minutes, I feel the weight of the gun slip off my leg and as the heroin streams through my blood, my eyes begin to close and my heartbeat slows to a sluggish rhythm.

THE NEXT MORNING

I wake up against the wall in an uncomfortable slouching position. I see the light peeking through the hole in the curtains, sneaking into my room. The light beckons in a chilling whisper, "It's almost time." I force my stiff body into an upright position and make my way to Max's room.

"Max, can I get a shot of heroin from you before I go do this? I don't want to do it sick," I plead.

"Sure," he says. "Come on in." His assurance strengthens my weakened mind.

I take my supplies back downstairs where Jackal is making up his morning shot. I go over next to him and start prepping mine.

"You ready for this?" I shudder.

"Yeah, are you?" he responds with a glare.

"As ready as I'll ever be."

After I inject myself, I feel my doubts fade away. I am bulletproof and ready for whatever anyone throws at me. I go back upstairs and wait for

Jackal. I'm watching the clock and I hear every tick of the second hand like it's a loud bang. Nothing else enters my thoughts other than the sound of the clock.

"Hey Max, give them a call. We're ready!" Jackal yells from the basement.

"Okay," Max yells back.

Hearing him say that sends a cold chill through my body. It's time. I grab my coat and head to the car. It's not cold enough for this heavy jacket but I need somewhere to conceal the pistol when I get out of the car. My heart starts to beat a steadier pace as we back the car out of the driveway. We are completely silent driving to the meeting point. No music. No talking. Just the barely audible sound of burning cigarettes.

We pull into the parking lot on Twenty-first Street and circle around to the far east side that is entirely vacant. I step out of the car and watch as Jackal pulls across the street and parks behind a large shed. I feel nervous and my palms are sweating. I have never carried a weapon with these intentions before. I decide to sit on a curb in the middle of the parking lot that borders some shrubs and large pieces of wet bark. A blue Ford Taurus with a missing hubcap and a faded yellow sticker in the back window pulls slowly into the parking lot. *This is it.* The driver spots me and circles around. He pulls into a parking stall about 25 feet away from me. As I stand up and walk to his car, I notice that he is alone. What a relief. I begin to breathe easy and calm down some knowing I only have to rob one person. I squeeze my left arm against my side keeping the long barreled gun from flipping out of my coat. As I approach his car, I try to keep the left side of my body blocked from his view without being too obvious. I open the door and get in.

"How many you want?" his thick Mexican accent slurs his words.

I reach inside my coat with my right hand and pull the pistol out. I cock the hammer and point it right at his face.

"Give me everything you got! Heroin, Cocaine, money! Everything! Give it to me or I will blow your head off!" I scream.

Could he tell I would never really shoot him? I just had to stay tough and crazy. If he were to call my bluff right now I would be in big trouble. There weren't any bullets in the gun. I was just hoping that my threat was believable and that I would walk away with what I needed.

"Okay! Okay! Jus don't shoot me man!" he stutters frantically gathering the goods. "Here, here! Take every-ting!"

"Give me your cell phone too!"

I shove all the money and drugs in my coat pockets as fast as I can. He hands me his phone and I jump out of his car. I run across the street and head back behind the shed were Jackal is parked. I throw the cell phone against the ground as hard as I can and I watch it shatter.

"Go! Go! Go!" I yell.

"Did you get it all?" Jackal asks in concern.

"Yeah, I took everything. His money, his dope, and his cell phone. Let's get out of here man in case someone saw me."

The ride home is much different than the ride there. We laugh and celebrate as if our favorite football team has just won the Super Bowl. I had taken one for the team. Now Jackal will move in with us and help us find clientele for Max's newly acquired business and I will have a never-ending supply of heroin at my fingertips. Jackal and I will be the drug runners. Whenever someone wants dope, we will be the ones who deliver it.

It didn't take long for us to have people calling and showing up at the house at all hours of the night. Within three weeks we had over 100 customers. Max's business had grown and was proving to be very profitable. It was nice not having to hustle everyday for money. But I knew all good things would eventually come to an end. Especially since my view of "good things" were illegal and incredibly harmful to myself personally and the community at large. The tensions between Max, Jackal, and I started building from the broken promises and unfair dealings to the trivial arguments and the drugs that would come up missing. It was only a matter of time before something had to give.

9

AND SO GOES THE SOUL

DALLAS

OCTOBER 2005

We had no idea where Dustin was during this time. We suspected he was surviving on the fringe of society and not hearing one thing or another from him during this time tore me up inside and wreaked havoc on Dustin's mother's emotional state. We could only hope that no news was good news, and good news in this situation was that of being alive. As I wondered what had become of my son, my mind reviewed my past interactions with him during some of our most turbulent times. Maybe it was less painful to not see him or know of his whereabouts.

Have you ever felt like you have talked directly to Satan himself? Reflecting back on many experiences speaking with Dustin, often in his panicked "I'm-ready-to-come-clean" phases, I now know that I had in fact NOT been talking or listening to Dustin, but rather exchanging words with the Devil himself.

I have looked into the very face of an individual our family had come to identify as one of our own. But, beneath this recognizable exterior, I could again hear that poisoned cadence in my son's voice. The one true mainstay that had come to serve as a warning and a validation that Satan was alive and well. The adversary had once again found sanctuary within our family structure.

There are several specific time frames our family had absolutely no idea of our son's whereabouts, nor could we assume anything good was going to come from whatever he was doing there. By this same token, Dustin's mother and I could only guess that these activities were purely of an illegal nature.

Setting these types of thoughts and emotions aside, the two of us would anxiously await word from our son. Had he found a safe place to stay? Where was he? Was he okay?

I had not known until our collaboration in writing this book the full extent of Dustin's hideous lifestyle nor of the horrifying events and numerous life-threatening situations he had not only witnessed but also, with great hesitation, now shares with the world.

As my son, my wife, and I continue to share, exchange, and bear witness to the many situations, circumstances, and hardships for which we all suffered during Dustin's life on the streets, I still find myself in awe and in total disbelief. My wife and I had not raised Dustin, nor any of our children, to think it acceptable to lie, cheat, or steal. So, I can't help but ask myself how can any individual (more importantly, a person of my own flesh and blood) be capable of finding happiness in this world based on evilness and wrongdoing?

Sadly enough, I have come to realize that for most addicts, not having a bed to sleep on or food to eat is only a secondary concern when reviewing each day's list of priorities. Obviously, if you recall my son's comments, an addict's priority list and daily schedule begins and ends with a syringe in one hand and drugs in the other.

There is no remorse, second thought, sadness or even trace of a conscience for what they do or how they live. Even more heartbreaking, is the fact that at one point Dustin admits he found excitement in the very thought of being hooked up. Dustin adds that deep in the trenches of his addiction he found an appeal to the spontaneity of living on the streets and the adventure of finding ways to satisfy his heroin lust.

While preparing our individual thoughts regarding this specific time frame in my son's life, I couldn't help but ask him whether there was ever a guilt or fear issue in his daily process of deceit and theft.

"You know Dad, it's really hard for me to look back at some of the horrible things that I was doing," Dustin confided to me during one of our many conversations. "I have to admit that at the time I was using, nothing mattered. As an addict, you don't care what it takes to get your fix and you definitely don't have a conscience. It's like I, the addict, receive this letter or invitation to go out and get wasted every day," Dustin added with tears of embarrassment rolling down his cheeks.

As I contemplated what my son had said, it came to my mind that addiction knows no boundaries and has no target demographic. Addiction knows not of your wealth or success nor does it only visit the young and helpless, but will seek out the old and the poor alike.

And, what about this invitation? Perhaps you or one of your family members has already received such a letter. I imagine it resembling the following:

(image on the next page)

My dearest friend,

I am writing you because you are important to me. Any time you need me, I will be there for you. All I ask is that you extend your arm to anything else that may come your way in this relationship.

You and I have become good friends and that is why I love to see you cry when I am not always with you. You have dedicated your old life in exchange for our devout friendship- and for that I owe you a lifetime of close connection and an endless devotion to our binary growth. Your depression seems to bring us even closer together. Don't forget that while your entire family pushed you out, I stood right by your side.

Although you did not know it, I was there when you were feeling sorry for yourself. I am glad you turned to me in your time of greatest need. You must admit we have a lot of fun together. I darn near laughed out loud when you and I stole your family's car. Do you recall how happy you and I were after robbing that convenience store?

I think that from now on, I am going to be with you from the time you wake up until the time you go to bed at night. How's that sound?

Did you know that you and I overdosed last night? I heard you almost died. I will make sure that I am there for you when you get out of the hospital.

By the way, if you do die, will you tell me someone else I can get close to?

Yours truly,
Your Addiction To Drugs

10

The Raid

Dustin

February 2006

J ackal and I have been helping Max with his business for about 2 months now and my tolerance to drugs has greatly increased. I am using about $200 to $250 in cocaine and heroin a day now. I've noticed that Max is starting to use more drugs than he sells. He makes up for that by shorting me more and more.

This past week I have been going to hardware stores and stealing whatever Max wants to help supply my addiction. If he wants a lawn mower or a chainsaw, I get it for him. It's getting easier the more times I shoplift. I find a newer looking receipt in the parking lot and put it in my pocket. I go to the garden shop, pick out the nicest floor model lawn mower and start pushing it towards the exit doors. I take the receipt in one hand and almost parade it like a flag as I exit the doors. I don't worry about the alarm going off because it has only gone off a couple times on me. When it did I just kept walking. One other time it had gone off, a lady called out to me but I continued to walk away like I didn't hear her. I think she was too timid to try and pursue me any further. I am going to get Max a gas powered leaf blower today. Jackal is bothered because I get things for Max and not for him. That doesn't make much sense because Jackal has never done anything for me and it's not like I owe him anything. He came up to me the other day and told me I'd better start bringing things home for him and Betty. I told him to kiss my ass.

I decide to head to a local thrift store to see what I can pick up there. As I meander the aisles of useless junk and hidden, scuffed up treasures, I think

about my earlier conversation with Jackal. For some reason I feel bad for
what I said to him. I decide to steal a few movies and a couple of baseball
caps. Maybe that will calm him down and keep him off my case. I make my
way back to the house with my finds and head down the shabby, dimly lit
stairs to Jackal's room. I pause at the bottom of the stairs listening to Jackal
talking to someone in his bedroom. I walk across the hall to his room and
show him what I interpret as my peace offering. He stares at the stuff, then
looks at me strangely with a contorted, angry smirk ripping across his ugly
face. He grabs the offering from me without so much as a "thanks."

Whatever, I think. *He's so messed up.* I ignore his lack of gratitude, turn and
go back into my bedroom.

I didn't even hear him walk up. I was bent over picking up my sleeping bag
when Jackal ran up from behind me and punched me in the side of the head. I
was startled, but not in any pain from the blow. It knocked me off balance
and before I could get to my feet he swung his fist again and popped me in
the mouth. I felt my lip start to swell as my tooth cut a small gash. Jackal is
right on top of me – his foul breath snorting angrily as he spits out his words.

"You bring me home this shit? Who do you think I am?" he rages.

"You ungrateful jerk. Nothing is good enough for you is it?" I yell back.
"You touch me again and I will mess you up Jackal!" I say trying to stand up.

Before I can stand up completely I feel another quick blow to my nose. My
eyes start to water and I feel the rage inside me building. One of my legs is
between his so I turn on my side and lock my foot around his ankle and I kick
as hard as I can to the inside of his kneecap. I hear a loud crack. Jackal hits the
ground screaming in pain. As I stand up I notice he is reaching into his
pocket. Before I can deliver another blow, he pulls out a switchblade. I jump
back as he points it in my direction.

"Come on you little pussy!" he says waving the blade.

"Fight me like a man you coward!" I protest.

Jackal hobbles into a standing position favoring his right leg. He begins to
walk towards me and I can see in his eyes that he has morphed into someone

who will kill. His eyes scream that he won't hesitate to stick that knife through my liver. It is like he is looking straight through me. Every second slows as I weigh my options. I have to withdraw. I can't compete with this maniac. An overwhelming anxiety washes over my body as he staggers over to me, trapping me against the wall. I can't get to the door without going through him – or his knife. I wipe the blood off my face with my hand as he approaches.

"You want me to cut off your fingers?!" he says grabbing my hand.

He puts the blade against my thumb and the blade rips my skin. All I can think of is how to get out of this. He pauses and takes the knife away from my thumb. This is my chance. I throw my right elbow across his cheekbone dropping him to the ground. I skirt his crumpled figure and dart out of the room as fast as I can. His shouts ring after me as I bolt to my only possible haven: Max's room.

"Max! Jackal is a psycho!" I panic. "He just tried cutting off my fingers!"

"What? Are you serious?" I can't figure why Max seems so calm and even doubtful. Obviously Jackal is a psycho.

"Keep that bastard away from me!" I demand. This seems enough to make Max get involved.

Max storms out of the room and stands at the top of the stairs, yelling down to Jackal like a mom scolding her kids.

"Jackal! Knock your shit off!" he screams. "You two just stay away from each other!"

Max comes back into the room and hands me a balloon of heroin.

"Here, go do this," he says with a crooked half smile.

"That's it?" I exclaim annoyed that he thinks my brush with a psychotic killer who is practically my roommate can be dismissed so easily.

"Don't worry he won't bother you again and if he does I will kick him out of my house," he says. I don't feel all that reassured, Jackal is a lot closer to me downstairs than Max is upstairs. How will I sleep at night constantly worrying that Jackal will mess me up?

1 Week Later

Jackal hasn't tried to do anything to me yet, but I keep close tabs on him whenever he is within 50 feet of me. Everything seems okay for the most part. Max left Jackal and me in charge of weighing out the dope and packaging it into small water balloons. As I sit staring mechanically at the dope, monotonously weighing, scooping, weighing, wrapping, my thoughts start churning. Max told me he would give me my share of dope after we finish preparing it for his buyers. He told me the same thing yesterday but he only gave me a third of what he promised. It will probably be the same today. Irritation at the whole situation starts brimming throughout my whole body. I am the one making all the runs and putting myself at risk of a long prison sentence. If he doesn't pay me everything he owes me tonight, I will take what is rightfully mine.

Sure enough, after my deliveries that evening, Max doesn't give me what he has promised. I wait for my opportunity while Max is gone and steal a large amount of heroin from his room the next day. I feel like it is rightfully mine to take. I don't have a plan. I take about 600 dollars worth of dope and leave his house.

For four days I roam the streets of Salt Lake with nowhere to go. I don't care about much of anything; I have my dope. When you are strung out, nothing else matters. I have been in zero degree weather before with not much more than a single layer of clothing and as long as I had heroin in my pocket I didn't care. I know I will run out of heroin soon. I know I have to make things right with Max. When I left, Jackal was left doing the drug running alone and I know he can't keep up with the demand. Max won't help; he thinks he is above running the errands. He sees himself as a king on a throne who watches his peasants cultivate his empire.

I can see the business falling behind from my safe distance on the street. After being gone a couple of days, Jackal falls behind with the deliveries so people just start showing up at Max's door for their dope. The amount of traffic at that house is staggering. It reminds me of the gas pumps at a popular snack mart. One car pulls out and two more pull in. Had I known this caused suspicion to the local task force, I never would have returned.

It has been four days though and now I am out of dope. I guess I should go back and fix things with Max. He needs me too much to be too angry. Plus, it was his fault for overpromising and underpaying me. As I approach Max's street I begin to wonder if this is such a good idea. I continue walking until I am two houses away. As I get closer, I see Max sitting on the porch. He looks over at me. I see the anger on his face but I keep walking towards him. When I'm only 10 feet away from him, he stands up, then suddenly charges at me yelling and ranting.

"What the hell? You think you are gonna steal from me?" he yells as he pushes me back with both hands.

"I was sick of you saying you would pay me man!" I stammer back defensively. "Look Max, I will pay you back," I blurt out. "I got 90 bucks from a gift card that I just sold. Just give me $20 worth and I'll give you 90 for it."

I can tell instantly he will accept my offer. I'm taking a $70 loss but I need a steady connection and a place to crash so I'm more than willing to make a deal with him.

"Yeah okay," he says. "But if you ever screw me again, that's it man..." he trails off and shakes his head in warning.

As we approach the house I notice a security camera hanging above the porch light.

"When did you install that?" I ask pointing at the camera.

"There are two more around front," he says. "All the traffic that has been coming here has me worried. I installed them yesterday. There are video monitors in my room so I can watch who is coming and going."

We walk into the house. We get to his room and he hands me two balloons of heroin and I hand over the cash. Relief starts to wash over me – I can't believe this went over so well. I really didn't know what to expect. I had never seen Max lose his temper on another person. I figured since he was capable of stabbing his forearm repeatedly with a needle, he probably wouldn't hesitate to stick one in the side of my head either. It is a morbid thought that makes me shutter but only reminds me of my other long-lost friend: Jackal. I'm sure he'll have a few choice words for me. The good news is I have somewhere to stay again and I am on speaking terms with my dealer.

I go back downstairs so I can do a shot of heroin. I get out my supplies and start getting it ready. My thoughts are at ease again and I am about ready to numb myself to the outside world. I am not happy but I am smiling. I feel more relaxed now that I got through to Max. I don't plan on biting the hand that feeds me again. After I prepare my fix, I put the rest of my heroin in the inside brim of my baseball hat. I keep it here often. It is convenient, close, and easy to tell if it is still there or not. I continue up the stairs and decide to sit on the couch in the living room. I look over at Mel. She is asleep. My body starts to feel the effect of walking the streets the past few days and my body is hit with a sudden rush of lethargy. Within two minutes I slouch over and fall asleep.

A loud bang wakes me up. I am disoriented, startled, and confused. My heart quickly changes to a swift hard thump and I am frozen in shock. I watch as the front door gets smashed through. The hinges are ripped off the doorframe and a loud voice booms through the entire house.

"Freeze! This is the police! Put your hands were we can see them! Get on the ground! Get on the ground!"

The rough texture of old stained carpet scratches against my cheek as two officers slam me to the floor. They tell me to put my arms behind my back as if I had an option. One officer buries his knee between my shoulder blades as he twists my arms behind me and bends my wrists at 90-degree angles. I am completely immobilized and can't breathe. The musty carpet wafts stronger and stronger through my nose.

Once we are all detained, the officers take us outside and begin to speak with us. They don't separate us, which I find strange. One officer starts talking to Jackal first. I can't believe what I am hearing Jackal say. He is talking like he has Down syndrome or a serious handicap. But I am equally impressed at how well he plays the part. Had I not known him, I would have thought he really had the thought process of a handicapped individual. Unfortunately for Jackal, the officers are pretty sure they knew who he is and aren't buying his story. They don't laugh at his act due to the false authenticity of it. Two cops grab Jackal and place him in the back seat of the running patrol car and then walk back up to Max and me. One of the officers ask for my information. I know I have at least 10 warrants out for my arrest right now, maybe more. I am too afraid to go to jail knowing how bad my withdrawals will be. The officer demands my name again. Without thinking, I blurt out the first name that I can think: "Kenny John."

Kenny is my older, much more responsible brother. He has a wife, children, a home, a business, and is a respective member of society. He always introduces me as "the better looking brother" when in fact, I look like an anorexic Kevin Bacon.

The cops run my alias and when it comes back clean they move on to Max. They found a gun in Max's room. The same gun I used to hold the Mexican dealer at gunpoint. The officers make a deal with us. If we tell them Jackal's real name, they will charge Jackal with the gun and let us go free. I rack my brain to dig up Jackal's real name, but realize I have never known him by any name other than "Jackal." Max speaks up quickly divulging the guarded name to my relief. There is no hesitation in his voice. I look over at Jackal in the patrol car and I can see that he knows he is going away for a long time. He must have a rap sheet longer than I imagined. Relief floods over me not having Jackal in the picture anymore. He has always been too unstable and a borderline psychopath. I have never trusted or liked him in the least bit. I was constantly worried that one day I would wake up to him plunging a fork into the side of my face. Max and I later discover that Jackal had been on parole in California and was on the run.

The officers' stand true to their word and after a short conversation with Max and me, they hop into their patrol units and speed away. We stand outside and watch as the police cars disappear. I can smell a difference in the air. It is more crisp and refreshing. I have dodged yet another bullet and I have a new appreciation for my freedom. I can feel my heart beat slowing almost to a normal, steady rhythm. The feeling of escaping the law once again is energizing. This feeling fades quickly and within a week of the incident, I start to feel more and more empty inside. I have already been completely hollowed out by my addiction but this is something turning my blackened heart into a heavy granite slab inside my chest.

Every second I sit in Max's house I feel it washing over me. My lifestyle is finally tearing me apart. Many times during the midst of my addiction-mired life, I would have these moments of brief clarity when deep within myself I would say, *This is NOT who I am!* However, this time it is something more. Something much more powerful. Through the numbness of the heroin and cocaine rushing through my veins, I feel the weight of what I have become trumping my dope-driven body.

The good and the evil inside my soul are at war against each other. It is a violent battle ripping my soul in two. It seems like my soul, and all the components that make it up are wearing heavy armor and wielding swords. They are charging toward an overpowering opponent, knowing they will lose, but determined to die trying to free themselves. As a last resort to save my own life, I watch my soul, my freedom, and my life running full speed towards the shadows of death. With failure no longer an option, the outnumbered infantry run into the indirect firing of the trebuchets' enormous flying boulders; killing dozens of warriors per massive blast. Thousands of fiery arrows blaze across the night sky stabbing through plated armor mercilessly and tirelessly. I watch as more of my men are pierced and scorched to their death. With dozens of torsion-powered machines and unlimited numbers of keen archers, I hear my demons echo laughter inside me. It reverberates through me until it hits bone. I know I don't stand much of a chance. I know right then, if I do come out of this battle sober and alive, it's going to be one hell of a fight! I can't endure this fight alone any longer. I have to get around people who love and care about me. I am really wishing I were home with my family again. Being at Max's is taking out of me what little I had left. I feel like I am in a snow globe that is slowly filling with water. Soon, I will be shaken and knocked off my feet and tossed in a swirling vortex unable to land, unable to breathe.

I have to leave Max's house. I am spiritually and mentally depleted. I need the comfort and love that only comes from my family. I must contact them. I hope they will allow me back into their lives. Something has to change. If I can't crawl out of this mess I will die. My soul is already jeopardized, I can't continue this much longer.

1 0

BEHIND THE SCENES

DALLAS

I knew the textbook definition of addiction. My family and I had heard stories – rumors really – of horrendous, far-off evils and the great lengths that addicts went to in order to keep their drug lust satisfied. We had even seen the direct results of addiction in the rubble of our son's ruined life. Yet somehow, we didn't really know how serious a disease addiction is. We figured if we could just get Dustin over the physical withdrawal hurdle, Dustin would magically revert to the old Dustin we used to know. We assumed his career ambitions would return and his desire to have a family and settle down would trump his wild fling with drugs. We couldn't figure out what we were doing wrong, and now our son had been absent in our lives for months and we could only wonder what he was involved in. We did not realize that addiction is not just a matter of willpower, but a full on debilitating mental illness.

Because of our own ignorance, my wife and I and the rest of our family, continued to "help" Dustin whenever he would surface. At least, we thought that's what we were doing: helping. In some ways, the love that we continually showed him was indeed a help as it gave Dustin something to hold onto in his darkest hours – like his time he spent living with his friend Max in what seems like to me a twisted, parallel universe to the real world of society. After only now hearing so many details of Dustin's affairs in these periods, I can conclude that to be a more effective intervener, you must understand what you are dealing with. While it may be impossible to know the exact extent to which your loved one is involved, you can start to piece together clues to form a rough guesstimate. In order to form an accurate approximation you should learn everything you can about the world of drugs that your loved one has succumbed to and how they function in it. Having a basic working knowledge of this will allow you to no longer remain naïve to where your loved one is disappearing to. While I can hardly recommend you go to the lengths my wife and I did at times, there is a multiplicity of resources available to educate yourself on the drug world on the Internet. For now, please start with my observations of the drug underworld.

Through my experiences with Dustin, I have come to learn that there are a number of people involved in a drug hook up. First, there are the suppliers. These are the faceless, often nameless shadows that obscure their identity at all costs typically working through a vast network of underlings. They supervise the supply and availability of illicit substances from their origination specializing in one drug or a variety of drugs. Suppliers are the stalk of the drug problem. For any plant species to thrive, it must produce seeds.

Drug users – the victims – become the seeds of the "drug plant." Users are the tiny seeds proliferating indefinitely, growing wherever they are planted: a rave, a bachelor's party, a skateboard park, around a campfire. There are hundreds of thousands of users and they keep the entire drug industry alive and thriving thanks to a fallacy in the human brain we call addiction.

While not much is publicly known about the supplier side, evidence of the user side is all too obvious in today's world. The direct connection from the user to the supplier is the dealer.

Dealers are the roots of the drug problem plant. There are thousands of dealers constantly digging their roots deeper to find more and more avenues to push the drugs in. If they hit clay, they re-route their growth to the side until they grow far enough to continue their downward journey, digging ever deeper to keep their profits piling up and to keep the suppliers healthy and ever expanding above ground. Dealers often employ drug pushers – the marketing department for the drug economy. In an attempt to build their own clientele, dealers either employ pushers to hand out free samples to teens and college kids or do it themselves.

Dealers almost always employ drug runners to make the actual deliveries. Dealers themselves like to limit the amount of transactions they personally participate in. It is too risky to be caught in public making an exchange. They know too much – their supplier could be compromised, and no dealer wants to fall into ill grace with a powerful supplier.

Many of today's drug dealers have specific hours in which they operate. According to my son, most dealers open and close their business at a specific time, the same way any respectable shopping venue would conduct itself. If you miss their office hours, basically your appointment, you go home withdrawing and empty handed.

There are two main different kinds of dealers. There are open dealers and closed dealers. Closed dealers limit their market to supplying only friends and acquaintances. These dealers often sell larger amounts to individual buyers and often specialize in one drug. These dealers rely on word-of-mouth alone and don't actively advertise for business. These dealers prefer a more secure location, often removed in a quiet area, to limit general suspicion from normal society leading to legal intervention.

Dealers running an open market are essentially open to the public. They often advertise with street markings, graffiti codes, or other telltale drug signs letting drug seekers know they are in the right neighborhood. I am amazed at how quickly Dustin can tell if he's in a drug neighborhood just from looking around. My untrained eye can glance around an area and assume it's just a little run-down, whereas Dustin can be standing beside me and from his highly trained drug-seeking senses, interpret several signs that point out right where drugs can be procured, what kinds are available, and when. Addicts can find drug sources through these "billboards" or word-of-mouth in every city in this country just from making some key observations about their surroundings and talking to the right people.

Open markets with stranger-to-stranger sales tend to operate closer to where people naturally congregate so that customer traffic is maximized and normal law-abiding citizens mask any illegal activity. Prime locations might include shopping centers, office buildings, schools, parks, or apartment complexes. Multiple entrance and escape routes are critical to open market dealers. They don't want to become bogged down if something starts looking suspicious or if they feel they are being closed in on. From my understanding, Dustin was typically dealing with an open market dealer, although during his time in Salt Lake living with Max, he had an inside track to that open market.

11

ENTRAPMENT

DUSTIN

MAY 2006

After a long, emotional phone conversation with my father about my "moment of clarity" at Max's house, I think my father is beginning to see and feel the honesty despite my highly addicted and altered ego. We came to an agreement on the rules at their house if they were to allow me back. We also spoke about how I plan on getting sober.

Unfortunately, I didn't have any answers for him. I truly wanted my old life back and I was running out of energy. My family and I were all hanging on to one microscopic particle of hope, but at least I had rediscovered that hope.

Because I have been defeated time and time again, I know in my heart that I am destined to fail. I told my father a sugarcoated version of my mind's battle scene because I didn't want to alarm him. I also didn't want to diminish any hope he still might have for my sobriety. I felt I had proven to myself and to everyone else in my life that I am in fact a useless heroin addict.

I know my family wants the old Dustin back. The weighted pit in my stomach is telling me that the old Dustin might never come back. I can't admit that out loud because it hurts too much. Knowing I will most likely die from a self-inflicted drug injection makes me hate myself even more. I can't grasp what I have become. Each time I have gotten clean, there has always been a common thought that reels through my mind over and over: "I will never go through that again!" Unfortunately, that would last about all of a day or two and I would sure enough find myself "going through that again."

My inability to establish continuous sobriety has been the most baffling life lesson for my family and for me. How could I not stay sober after seeing first-hand and having such a literal knowledge of what drugs do to my life and to my family? That is the question of all questions. That question is perhaps the driving nucleus of this entire book: how do you defeat addiction?

Millions of people are continually baffled by this question. The answer that makes the most sense to me is that my addiction is stronger than me. This concept has been generally acknowledged by thousands of addicts. Had I known that fact prior to the "weaning off" idea, my family and I would have known that I would fail 99 percent of the time. Because none of us realized this in the midst of my throws with addiction, everyone, including myself, assumed I just needed to muster the willpower to temper addiction.

Addiction and willpower are in no way connected to one another. Both drug and alcohol addictions are not willpower issues. That is a common, outdated belief based upon individuals wanting to blame the addict. Observing an addict in behavioral therapy leads people to believe it is all a matter of self-control. That is just simply not the case though.

Addiction occurs in a different location in the brain than the self-control area. The mesolimbic dopamine system is the area responsible for addiction. This area of the human brain is not controlled by the conscious mind; therefore, self-control and willpower have nothing to do with staying clean. Like any mental disorder, it cannot be consciously controlled or flipped on and off with a basic desire to stop or change. This is what separates addictions from habits. Addiction is a disease and it must be treated as one.

Even though I did not understand this concept fully at the time, I knew I had to try something different. What I had done in the past had not worked. After a moment of assessment, I had some inspiration. *Maybe if I wean myself off the heroin, I can get through the withdrawals,* I think. Quitting cold turkey has proved itself unsuccessful time and time again so maybe this will work! I know if I can gain my parents support with this plan, I can talk them into driving me up to Salt Lake to get my heroin. I hope that if I tell them they can have full control over monitoring my dosage, they just might agree to my plan.

You may think that I am a crooked little jerk for trying to pull one over on my loving parents. If you are thinking this, I can't blame you for such thoughts. However I would like to add that despite my manipulating lies and deceit, there was never a thought in my head that said "I love screwing over my family" or "I wonder what I can do next to hurt them." At that time, I desperately wanted my idea to work; yet deep inside me, I knew I would probably lose the battle. I started seeing just how powerful my addiction was. Knowing that something was controlling my every move made the "real Dustin" slowly give up over time. I knew I was defeated, but I knew I needed to keep trying. It was quite the predicament mentally and emotionally to be constantly torn between such opposing thoughts. The only thing that absolved my intense feelings of guilt and shame was the same thing that was causing it: heroin! I just wanted out of the life I had made for myself. I was incapable of escape and the demon inside me knew it. He took this opportunity and ran with it.

After I discuss my idea with my parents, I can tell my mother is more willing to accept my proposition. My dad finally accepts, but with much more concern and doubt. The agreement is that my father would drive me up to my dealer this first time. He makes it clear that he will not under any circumstance get out of the car during the transaction and I agree. I know that the dealer will not meet me if I am with a stranger driving a strange car, but I wait until we are moments away from my dealer before I mention that issue.

A couple minutes before the dealer is to drive past, I begin to explain the hang-up we will have with my father being in the vehicle during the transaction. I calculate the time investment we have made of driving an hour to my dealer against my father's desire to remain in the car. If my dad doesn't trust my plan, we've driven all this way for nothing. The only thing for him to do logically is step out of the car briefly while I meet up with my dealer. I explain the simple process to my dad.

"The dealer will drive past us and pull over down the street. I'll follow him in the car, jump out of our car into his, score the heroin, and then drive back to you." With that explanation, my father begrudgingly obliges.

"I'll wait for you over here – hurry up," he adds, not too pleased about any aspect of this predicament.

Just moments later, I spot my dealer pulling around the corner. As he passes, I put the car in gear and merge in behind him. I follow him to a more discrete area. This time, the dealer drives a lot farther than normal. I continue to follow my dealer despite the ironic distance it puts between my father and me. Once my dealer finally pulls off the road, I am relieved. Not only because I am scoring heroin, but also because I know I have to hurry and get back to my worried father.

Had I known there was a fatal shooting a week prior on the same corner where I left my dad, I would have never left him there. The neighborhood had been experiencing a higher volume of delinquency, but I had no way of knowing that at the time. I sped back to the corner where I left my dad standing only to find he had disappeared.

I begin to panic. I park the car haphazardly by the side of the curb and run into the gas station kitty-corner from where we had last spoken. I ask the attendant in the station if he has seen anyone come in recently with my dad's distinguishing physical traits: a handlebar moustache and baseball cap.

"No sir, I have not. I did hear some commotion outside about 10 minutes ago but I didn't think anything of it. Then two cars came flying around this corner right here, tires just a squealin'," he says pointing out the window. "Didn't you hear it?"

"No, no I didn't. I just got here. Umm, thanks for your help sir."

I bolt out the door scared and in a shaken disbelief. *What have I done? What have I thrown my father into?* Tears fill my eyes as I imagine what I could have exposed my father to. Thinking of the worst possible scenario, I run across the street to the car mustering all the composure I can find to cover my panic. Bewildered and worried for my dad, I decide to drive around the block. Before I can turn the car around, I notice a faint silhouette at the end of the block walking towards me. I can't decipher the person's identity because of the streetlamp light behind him, but I had seen that walk before. As I pull onto the road and drive towards the person, my panic turns into joy. I know that walk all too well. It's my father, just in time to sedate my worries once again.

Unfortunately for me, my father is not as happy to see me as I am to see him. There are no tears of joy or hugs that evening in the slums of Salt Lake. The ride home is not a quiet one. Apparently shortly after I left my father on the curb, a couple rowdy teens were racing down the street yelling and cussing at passersby from the window of their car. When my dad saw them being so reckless, he decided to walk to a store around the corner.

Although my apologies were abundant, they were vacant. They had worn out their welcome years ago and the hollow "I'm so sorry" held no sway because even if my emotions were apologetic, it would not change my betrayal in the future. The most painful part of this situation in retrospect was that despite what happened that night and the imminent danger I exposed my dad to, it didn't stop me from having my parents take me many more times to meet up with my dealer. How could I not understand that I was weaker than my addiction at this point?

Knowing I had pushed my father over his limits that night, I knew my parents would not allow me to kick one of them out of their own vehicle again. Despite the pain, distrust and lack of respect I had just shown to my parents, I wouldn't stop there. I knew my mother would be more accepting to drive me if I promised not to make her do what I did to my father on the previous trip to the big city.

My mother becomes my typical heroin chauffer after the scare I gave my dad with the first exchange. Because my family is not as willing to risk their freedom as recklessly as I am mine, I have to fabricate more and more stories to get me to my dealer. My mom and I have made about 15 trips without any hitches. My parents are realizing my drug is not in fact weaning off though. I am still using the same amount, if not more heroin than before. We have another family discussion about my lack of ability to use less heroin. My rides to my dealer are halted for more than a week. I am devastated. I have to come up with another plan.

Asking my parents if they will drive me to Salt Lake again will not be an easy request. They are stung from my failed "weaning" and seem more determined than ever to avoid abetting their criminal son. I know I have to come up with something that makes a whole lot of sense, and more importantly than making sense, it has to be a plan that gives them hope for my sobriety. Then it hits me. I can play up the hope idea big time. What if the sole purpose of the rides to Salt Lake are to get pills that help me quit heroin? That's a great plan, right?

So here's the plan I propose to my family:

I know a guy from Salt Lake that is selling pills. These pills help with heroin withdrawals. They are pretty expensive, but it will be a lot better than me shooting heroin into my arms. They are herbal pills so they are non-addictive. Within 3 to 4 weeks I can be entirely free of heroin! The only issue is Salt Lake is the only place I know where to get these pills. I won't have to go through painful withdrawals anymore and I may soon be completely sober!

Here's the same plan translated in my mind:

I know a guy from Salt Lake that is selling heroin. Before driving to Salt Lake, I will put a handful of random herbal pills into my pocket. Once we get to Salt Lake, I will meet my dealer and act like he gave me herbal pills. If my parents would like to see the pills, I will gladly show them my pre-selected props. I will have purchased heroin instead of herbal pills but no one will know that. I know my parents will eventually see through this as it cannot work forever, but at least I won't have to go through painful withdrawals tonight.

Somehow, my conniving plans to continue the heroin runs work with my parents and my mother agrees to take me to buy the "herbal pills." I think at this point my father has given up on my sobriety. I don't think he believes even one word that comes from my mouth anymore. I'm sure he is just too tired and angry with my addiction and not willing to let it tear him and my mother apart any more than it already has.

2 WEEKS LATER

As my mom and I head up to Salt Lake for another "herbal pill purchase," everything seems to be going as planned. After all, we have made this trip many times now. However, when we get to the call location (a nearby pay phone), my dealer isn't answering his phone. This has happened in the past but not very often. When it would happen, it would make me sick to my stomach. I would wonder if he had gotten busted or if he ran out of heroin and didn't want to answer the phone. It was so bothersome only for one reason: I desperately needed some heroin. I have to find a way to get some heroin before we drove home. But what will I do with my mom in tow?

I know several different meeting places for different dealers and I am willing to ask my mom to go these places. They are random spots like grocery store parking lots and gas stations scattered about the city. After convincing my mother, we drive to a few of the "hotspots." Hours pass without a potential dealer surfacing. Withdrawals start to break through my body and I feel the desperation for a heroin fix increasing quickly.

Finally after 4 hours of driving all over the large city, I spot a man who looks to me like a heroin dealer. He is Mexican and trying extremely hard to look innocent all while sweating bullets and holding a mouthful of heroin and cocaine balloons. So, if you ever happen to pull up next to a car being driven by a happy-go-lucky sweaty squirrel with a mouthful of nuts, it may be a drug dealer. He drives past us real slow and stares at me with a questioning look on his face. He raises his eyebrows as if asking if I need something. I know right then that he is our guy.

"Follow that car mom! Keep up with him and don't lose him!" I blurt anxiously.

"Okay! Okay! Settle down," she hollers at me in disgust.

As the tires of the car squeal against the asphalt, my head sinks into the headrest. I allow my body to freely sink back from the forward gravity as the car lunges forward. I begin to feel relief rushing over me. Before seeing this potential heroin dealer, my body had begun preparing for the worst knowing it would inevitably be in experiencing heavy withdrawals. With the herbal pills rolling around in my pocket, I begin to finger them so I can easily show them to my mother after the real switch takes place: money for heroin. I don't want to have them in the same pocket with my heroin. That would be disastrous trying to fiddle around and only grab the pills and no balloons of heroin. Nonchalantly, I switch the herbal pills into my left pocket. We approach the dealer's bumper, which has just pulled into a newer apartment complex off the main road. Before we are at a full stop, I reach for the door handle and bolt out of the car running towards the dealer's passenger door.

"What you need?" he sputters in broken English.

"Gimme three blacks," I order. Three balloons of heroin are enough to get me by until tomorrow night. I wish I could buy more, but not a dollar of the money is my own. My parents have been "loaning" me the money for most of my runs and $30 is all they could spare this round.

He hands me the three tightly wrapped small red balloons and I jump out of his car. Now that I have the heroin in hand, my withdrawals are completely nonexistent. Re-entering my mother's car again, I slide the balloons into my back pocket. I close the door and see the taillights of the dealer's car go behind one of the apartment buildings. Then glancing in the side-view mirror my body floods in fear. I can hardly believe it. We are suddenly completely surrounded by the DEA: the US Drug Enforcement Administration. Within seconds, the complex parking lot fills with numerous black Suburban SUVs and Black Dodge Chargers. My mother has no idea what is going on. She starts to put the car in reverse to continue on our way, but my shouting interrupts her thought process.

"Oh crap mom, we are busted! They have us surrounded!" Why is this happening now of all times – with my mother in the car?

"Well, what do I do?" she hollers.

"Nothing mom. Let me talk to them. Don't say anything," I answer. *How am I going to get out of this one?*

"But I have a gun under the seat Dustin!" she exclaims as she weighs out the repercussions that could be coming her way. "I just got my concealed weapons permit! I am so screwed Dustin!"

"No you're not mom! Calm down!" I don't know if she can follow my orders, but her panic is mounting, and that will be a dead give away.

"Dustin! You don't understand! I just got my nursing degree and now I am going to prison! How can I calm down?" She is exasperated.

"Listen mom! I will talk to them. I will take care of it okay," I reassure her.

Spotlights and sirens turn the softly lit parking lot into a mid-day arena. With assault rifles drawn, a voice yells for me to step out of the vehicle. I step out of the car with my hands above my head. I am directed to walk backwards towards the blinding spotlights. A deep voiced man probably in his late 40s meets me. The rest of the force keeps their distance except for two men who approach the driver's side of the car where my mom is sitting. The man reaches for my wrist and places my hand behind my back placing one handcuff on, then the other. His mild approach seems odd to me and definitely unexpected. Once the handcuffs are in place, he asks me to turn around. In blue jeans, T-shirt and an unzipped DEA jacket, the man fiddles with his leather-covered credentials that hang from a bead chain, low off his neck. Then from under a perfectly trimmed Tom Selleck moustache I hear him say, "Tell me what's going on here."

Still staring at his federally issued leather-bound identifier, I begin to shakily explain. "Okay look sir, my mother has no idea what's going on okay. I lied to her. I needed a ride here from Utah County to get heroin and I told my mom I needed some bogus herbal pills to help me quit heroin. I got heroin but she thinks I got herbal pills. The pills are in my front left pocket and the heroin is in my back pocket. Please don't allow this to get her into any trouble officer. This is all my fault," I blurt.

"Are you serious?" he asks reaching into my back pocket and looking at me strangely. I guess he hasn't heard this one before.

"Yes I am serious," I assure him. "Please don't tell her I am lying to her. I think she has heard enough lies from me already."

"I am not concerned with that," he says all business. "I am more concerned with the heroin. Is this all you have?" He puts the balloons in his jacket pocket. "Yes. That is it."

"Okay then, get back in with your mom and go home now. I don't want to see you around here again." He lectures me sternly.

"Okay, but one question," I seriously inquire. "Is there any way I could have one of those balloons back? I'm going to be so sick and that is all I have."

"No. That will not happen. Now get in the car and go home before I change the outcome of all this!" he threatens with a piercing stare and a deep furrow in his brow.

On the drive home I feel the disgust my mother has for me emanating throughout the car. Not only should I have shown more concern for what happened, but I also shouldn't have asked if we could have tried another known drug spot after dodging both of our prison sentences. I was more concerned with how to stop my withdrawals than anything else. Nothing deterred me from stopping the pain of withdrawals. I would ask anyone anything and go to whatever lengths I deemed necessary to accomplish my plan. The fact that we still had our freedom only allowed me to continue feeding my addiction. I can't imagine how petrified my mother must have been that night – and all I cared about was getting another fix. I remember saying to her on the drive home, "Now what am I going to do? I have to go all night in withdrawals!"

Once my father found out what had happened, things took another turn for the worse. My parents decided they could no longer allow me to live with them. The herbal pill stunt I had pulled was the straw that broke the camel's back. They had had enough. I had all but destroyed my parent's relationship as well as our entire family dynamic. I had screwed them over for the last time. Having no clean and sober friends who would take me into their home, I knew of only one place to go. Deep inside of me, I didn't want to go back, but the devil that was driving me was my only friend and he was more than pleased with the idea. Once again, I rounded up what little belongings I owned and took the next bus to Salt Lake City. I was on my way back to Max's.

11

Aiding & Abetting

Dallas

May 2006

As parents, my wife and I were willing to go to any length to try to save our youngest boy. It is important to realize that not all individuals or family members will respond to each and every situation in the same manner. You will be surprised to find out just how far you will go and how much you will endure in order to save a loved one from today's lethal drug market.

Several months had passed without word from Dustin. While my wife and I had taken another oath that we would not allow our son to use our home as a refuge ever again, I soon found myself sitting on our front porch next to a bedraggled Dustin.

With heavy tears of sorrow rolling down my son's face, Dustin's thin and worn-out t-shirt began to soak through. As I glanced a bit lower into his lap of skin and bone, his wet and worn out jeans had taken on a perfect match to his faded t-shirt.

Although I had listened to just about every excuse in the addict's playbook, for some reason, I found a strange but conforming belief that only the "truth" had the ability to lay down such a cloudburst of tears.

Rain or no rain, this kid needed my help. What kind of parent could walk away from the damage resulting in this kind of monsoon? I figured if he was in fact being truthful and was starving to find himself again, what kind of parents would simply turn him away due to their own ailing health – which we viewed to be the dehydration of our own mental and physical being much as a result of the stress and worry we exerted in Dustin's behalf.

Having convinced us once again that he was willing to do whatever it took to change his life, Dustin once again committed to stop using. Although this meant he would again be facing several days of painful withdrawals, he promised with a little help from us that he could in fact get clean. Knowing that Dustin had tried to come clean many times before, both my wife and I were hesitant to lend our support. Nevertheless, after several hours of heated discussion between Dustin, my wife and I, it was decided that we would give it another try.

Then Dustin threw in the kicker: "Dad, I know that you and mom have agreed to help me get through this withdrawal period again and I don't want to fail." Dustin's words spilled out shiny and slippery off of his silver tongue but somehow tinged with honesty.

"So what is your point?" came my sharp reply.

"Well, we all know that I've tried this many times before, getting sober and staying clean, but it's never completely worked," Dustin had us paying attention if he had some new light he could shed, some miracle cure that we had overlooked. "I think the biggest reason for my failure has been that I've always tried to stop cold turkey. If you and mom will agree, I'd like to try getting off the heroin a little at a time."

He looked at me. He looked at his mother. He was serious. I couldn't believe it. Maybe I had misunderstood. "So, again - what is your point? What is it that you are saying?" I asked for clarification. It had been a long day and through all the emotional turmoil, I had surely mistaken his brilliant fix-all plan.

"Well... Do you think that you could give me a ride to Salt Lake? If I could just get me enough stuff so that I could gradually work my way off the drugs, then I think that I will be successful this time. It will make my withdrawals a lot less painful. Also, by doing it this way you and mom would have full control over the amount given and when. I know that if you will do this that I can make it," Dustin said with tears rolling down his face.

Sitting across from my son, I found myself in total awe. *Did I just hear what*

I think I heard? My son was asking me to be his transportation so that he could in fact find his next fix. My first reaction was to punch Dustin right in his fricken' mouth for even suggesting such as thing – and the next minute, I somehow found myself sitting at a gas station in South Salt Lake.

Now before placing judgment, know that if you have not had the misfortunes of being placed in this position that you can not say with absolute certainty that you as a parent or loved one would not have done the same.

I know that as you follow along in this book you are going to recognize the redundancy that we continue to go along with our son's pleas for help. While it seems simple or perhaps ridiculous, I assure you, it is not. I am not trying to justify my own stupidity, but rather point out that loved ones of addicts often don't know how to help. They don't know where to turn. They don't know if they are making the wrong move or the right one. Are they enabling the addict by sheltering him or her? Or are they making the addict more mired in addiction by turning their backs to them?

There may not be a right or wrong answer. It is entirely case-by-case, dependent on the individual, their level of addiction, and the family circumstances you find yourself in. You must consider your own mental and emotional health as well as the strain and stability of your family relationships first and foremost. You must consider if there are other children at home who could be influenced and misled by an addict's presence. There are a number of variables that must be weighed out and carefully reasoned with. We have found that the more we know, the more prepared we have been to deal with and recognize our son's self-deprecating habits. Obviously, it took us many years and many failures to learn enough to truly help our son.

I am assuming that many of you don't feel that my wife and I should have repeatedly helped Dustin. Let us consider this scenario and suppose that our family did in fact do nothing to help Dustin:

A family member or perhaps one of your best friends that you love very much is sitting in front of you. In that person's hand is a syringe filled with a deadly poison. It could be heroin, cocaine, meth, or any mind-altering substance. They have tightly tied off the upper part of one of their arms and have now placed the needle into one of several protruding veins. Remember, in this scenario, you are only a witness and can do nothing but sit by and watch. Now, the addicted individual slowly pushes the toxins into their bloodstream. At best, this individual will drop to the floor. After five minutes or perhaps as long as 30, they regain consciousness. Their mind is now mush and for the next several hours this person is completely incoherent and oblivious to his or her surroundings. Having a case of blurred vision would be potentially dangerous or in fact deadly if this individual is allowed to get behind the wheel of a vehicle. What do you do? Oh, you can do nothing, you are not really there. At best, this individual may regain most of his or her faculties but only just prior to having yet another insatiable craving to do it all over again.

In a worse case scenario, the drug in the syringe is pushed directly into the vein: an addict's paradise of unfeeling bliss. The drug has been mixed too strongly or perhaps it is contaminated with rat poison or another deadly filling agent. Within minutes, this individual - your son, your daughter, a friend, your father, your mother – dies.

The fear of truly losing Dustin and never knowing his exact demise or whereabouts is why my wife and I, along with Dustin's siblings and other extended family, have repeatedly found ourselves so willing to help Dustin. We have hope that he can overcome this demon. But he will not do it unconsciously in a gutter in the dead of winter with only snow to bury him.

Before we reach the end of this book, you will learn from our family's experiences that you cannot – no matter how much it hurts – continue to assist or enable the so-called addict. Indeed, Dustin was only saved as we took a more hands-off approach. But I believe it was only successful because of the time and love invested in him that he was able to find the desire to truly overcome. If an addict feels he or she is nothing, worthless, trash, they will never be able to find the inner strength to crave anything other than their next fix. They will never get over that mental hurdle and that is how addicts end up dead instead of recovered.

Looking back on the day I decided to drive Dustin to his dealer, although I knew in my heart it was all wrong, I did it based purely on my love for him and the glimmer of hope I had for his possible recovery. Now, I am not advocating that all who know an addict should be their resource for drug supply, but you must determine in each situation how you can keep your faith in your addict's recovery so they will believe it themselves.

Our family needed to have the real Dustin back in our lives. And so, we found ourselves oblivious to relinquishing that hope and constantly extending our love to him. Sometimes we had had our last straw and he was out. I think that is called "tough love." Sometimes we believed his stories when we shouldn't have. Sometimes we should have been more suspicious, more probing, perhaps set firmer consequences. There are a million ways of second-guessing what we could have or should have done. The fact is, we will never know. All we know is that we loved Dustin and knew – I don't know how we knew – but we knew that Dustin could be Dustin again. While that belief is always enough for everyone, for whatever reasons, it worked for our situation.

As I sat in the gas station parking lot that afternoon waiting for Dustin's dealer to show up, I found myself contemplating my involvement in what was about to take place. Perhaps I was trying to justify my actions, but all I could think about was the past. First and foremost were those days and nights that my wife and I spent fighting, crying, and worrying about whether or not our son was dead or alive. Just hoping that Dustin's face would not appear on the morning or evening news. Indeed, we had watched the news with bated breath during the periods of Dustin's disappearances. As I reviewed these experiences, I came to the conclusion that I needed to put an end to all this turmoil. I had to find a way. Surely there could be something more I could do.

I knew that if I gave up on finding a way out for Dustin his only option would again be to carouse the streets, scavenge for food, and sleep in empty dumpsters. This kind of lifestyle does not bode well for the homeless, especially in winter months when temperatures reach well below freezing. It seems a bit ironic, but much of our son's street time could be blamed on our unwillingness to not let him stay within our own home. We had already allowed Dustin to return home many times, all of which left us paying a stiffer penalty with each consent.

I asked my son several years prior: "Just what is it about Heroin that keeps you going back?" He simply replied: "Heroin puts me in a world where there are no hassles and no problems. You know all those bill collectors out there that are constantly threatening me? They just all melt away. When I'm straight, all I can think about is the pain of my failed marriage. Getting a hit of Heroin removes all of that. It is a place where all of my aches and pains just float away. I guess you could say it seems like a perfect life and one of true euphoria."

And so, Dustin duped both my wife and I into many more heroin runs before we ever wizened up to what addiction really is. In most of the runs that I taxied Dustin to, we would aim to reach the exchange point between 8 pm and 8:30 pm. According to my son, dealers stop pushing by around 9 pm. Only a few minutes prior to reaching our exchange point, my son would always direct me to pull the car over so to make a call from a public phone booth. The phone number is never written down or verbally tossed about. It is kept only in my son's head. It is the phone number to his drug dealer and it is guarded with his life. According to Dustin, that's what it would cost him if the phone number escaped through him: his life.

After making the phone call Dustin would give me instructions to the location we are to drive to and wait. The phone call also informs Dustin as to all the information for recognizing the drug runner: the make, model, year, and color of the car. This waiting period is where things would tend to heat up between Dustin and me. As the so-called taxi, I have no idea who or what I am looking for. All I know is that when Dustin sees the runner drive by, he begins to yell and scream at me: "Get Out! Get out! I've got to catch up to him. He will not make the exchange with you being in the car. Get Out!" With that, I would often be left trying to catch my balance on the curb watching my son speed away in my car.

In each of these exchanges, I would never know whether or not my son would come back or if I would have to call someone to give me a ride home. There have been times where Dustin has left me standing in the cold – sometimes only 18 degrees – for more than an hour. On several of our first trips, I had no idea what to expect and would find myself standing in below freezing temperatures without as much as a thin jacket. I simply hadn't bargained on being evicted from my own, warm car. Despite my fears, each time my son did return with my vehicle – usually with a huge smile all over his face. At this point we would return home before coming back the next day or perhaps the day after.

Although our family will tell you no matter how hard it hurts you cannot continue to enable the so-called addict, often times the fact of the matter is that you feel what you are doing, following the addict's instructions, is the only way to save this individual in the long run. The crucial factor to determine if you are really helping the addict or just enabling the addict is if the individual you are trying to help recognizes he or she has a problem with addiction. If the individual knows there is a problem and they are choosing to ignore it temporarily, but long-term sees themself escaping their addiction, there is hope. If they cannot recognize they do indeed have an addiction no matter the size, you will never again enjoy the individual you once knew.

After acknowledging the problem, an addict can only get clean by overcoming the next two processes. The first challenge is physical. Here the addict experiences extreme fatigue, muscle pain, and many other flu-like symptoms. The simple act of walking or any kind of body movement is almost unbearable. As the withdrawal process continues, the absence of the drug causes cold sweats and hot flashes. According to Dustin, your feel for reality becomes questionable and in some cases your vision may even be impaired. Other ailments included periods of vomiting and severe diarrhea.

The second stage of this terrifying battle to stay clean is more of a mental challenge. While Dustin has proved victorious several times over the physical withdrawal stage, it is here in this second process that most addicts fail, including my son. According to Dustin, the need to experience that "feeling of euphoria" Dustin described resulting from drug intake can be blamed for the failure of most drug-addicted individuals. According to him, the need to find that chemical-induced high will never fully go away. Because drugs disproportionately stimulate the pleasure sensors in the brain, true pleasure is downgraded. Normal joys are disparaged. Simple daily happiness has been depreciated due to the brain's memory of a synthetic bliss that can now never be matched or exceeded by reality. For the addict who truly desires freedom from Satan's "tool of choice," these individuals must somehow find the strength to ignore those promises of ecstasy and enjoyment being offered in the form of addictive substances. Dustin acknowledges that this daily battle persists until you and your aching body finally cave in. And so, it is not necessarily getting clean that is hard, but staying clean once you get there.

Not only did Dustin's plan of gradually withdrawing from Heroin not work, but it left my wife and I feeling stupid and very angry that we had actually enabled our son in getting yet another fix.

The fact that our son was back on the streets and looking for that so-called cool feeling of euphoria took second stage to the anger and self-disappointment that was going through my mind at that particular moment. I needed to be alone. I needed to think.

"Okay, let's just think about this for a minute," I said aloud after parking my car up a nearby canyon. "My son is on Heroin. My wife and I are aware of that fact. He asks for our assistance in getting this drug. We accept! Duh!"

At this point, my exasperation knew no boundary. I felt that we did not deserve these problems, and we had now become accomplices to his crime.

Love is a powerful motive and it makes all of us do crazy things, but the fact of the matter is that not only should our son be in jail, but so should his idiotic, beside-themselves, love-crazed parents!

And that's where my wife, Kris, found herself on that "herbal supplement" run that Dustin just detailed in his last chapter. May the Lord have mercy on us as parents for having so much hope, faith, and stupid trust in our son we wanted to see saved from himself and his addiction. Surely my wife's intentions merit a special blessing for the love she has shown for her drug-crazed son. Kris had just finished her Nursing degree and received her diploma the very afternoon she found herself driving Dustin to pick up his next so-called detox pills. She put her career and her life on that afternoon.

When I asked Kris about her thoughts when five undercover officers surrounded them after pulling into that parking lot, she says she immediately felt that her life had just come to an end. She thought she would lose her Nursing degree, she thought they would impound the car, and that she would be in jail for the rest of her life – all while having no idea that Dustin had again lied regarding his true intentions about that day's drug pick up.

Although I cannot speak for my wife, I can now see in retrospect how stupid and embarrassed we should be for putting our own reputations and lives on the line – be it for love, faith, stupid trust, or anything else in this world.

Our account might have many readers noticing our sheer stupidity with all the undeserving faith we continually invested in Dustin and the hope of his recuperation. Although a betting man might wager that both my wife and I have the word "STUPID" stamped all over our foreheads in caps, in fact, we do not. Instead, I would hope that each of you would try and substitute the word "LOVE."

As you might suspect our attempt to gradually work our son off the Heroin did not work. Although there would be no miracle, we were able to get him through the seven to ten days of painful withdrawals only to lose him to the streets once again within a month's time.

12

STING-OP

DUSTIN

JULY 2006

As the sun sinks below the horizon, the sky fills with loud bursts of neon sparks. The pungent smell of gunpowder fills my nose as I trudge along the uneven sidewalk. The tree roots lift the concrete in broken fragments and weeds grow through the busted walkway. Spent firework casings litter the street. I am headed to a grocery store when the aroma of backyard barbecue hamburgers captures my senses. I imagine every morsel of the toasted sesame seed bun loaded with grilled Angus beef topped with gooey cheddar cheese, a juicy tomato slice, pickles, crisp lettuce and tangy mustard. A Hispanic family launches fireworks and serves up their delicious summer meal oblivious to my atrophied figure lurking beyond the shadows of their backyard fence.

Memories of family festivities flood my degenerated mind. I pick them out and savor them morsel by morsel. Gathering with my family on my dad's fresh-cut grass, his manicured lawn providing a sanctuary for enjoying an array of summertime foods. Throwing the football with my brother and chasing his kids around our backyard. All of us smiling and having a wonderful time. Laughter. Sighs of contentment. Relaxation. Second helpings of dad's macaroni salad and maybe another hot dog or slice of watermelon too. Peace. I skid the memories to a stop, refusing to give myself such false hope. Jerking my mind to the present, I force myself to accept that I will never enjoy those activities with my family again. The pain limps through me. It wants to hurt, but it is too dull to shock me into a definitive emotion.

Perhaps I should call my mom and dad. Seeing all the families celebrating the holidays together makes me miss my family more than I have in a while.

I continue staggering down the street, passing several other happy homes when a human-like silhouette catches my attention. As I draw closer, I begin to see what it is. Behind the metal-barred screen door of the home I am now in front of stands a little boy. Something about this boy keeps my attention. The boy is staring directly at me. With his hands holding the upright bars of the screen door, the idea of a jail cell comes to mind. Thoughts pour into my psyche. Once again, I am mesmerized by a young boy. An unspoken message between us turns this young boy into a much wiser, older man in a young boy's body. I get the sense that he knows something about me that he shouldn't. *Is he a messenger? Is this the same boy I saw that day on the bus? Am I am being prompted?* A cold bolt streaks through me and brings the chill of fear. *Why is this happening to me? What is he trying to tell me? Does he know that I have become a soulless being controlled by heroin? Am I in danger?!* The boy closes his eyes. He begins to shake his head in a slow, back and forth gesture. The hair on the back of my neck stands on end and the electrifying chills pulse through me. I continue to stare at the boy and watch his every move. He finally stops shaking his head back and forth but closes his eyes. He stands there, perfectly still. I can't see anything else but this little boy. My world stops to witness an unspoken message between us. I see nothing but the door and this boy. No noises. No movements. Nothing. My brain closes off to everything but that front door and the mysterious boy who stands behind it. Time stops as the boy stands motionless, eyes closed. Then finally, with a quick movement, the boy opens his eyes. I can't see any color at all. His eyes look like sunken black holes. There is no white in his eyes, just big black spots where his eyes once were. The blackness is much larger than that of an eyeball. It terrifies me. As afraid as I am, I cannot break my gaze from this freakish child. I am immobilized. I blink but he is still there. I close my eyes and rub them with my hands. I look back up at the door and only the cast iron bars remain. The boy is gone.

Shaking off the alarming image of the boy behind the bars, I meander along the sidewalk still in an obvious daze. The brilliant flashes from the fireworks light the sky above me. Loud booms echo in my head as mortars explode in the distance. Before I realize it, I reach the supermarket. Visuals of the boy with black empty eye sockets invade my mind as I enter the store. Something doesn't feel right. Something is definitely wrong with tonight. I am trapped in a surreal world between reality and subconscious. I am a ghost and everyone seems oblivious to my presence. I find the large boxes of fireworks on display in the store. Even though I feel like no one can actually see me, I still scope the area to ensure sure the coast is clear. Through the aching hollow pit in my gut, I know something isn't right. I pick up the large package of fireworks and walk towards the automatic doors where tonight's heroin score awaits my arrival.

That score of heroin is still patiently awaiting my return. Waiting for me to stop by and say hello. I never made it out the doors that firework-filled night. Well, I did make it out the doors but I was wearing nice new shiny bracelets. Some people call them handcuffs. Ironic that for all the felonies I had committed and all the illegal activities that had become my life, I would only begin to regain it from a petty shoplifting violation. At that point in my life, I had truly hit my rock bottom. If I had sunk any lower, I would have been a corpse buried in a box somewhere. I was the kind of addict that would continue to use until I died. This was the turning point in my life. I was incarcerated in the Salt Lake County Correctional Facility from July 23rd 2006 until July 8th 2007 where I was then transported to Utah County Jail to serve my warrants in the Utah County Correctional Facility. I stayed in that jail for 3 weeks and was then released to the streets on July 18th 2007. It was a total of 13 months without my freedom and without a drop of heroin. I used that time without my freedom to reevaluate and rebuild the life that I had totally destroyed. I would slowly rebuild trust and friendships again with my family. While I was incarcerated, I learned things about myself that I never knew. I also found out who I was and what I wanted from my life. Figuring out the cause of my continuous relapsing was the biggest and most important thing of all. After my recovery, learning how to STAY sober started to make perfect sense.

While sitting in the back seat of the patrol car I think of any way possible to avoid the jail sentence I know I will face. I think of any and every way to convince the officer that I am not who he thinks I am. Once the officer pulls me into the jail premises, I try to convince him that I am Kenny John and not Dustin. The officer turns and looks over his shoulder at me and says, "Nice try Dustin. Your father told us exactly who you are."

The lingering stench of damp basement mixed with urine-soaked carpet is making me dry heave. The cold, dim waiting cell is packed like a sardine can. I couldn't even hurl in privacy if I had anything that would come up. The walls are bare except for the layers of thick paint that covers the cinderblocks. Towards the back of the 9x15 foot cell is a sink-toilet combo. The steel toilet juts out from the side of the sink as if it was molded as one piece during manufacturing. A hideous thought begins to form inside me as I connect the pieces of my last phone call home just prior to my arrest. *Is that*

why dad asked for my address when we talked on the phone? Rage boils up to my eyeballs. *Did my parents really turn me in?* Entertaining the thought that my family is the reason for my arrest makes my stomach churn even more than the putrid circumstance I find myself in.

Withdrawals are already starting to take over my body so I know I have to calm down. Anger will not help them subside. The emotional turmoil of my family doing this to me is too much to handle in my poor condition. *I hope I don't have a bad diarrhea attack with all these other inmates in here.* I am terrified. There is no stall. There are no walls to give me any privacy. If I need to use the bathroom, I will just have to do it in front of everyone. In any other situation, this wouldn't be so difficult. The problem is I am coming off of heroin. The cramping and intestinal pain that takes place when detoxing is nothing less than horrifying. Diarrhea will last 5 to 6 days. Being in a tiny cell with a bunch of burly inmates, I sure don't want to be the one making everyone smell my crap. I am terrified.

There are about 25 inmates in this single holding cell and the volume level is deafening. Listening to everyone talk over the top of each other has my nerves completely disheveled. I listen to their ridiculous stories about how much money they make slanging dope and how much meth or cocaine they can do. They brag about how they boss around their women at home and hit them and call them the "C-U-Next-Tuesday" word. I quickly realize that I am one of them because I am a criminal. *I will never become one of them.* Listening to them brag of completely demoralizing things as if they are proud to slap their wife sickens me and begins to enrage me even more than the thought of my parents sending me here. These brutes repulse me. The way they talk, they way they carry on, and worse how proud of their malicious actions they are. I hate being here. I want to get out of here and never come back again. Deep remorse and sadness for what I have done to my life and what I have become rushes over me. Between the cold concrete walls and the rancid smell of urine, I become nauseous again. The onset of withdrawals eases its way to my bones. I shiver. A tear drips down my cheek and I whisper, "If I make it out of here alive, I am never coming back."

I am transported to a concrete and metal cube that will be my home for the next several months. I can see I will have plenty of time to do some deep thinking here. So many emotions that I have not felt for years course through me. I feel true sadness, real remorse, genuine loneliness and anger. I feel like my body is going to quit on me. The intense pain is almost too much for my frail, emaciated form. Knowing I am many days from any sort of relief, I try to keep positive. This proves to be much more difficult than I had hoped. I begin to lose hope. Not sure if I can handle all the obstacles in front of me, I begin to think of an easy way to end it all. I've already heard of many successful inmate suicide stories. This is the second time in my life that I know I could actually take my own life. The thought of jumping off a tall building headfirst seems far less scary than trying to overcome what I have created: a life of complete misery and anguish that bleeds far past my weakened grip.

I begin realizing the amount of damage I have caused; not only to my health and my well-being, but also my friends, colleagues, and my loved ones. The idea of reuniting with my mother and father do not exist. I have ruined any chance of a relationship with my family. They will never want to see me again – and who could blame them? The repeated lies, cheating, and stealing from them has completely demolished any connection for trust there may have been. On the other hand, I don't know if I can ever forgive them for turning me over to the law and landing me here. I have never felt so alone and lost in my life. *What am I? Have I truly turned into a life-long, hardened criminal who lives only to destroy loving relationships and trusted bonds between people? Will I continue to stick needles in my arm when I get out of jail? I've tried to get over this so many times, how will this be any different of an approach? How many times will I go through this? I am worthless. I am nobody. I have dug too deep and I no longer have the strength inside me to find any freedom or happiness. Survival is not even an instinct anymore. All this worry, all this loneliness, all this sadness, it can all go away if I just allow myself to sink. I have been swimming for so many years and I am tired. The boulders I am carrying are pulling me under. The weight is too much for me. I want it to all be over. I am ready to take my own life. It is time to quit swimming. I give up. It is time to end all this misery and heartache for myself, for my family, for everyone.*

At that point in my life, I was ready to call it quits. The combination of the heavy withdrawals mixed with the surfacing emotions I had been running from my entire life was too much for me. I had suppressed my emotions for so many years and when they were finally allowed to emerge, since drugs weren't there to keep suppressing them, they were so jumbled and unstable that I lost all control. When you begin to use drugs, your emotions and your mental state come to a stop. Today, I have the emotional and mental capacity of a 21-year-old. I am 33. My drugs and street time probably make me look much older than that though. I didn't take my own life that painful night in jail. I didn't sleep for the first 12 days in jail thanks to another, and one of the most difficult symptoms of opiate withdrawal. I would sleep for 10 minutes here and 15 minutes there and when I would wake up, I would be in an alarming state of panic, usually drooling profusely and covered in horrible smelling puddles of sweat. I didn't eat for the first 5 days other than a tiny bit of bread and some milk. Everything else I would just throw back up. After 20 days of extreme leg cramping known as restless leg syndrome, cold sweats, insomnia, cold chills, blurred vision, vomiting, and diarrhea, I started to feel somewhat more like a human. I still didn't have any energy and taking a couple laps around the small day room provided for us to recreate in, I would be out of breath and very fatigued. After 30 days in jail, things started to look up for me. I could actually smile again. I started sleeping 4 to 6 hours a night and my vision started to improve.

"Dustin John! You have court!" the intercom screeches.

"Good luck!" my cellmate offers as he slaps my shoulder passing by me.

"I'm here for a while still, but thanks," I respond knowing no amount of luck will change my fortune for the time being.

Being transported to court was always exciting for me. It was a chance to get out of my jail cell and see the outside world again. The sun shines so much brighter when you are in custody. It didn't matter what song was playing in the transport van either. Just the sound of music was enough to brighten the rest of my day. It was these small things I started to notice that began to have so much more meaning than ever before. When I was living on the streets I don't ever recall even looking at the sun let alone taking a second to enjoy its warmth and beauty. I never liked oldies music. Now I am realizing its greatness because oldies music is music, and that is profound to me. It is these small epiphanies through my clean and sober mind that is building my inner strength to succeed and become someone I am proud of, someone my family can be proud of. That reminds me, I should probably write to my family. I haven't written them or spoken with them for almost 3 months. I knew it would be a bad idea if I were to write them too soon. I am actually quite scared to write to them. I am scared of not getting a letter back. I am scared of what they might say if they do write back.

After all my court appearances, I am sentenced to do 365 days in jail without the possibility of early release. Once I accept this and quit fighting against something I can't control, the jail time goes much smoother. I decide to take this time I have and make the best use of it. I apply for the C.A.T.S. Program. This is a 90-day program offered by the jail. It helps inmates learn about themselves and learn about addiction. I take the program very seriously and I also attend every Alcoholics Anonymous and Narcotics Anonymous meeting I can.

I once had a major issue with AA and NA. For years, I believed that counseling – especially in a group therapy format like this – could never benefit me. Counseling was for crazy people, and AA was for complainers. That's just how I viewed them. It took being stuck in jail with little to do to open my mind and try something that I had previously misunderstood.

Throughout these courses, I did a lot of spiritual searching as well as reading spiritual literature. This was the real turning point in my life. These courses help me to build a firm structure underneath my once shaky foundation. It didn't take long to feel the growth and self-achieved happiness that spread throughout my thoughts and feelings. I had finally done it. I had beaten my demons. I knew inside, these feelings were genuine and the strength that I assembled against my enemy, had overpowered the beast. Despite my successes, it took a long while longer to realize that I myself had nothing to do with my victory. Although I had humbled myself and opened up to empowering concepts taught in AA and NA, I found the ability to stay sober and I was given my life back. In challenging my core beliefs, I began to grow. Time and time again I have proven that when I try to take control of my life, I lose all control. The only way I have learned to stay sober and live a happy life is by letting go life's steering wheel ever so slightly. No longer will I insist that I am capable of controlling every aspect in my world. I am but a speck co-existing in a much larger universe. I will always come up against new challenges and I must seek the help to overcome them. That is part of the learning and growing process. The nature of humankind is to learn, adapt, and overcome in order to survive. That is what AA and NA gave me the tools to do.

12

THROWING IN THE TOWEL

DALLAS

JULY 2006

Our family had been fighting this nasty war for years now. I always thought nothing could last forever, but I was beginning to doubt even that rational. Despite our efforts to save the son we once knew, we were losing. More importantly, the thought of losing even one more time left my wife and I emotionally, mentally, physically, and financially exhausted. I remember thinking, "We can't lose him, what more can we do?" We had already crossed the legal boundaries of right and wrong when we allowed ourselves to serve as his transportation to pick up his drugs. Our love for our son and our determination to free him from this world of filth was backfiring. We had done everything we could do except for one thing. We had to let go.

My brother-in-law had spent more than 20 years in law enforcement. I'm sure he has seen and done just about everything. At the time, he was serving as a Probation Officer. In this position, he kept tabs on a long list of ex-convicts. In an effort to ensure that these individuals stay within their legal bounds, each of them is required to report to him each month. He is their leash.

Growing weary of dealing with our situation each and every day for over a decade, Kris and I decided to pursue alternative actions if it could produce any kind of a remedy. We decided to consult Kris' officer brother. We were fortunate to have a family resource to talk with first to test out the waters since we were both so unsure of the legal ramifications that would be imposed on our son. Not only did my wife's brother have the answers we needed, but also we knew he was an individual who cared about us personally as a relative does. Although he had shared his knowledge many times over during the past 10 years of struggling, we as parents did not want to hear what he was telling us. If we wanted to put an end to all this pain and suffering, all we had to do was open our ears to the advice my wife's brother had been so kind to share with us many times over. So, what was his advice?

"If there's a chance for you to get your son back, a couple of things must take place," he told my wife and I as we sat in our living room. "First of all you guys have got to stop trying to help him. Unfortunately, you as parents are too close to this case. You need to let the law help you take care of Dustin. I've looked into Dustin's history," he continued. "Our records show that he currently has a couple of warrants out for his arrest. It would appear that the warrants have to do with retail theft as well as drug possession and drug paraphernalia. With these kinds of charges, the judge could possibly put Dustin behind bars at least a year. Just think about what I am saying. Your boy, although behind bars, would at least have a good warm place to stay and what better way for him to get clean than to serve 12 months or so in jail?

"As I had mentioned earlier, there are two parts to this equation. The second thing that needs to take place in order for Dustin to stand any chance of turning his life around is that he must first hit rock bottom. He has to reach that time in his life where he can no longer continue with life as he knows it. Having to spend 12 months in jail might just be that low point in his life he needs to hit. It could be his ticket to a new life," he finished.

My brother-in-law's comments left me with a hollow spot in my stomach. It was a sickening feeling of betrayal. What my wife's brother was asking us to do was to turn Dustin in; turn him over to the law. How could I do that to my own flesh and blood? How could we help the law put my son in jail... perhaps for as much as a year? Why did Kris' brother think this sounded like such a good idea? Despite the pain of this horrendous hole in my stomach, I knew my wife's brother was giving us some very sound advice. After all, we knew these words were coming from a professional, someone who had been working with issues such as this for many years. The question now was: Would we take his advice? Would we turn Dustin in or would we continue to do things our own way?

Our past strategies had not worked and even though this was going to be one of our toughest decisions we both knew our next play was going to land our son in jail.

First of all, we didn't know a thing as to where our son was staying. Recent calls indicated he was residing with some piece of trash in the west portion of Salt Lake City.

Over the next few days, my conscious began burning a hole in my stomach. I have never made it a habit to lie to my son, but I knew that during our next phone conversation I would be setting him up to take the big fall. I felt this phone call coming much too soon. I didn't feel rectified yet in betraying Dustin.

"Hi Dad," came Dustin's scratchy voice over the pay phone line he was calling from. "How are you and Mom doing? Have you guys got any big plans for the Fourth of July? I guess my friends and I are going to grab some fireworks and set them off on the front yard of our house," Dustin continued the excitement in his voice mounting.

Holding back my tears, I did my best to hide my feelings for what I was planning to do to my son. Not only was he going to have his holiday party ruined, I was about to take his freedoms away for possibly a year or more.

"Where are you at? Who are you staying with?" I asked.

Although Hesitant, Dustin responded, "I'm staying with my friend Max." He then proceeded to tell me the address.

Little did Dustin know that his happy tone and willingness to share his friend's address had just driven the final nail into his own coffin. After a quick call and brief conversation with the police, they now knew where to pick up my son.

Tears began to roll down my face as I realized I had just pulled the trigger on my own flesh and blood. The look on my wife's face told the whole story.

We had just become traitors, something no one could be proud of... or could we?

Over the next few days we waited to hear from a member of the Salt Lake City Law Enforcement. We finally received word of our son's arrest. I would later find out that several law enforcement officers managed to put the cuffs on our son as he was caught stealing fireworks the same evening we had talked on the phone.

Although most of you reading this book would congratulate my wife and I for finally making the right decision, we on the other hand felt a tremendous sadness. It was a painful decision and we faced the outcome of a forever-strained relationship with our son who would spend over a year in jail.

My brother-in-law assured us we had made the proper decision albeit a difficult one. A world without consequences is no world at all, he pointed out. Until there is an equal and opposite reaction to his actions, he will continue to live, and possibly die, in an unbalanced world that he can never escape from or find happiness in. Justice has to be permitted to take effect for mercy to have sway. That is the formula for change and real growth for all of us. Dustin is no different. Until he had time – even though it was a forced time – to be clean and truly think through his life and what he wanted, he could never find the motivation to be anything other than what his addictions told him he was. Despite all of his good intentions, he had to learn how to cope, how to deal, how to live. Unfortunately, he had learned the wrong way to deal with life and it led him on a slippery slope of hard addictions that spiraled him ever downward to feed it. It had become a disease that controlled Dustin to the point that he was no longer Dustin.

Although Dustin's jail time, particularly his withdrawal period, was some of the harshest physical, mental, and emotional turmoil he has ever had to deal with, it did indeed force him to get clean and stay clean for the longest period Dustin had ever known in his adult life. If Dustin would have been sentenced to prison instead of jail, the outcome may have been different. In previous conversations that aided us in writing this book, I have learned that there is quite a difference between jail and prison. Although there are many differences, the simplified distinction is jail is a short-term correctional facility where inmates spend anywhere between hours and days up to five years and prison is a long-term facility holding convicts between 90 days and life. The length of sentencing and severity of the charges are the factors a judge takes into consideration when deciding which facility is best suited for an inmate. Fortunately, Dustin landed in the local jail, which means he wasn't surrounded by as many hardened criminals or getting himself into further trouble behind bars.

In fact, Dustin's jail time accomplished something that our love, disappointment, occasional assistance, and frequent tongue-lashings had never been able to.

Our officer relative, sums it up the best: "Having this happen has really been a blessing and it is now up to Dustin whether he will decide to make the right choice in staying clean."

13

RECOVERY ROAD

DUSTIN

JULY 2007

"J ohn! Roll up!" An omniscient voice shouts over the jail cell speaker. "What?" I think in disbelief. I'm surprised to hear my name, and even more surprised when I see the time. "I can't leave here now! Its almost 1 in the morning! Where will I go? What will I do?"

Leaving the Correctional Facility after almost 13 months was scary to even think about. The only thing I knew was how to find drugs and make friends with all the wrong people. I had nothing. No place to go. No car. No job. My only possession was a small bag full of useless, dingy items that had sat in the bag for over a year. I guess this was it. It was time to give life a final try living in society once again, the way normal people do. I am destined to fail. The odds are stacked against me.

The Correctional Facility I was in doesn't allow inmates to walk out of the jail once released. There is a 12-hour window for the inmate to be picked up by a friend or family member. If unclaimed in that period, a little after midnight an officer drives the inmate about 10 miles away from the facility. No one has come for me. I have no say in where I will be dropped off. My body trembles as we approach the freeway exit that must lead to my drop off. The stench of my year-old, unlaundered street clothes fills the cab and doesn't ease my restlessness. The sensation of my worn out Reeboks perfectly conforming to my feet is a welcome, relaxing feeling through all my anxiety and flashing thoughts of what is yet to come.

The nervousness in my stomach expands as the police cruiser drives on. He seems to be driving deeper and deeper into the "red-light district" of town. Run-down motels known for heavy drug activity are the main buildings along these blocks. The street is busy for this time in the wee early morning hours. Although not crowded with people, it is obvious that the few individuals loitering about are peddlers, drug runners, prostitutes, transients, and the like looking to find their next deal.

Sure enough, the cruiser stops in the middle of this web of temptation and I am truly a free man. I inhale a deep breath of fresh air, savoring the freedom of it. As my lungs expand and the fresh air circulates through my body, I feel invigorated. I begin walking on free ground feeling more and more alive with each step. I am all too aware of my surroundings though. Is this supposed to be the ultimate test? It requires all my mental capacity to ignore the obvious signs that would throw me back to the mercy of my vices. I can't help but wonder if I am some kind of lab rat challenged to navigate my way through a maze without succumbing to my many weaknesses presented on every corner and often in between. Is someone watching me just waiting to throw the handcuffs back on the second I take a misstep into the wrong direction? Or will they wait until I'm pushing a plunger into my arm to throw the irons on? Slightly bewildered at the paradox I find myself walking through, delivered by the law into the bane of society, I continue onward trying to formulate a plan.

You'd think after 13 months with very little to occupy my mind, I would have formulated a stellar plan of redemption. The fact is, although I hadn't made concrete plans, I knew what I wanted. I just had to figure out where to start. Apparently, the officer chose this as my starting place: in exactly the atmosphere I left off. But this time, I felt different. I can't pinpoint the feeling exactly, but I know I will be okay. For the first time since I started using drugs, I feel genuinely good about myself. I feel my confidence grow as the morning dissolves the darkness of night. Suddenly I realize I am no longer in the midst of the rough side of town. I walked through it unscathed. The faint lights and shadows of the part of town that used to beckon me have held no allure today. They are long gone in the distance. A smile sneaks across my face as I turn my back to it and keep going. The more distance I can put between us, the better.

It is still too early to catch a bus ride to my parents' house and I sure don't have any money for a taxi. It is 2 am. I continue walking north towards a street corner I remember has a bus stop on it. I guess I will just wait on the bench until sunrise. Maybe if I'm lucky I can catch a couple hours of sleep. I smile as the bus stop comes into view and I pick up my pace to reach it sooner – as if that will keep me safe from whatever weakness I might suddenly fall prey to. I approach the simple roof-covered bench and am relieved I don't have to share it with anyone else. I am exhausted, and it feels so nice to be truly free from both the physical restraint of jail and the mental restraints of drugs. I sink onto the hard metal bench. My eyes eagerly shut and relief washes over me as my body relaxes. Within minutes, my peace is disrupted by a speeding car hurtling towards me. The headlights cast a moving shadow around me as my heart began to thump. Zooming up to the front of the bus stop, the car brakes to a stop.

"Hey buddy! Did you know there aren't any buses running this early?" hollers the man.

"Yeah, I was just going to wait here until they start their routes," I explain.

"Well, do you need a ride? Where you headed?"

"Well, sure," I hesitate not knowing quite what to make of this stranger's generosity. "I need to get to Payson. It's about 20 miles south from here."

"Hop in!" he says waving his hand. "I'm headed that direction."

I am a little wary to take him up on his offer, but how can I refuse? I mechanically stand up and walk to his car. Once I am settled into the passenger seat I survey my surroundings. The car is a bit dirty and smells like mildew. The man's appearance seems normal. Normal meaning he doesn't look like a serial killer. I try to act as if I'm not bothered by the situation, but the man can tell I am uncomfortable. To ease things a bit, he begins to ask me some basic questions about what I do for a living and what I like to do for fun. I'm not exactly sure how to answer, so after stumbling over a few hesitant mumbles, he interrupts me.

"Why are you so tense?" he says as he puts his hand on the inside of my leg.

Oh. Now I'm starting to understand. I am in a bad situation. How do I deal with this one? I've never had to figure my way out of something like this before. Should I risk going back to jail and punch this guy? Should I tell him to pull the car over? Should I try to talk my way out of this? My thoughts are racing and I can't decide my course of action quick enough. While contemplating my next move, the man slides his hand up the inside of my thigh. I grab his hand and throw if off my leg.

"Pull the goddamn car over NOW!" I yell.

"It's not a big deal," the man replies while continuing to drive.

I clench my fist and swung at the man's face. The cracking noise echoes in my head. Red splatters across the dash from his nose. What have I just done? Unable to see, the man veers the car off the road and comes to a stop on the shoulder.

I get out of the car and slam the car door. I run across the street to a truck stop hoping to wash the blood from my soiled clothes. I lock the bathroom once inside and tear my shirt off to scrub it in the sink. My heart is beating so fast I can feel it through my entire body. I can't believe what just happened! I have never been a violent person. I don't just hit people! Not even two hours after being released from jail, I already feel like I am running from the law once again. I splash cold water in my face and gaze into the small scratched mirror above the sink. I freeze. I can't stop staring into my own eyes. My pulse begins to slow and a calming sense of satisfaction flows through my body. Finally, I wave my hand in front of the towel dispenser and swiftly rip the paper from the machine. I dry my face and hands and throw the wad of paper into the trash and walk out the bathroom door.

I exit through the front doors of the truck stop and sit on a nearby bench under a small awning intended for workers and truckers who need a quick break. I look for the creepy ride-offerer. I scan the street and see where his car had pulled off the road. I see nothing. Just tall weeds and pavement. The man must have driven off. That is a calming thought. I notice an ashtray with some half-smoked cigarette butts that have been smashed out not far from me. I haven't had a smoke in 13 months, but for some reason I feel like I need something. Even though I've been smoke-free for so long there is still a mental push directing me to smoke something. I grab the best looking malodorous cigarette and light it with one of few things I do have in my possession: a lighter. As I draw back on the bent smoke, a man begins to walk toward me. *Good Lord not another stranger.* I can tell by the way he's dressed that he is a truck driver. His unkempt red flannel shirt is greasy and dirty. His sleeves are halfway rolled up and his stringy hair covers his left eye and flows past his shoulders. He is an overweight man and it looks as if he hasn't slept in weeks. As he approaches the bench table I'm sitting at, he reaches into his chest pocket and pulls out a cigarette.

"You from around here?" I mumble.

"No, no," he replies with a smile. "I'm from Michigan. Just traveling through. Say, you want a real smoke?" he offers as he watches me digging around some more in the ashtray.

"Sure," I laugh at my own desperation, relieved to know that he seems to understand. He doesn't judge me for it, he just hands me a smoke.

We talk for another ten minutes or so and it is a conversation I need. He speaks to me like he knows somehow what I'm going through and where I am meant to go. He assures me that I will make it through whatever I am struggling with and that I shouldn't worry. The funny thing is I never told him anything about what I was up against. I needed to have that conversation and to this day I know he was meant to help me figure things out when I was starting to get all kinds of confused just hours into my freedom.

Since my encounter with touchy-feely ride guy, I decide not to trust anyone for rides. It will be a long 20-mile walk, but it is a beautiful day. I wave goodbye to the kind trucker and start my long journey south. The sun beats against me in all directions. I don't make it more than a mile before I have to take my shirt off. Luckily, I am already wearing shorts. I tuck my wadded up shirt into the waist of my shorts and continue on. I come across a few areas where I have to take shortcuts through fields and jump over fences and walls to avoid the main interstate. The feeling of confidence swells within me again as I navigate closer and closer to home. I have never felt it as strongly as I do now. At last I am free. I am finally okay with who I am. I feel happy.

I don't have a watch but I know I left the truck stop at 10 am. I watch the sun throughout the day and keep track of the time by how far it moves across the sky. It must be getting close to 4 pm. I'm approaching my hometown and the thought of facing my parents once again after all that has happened is making me nervous. I decide to stop by my sister's work instead. It will save me a walk across town to her house, about an hour, if I can make it to my sister's work before she leaves for the day. As I approach her worksite, my mind starts racing with thoughts and emotions. I am so excited to see my sister and I just hope she will be happy to see me too. My sister has always been in the loop of all my mishaps and mistakes. She knows that I have spent the last year in jail. Although it's not quite a relief to think of your loved one behind bars, she has known that I have had somewhere to stay and that I was alive. There's a chance that she will be unsure of seeing me and I'm not sure if showing up so randomly at such a public place was the best plan. I just don't want to disappoint her. I'm nervous and excited, and I can't wait outside her office any longer.

I open the door to her office and hear muffled sounds of people talking in distant hallways. I hear footsteps approaching and my sister walks through the doorway across the room and looks right at me.

"Hello!" I say nervously.

"Hi!" She exclaims, clearly caught off guard. "What are you doing?"

"I was released last night. I wasn't supposed to get out until they found me a bed in the rehab facility. I didn't know where to go or what to do so I came here. I need to contact the courts and tell them what happened so I can try and get into rehab."

"Oh. Okay. Well it's good to see you!" she says hugging me. "I'll take you home with me when I get off work. You can stay with me for now Dustin, but only until you get into the rehab place, okay?"

"Okay! Thank you Stephanie!" I can't believe she is so okay with seeing me just walk in like this after so long and everything that has happened. I am so grateful for family. I don't know why family always seems so willing to love, forgive, and ignore our stupidity, but I'm not about to question the benefits of blood relationships.

"You're welcome. Now just wait here and I'll be right back," she directs. "I just need to finish up a few things and then we can go home. My daughter will be so happy to see you Dustin!"

Arriving at my sister's house and seeing my niece was such a great feeling. I couldn't believe that my family was willing to accept me back in after all I had put them through. My family had loaned me thousands of dollars over the course of my addiction, not to mention all the times I had lied to them, stolen their belongings, and put them personally in harm's way. Yet, they were still right there for me when I needed them. I began to realize how evil of a person I once was. I also began to realize the strength of my family's unconditional love for me. Their love was a great assurance - especially because at this point in my life, I needed it more than ever. When I would think about how much they each still believed in me and supported me, I would get emotional. I didn't want to break down so soon and I knew I had a lot of work to do still.

I began the first step of my recovery. I called the court and scheduled a court date one week away. Spending a week with my family helped me see that there was life after all and that life can be good again. I went to visit my parents before I checked into rehab. The ill feelings I once had towards them had long ago vanished. Having a clear and sober mind makes you see things in a much different light. There is no doubt in my mind that what they did was the right thing. What they did saved my life and I am forever grateful to them. It was such a wonderful feeling reuniting with them after being gone for so long. The truth is, I had been absent for a lot longer than just the year-long jail sentence. The real Dustin had finally returned.

I still had a long, hard road ahead of me including a 6 month in-patient treatment program, getting a job, a driver's license, a car, re-building trust with my family and society, figuring out how to pay the fines, fees, back taxes, old bills, debts I had racked up, not to mention sorting out my court dates and repairing my wrong-doings. The biggest thing through all of this mess I had gotten myself into was to stay sober; to not cave under the overwhelming rebuilding process and just walk out on it all again. Just thinking about the mess I had caused myself was usually enough to drive my sobriety into a tailspin, but not this time. I was determined to stick it out. Despite a few minor setbacks, things went really well. At least for a long while...

The hour-long drive from my sister's home to the rehab facility seemed to only take 5 minutes. I was nervous but excited. I always hated making new friends and my social anxiety was already starting to build up. The thought of being in a closed facility for another six months was terrifying. After all, I had a 13-month jail stay under my belt just one week ago. Underneath all my fears of this uncharted place, I was willing to go through with it. I knew I had to. I was spiritually fit and I knew at this point in my life, I had to do it.

The lobby carpet was matted down and worn from the constant traffic. I imagine people were coming and going often. I also knew that many who left were leaving prematurely. I was committed to finishing the program to the end. I had no doubts. This place was like the Hilton compared to jail, even if it did smell like sweaty socks and maple syrup.

Once I got settled in, I was offered all the coffee I could drink. The majority of the men there were quite friendly. They all made me feel welcome and that was a relief. On top of that, there were a couple guys already there whom I had shared cells with while incarcerated. Seeing a few familiar faces made a lot of my anxieties fade away. One of the guys was named Rick. He was a cellmate of mine for almost four months. He got into a fight in jail with a man who was 6'4" and weighed about 245 pounds. Rick isn't a small guy. He is about 6'4" too but he is lanky and uncoordinated. That day, Rick took a pounding by a hulk of a man, and he took it, and he fought back. Rick was pummeled with pride. When the brawl was over, Rick had a smile on his bright red, bloody face. Since that day, I've called him retard-tough. I would later become roommates with Rick.

There was much work to be done while staying in rehab. It was far from a free ride and a free meal. There were classes every day: Bible study, learning courses, Alcoholics Anonymous meetings, Narcotics Anonymous meetings, and peer groups. Then, we each had to work an 8-hour shift at a thrift store or in the kitchen. Luckily, I was stationed at the store the majority of my 6-month stay. We worked for free sorting shoes, building furniture, picking up donated items from people's homes along with a variety of other chores around the facility. The first 30 days I wasn't allowed to leave the premises. As long as you kept your nose clean and did what you were supposed to, you could qualify for a 24- or 48-hour leave pass to a family member's house after that. We were not allowed to fraternize with the opposite sex while staying at the facility, but that was a difficult rule to enforce apparently. A lot of "fraternizing" was taking place, myself included.

I had more opportunities during my stay in rehab than I had had my whole life. We went on three trips to Colorado were we camped out in the beautiful Rocky Mountains in cabins owned by the Rehab Center. I went to two symphonies and never realized classical music could be so calming and beautiful. I participated in a rescue mission working to free some mine workers from a collapsed cave. I got to do so many things I never would have had the opportunity to be a part of.

During my stay in the facility, I was ordered to Felony Drug Court. If I successfully completed Drug Court, the courts would dismiss my felonies and several of my misdemeanor charges that I had been slapped with when I was picked up by police resulting in my yearlong sentence. Drug Court was not an easy route to take. It was a minimum of 18 months long. The average person finishes it in about 24 to 30 months. About 95 percent of people go back to jail for missing a class or having a dirty drug screen. Depending on your track record in drug court, you can get put back in jail even if you show up late for a required class. However, being in the rehab facility at the same time as satisfying my drug court requirements made it quite a bit easier for me. Instead of doing the mandatory classes the Drug Court required, I received credit for the ones I completed in rehab. In rehab, I had to take random drug screens and had to blow into a Breathalyzer every day – usually around 2 am. That way, you couldn't sneak any booze, even late at night. The sad thing is, even with all of us knowing about these random drug screens and "sneak" Breathalyzer tests, some guys would still get kicked out of rehab for being drunk or high on drugs. Seeing how people still didn't understand how to stay sober after so many opportunities made me sad. I knew that if I could do it, anyone could. I've always known that I possess very little innate self-control against addictive substances. It was a blessing for me to go through rehab because it made me realize that I was not alone. Many people had the same exact issues and problems as me. Part of my depression used to be that I envisioned I was the only failure and hence unfit and undeserving of anything better in life. It was here that I realized that was a lie. I now knew that there were hundreds of thousands, maybe even millions of people who were stuck in the rut of addiction. What was more though is that there were hundreds of people all around me conquering their addictions and living successful lives. It was a good feeling to realize I was not so alone. To realize it was a hard thing to do, but that it was do-able. All I had ever wanted was to feel like I fit in with everyone else. I can now say that I do.

During an in-house AA meeting I met one of my best friends. As the meeting started, he sat down next to me. There was a man talking who was extremely cocky and self-centered. You could hear it when he spoke and to say the least, it was annoying. My new friend leaned over to me and said, "That guy is a pickle smoocher." I started laughing out loud. I couldn't help myself. From that day forward Brian has been one of my best friends.

Before I knew it, months had gone by. I was now one of the senior members at the rehab. I would see new people coming in the way I did months before. It felt so good seeing the rapport I had built with so many people. I knew my duties at the house, and all the ins and outs. We called rehab a house because we lived there, slept there and after a while, it kind of became a home.

Soon, it came time for my transition time from the house. I had successfully completed all of the rehabilitation center and court requirements and was now ready to begin my transition into society. My assignment was to find a full-time job in the next couple of weeks before leaving. I was very motivated and had set specific goals for myself. Having a clear idea of what I wanted gave me the focus and drive to not allow myself to become distracted or disheartened and seek comfort from my addictions. Nothing could stop me. Years before I started using drugs, I had worked for many different printing companies. I was looking forward to finding another job in the same field. I knew it well. I could operate almost any printing press without being taught how. Since I owed so much money to the court system in Salt Lake, I knew it would be best to live in Salt Lake. Plus there were many more options for work than in my small hometown. The transit system in Salt Lake could take me almost anywhere, and that is a good option for someone with no car and no driver's license. My journey into the real world was about to begin.

Starting my life over at 26 and having to do it with so much baggage could have been awful. I did not feel humiliated though. I felt a sense of accomplishment and freedom that I had never experienced before. My integrity and humility had been restored and having an intact moral compass made me strong and confident. I could look my peers in the eye. I knew I was an addict, but I also knew I wasn't alone. All the years that I had thought I was "different" was one of the biggest problems in my life. It was such a profound finding to finally realize that so many other human beings were faced with the same troubles as me. I was so afraid to reflect on all the horrific things I had done in my life. After hearing other people's journeys through AA and NA, my story didn't sound so isolated and horrendous. I let go of everything I was trying to control and relied on faith to take care of it. It was invigorating to finally cleanse my tattered soul. It wasn't the faith in God I relied in, but it was a faith in a Higher Power, just something bigger and stronger than me. Something I didn't understand. Something I didn't need to understand.

Within two weeks, I secured a job at an envelope printing company. I did some research on the company prior to my interview and wore the only suit I had: one that was donated to the center. It was decent, and nobody could tell any different. I later found out that I got the job because of that suit. So I guess it was my lucky suit. Whoever donated that suit will have my unknowing appreciation for the rest of my life.

I ran into my old cellmate and rehab friend Rick yesterday. He is living in the Avenues now, just blocks from the rehab facility. He walked out of rehab before he finished the course but he seems to be doing well. He told me that his roommate is smelly and has 15 cats. All I could do was laugh. I've never been very fond of cats, or smelly people. In talking, we decided that getting an apartment together would be a good idea. We will split the rent and food costs. We decide to meet at the library later on to find apartments and goof around on MySpace. The library and a nearby coffee shop are regular hangouts for us rehabbers. Since we weren't allowed to talk with women while in the facility, these two places are perfect. They are both full of women.

Rick and I searched and searched for apartments. We spent several days riding the bus or walking through town to check them out and fill out rental applications. We finally found a fourplex in the Avenues that would suit us perfectly. The lease agreement is favorable and we will become the maintenance men for the complex as well. We are to be in charge of watering the lawn and fixing light fixtures and the like. For fifty bucks off our rent, how could we refuse?

Within two weeks, the grass is dead. Rick blames me. I blame God. After all, it has been in the triple digits for almost a week. Inside, we both know neither one of us even attempted to water the lawn. We are fired from our maintenance positions but we don't care. All the extra work isn't worth the fifty-dollar discount. Unclogging other peoples' toilets twice a day wasn't what I had in mind when I took the job. I think one lady was clogging the toilet on purpose. Every time I would go upstairs to her apartment she would try and flirt with me. She would stand in the door opening of the bathroom and lean against the wall just smiling at me, toilet water splashing all over the place. It was awkward. Plus, she didn't speak much English, which made it even more awkward. I was relieved I would never have that responsibility again.

Brian invited me to a Stone Temple Pilots concert on Saturday. I am excited to hang out with him again. Rick wants to come with us, so it should be a lot of fun with the three of us together. The closer Saturday gets the more nervous I start to feel. This concert will be the first big event I go to since being out on my own. I know that some concerts are full of women, booze, and drugs. Just thinking about it gives me butterflies. For a brief second, I doubt my sobriety strength. Once I realize I will be alongside two sober friends as well as Brian's fiancé who hates drugs and alcohol, I know everything will be okay. I'm not too concerned with women at this point. I know I'm not ready to have a relationship so I'm not even looking for a woman. I have gone over two years without feeling a woman's touch or having a romantic night out on the town with one. I miss that joyous feeling but I know I'm just not ready for such a large emotional attachment. After all, my record shows that after every breakup I've had, a relapse has followed closely behind. Whether or not the two are directly connected is unknown. Nonetheless, I want to steer clear of such roads for now. I figure that if I go to the concert and not even looking for a girlfriend, there is no way I will find one. It is a fail-proof plan. I think.

13

RECOVERY: A FAMILY AFFAIR

DALLAS

JULY 2007

"**D**ad, I just wanted to call and let you know that Dustin is finally out of jail," my daughter told me through the telephone. I didn't know how to respond, I just paused and finally thanked her for letting me know.

Because Dustin had so many warrants each with a different sentence attached to it, we were unclear of Dustin's exact release date. In some ways, it was easier for me that way. It had been 12 long months since that day we helped the police find and arrest our son.

My daughter's news that Dustin was now out of jail left me with a feeling of joy, but also a feeling of guilt. After all, it was my wife and I that had helped put him behind bars in the first place. Dustin did not know this, as far as I knew at the time, and as I sat pondering what I was going to say to him, I decided that that was not going to be one of my confessions.

The past 12 months had gone by very slowly and as I look back on the time my son spent in jail I felt not only sad, but also embarrassed. I'm not quite sure why, but during this time we had only gone to visit him a couple of times. As I contemplate my reasoning for not going to visit him more often, I believe it was simply a feeling of guilt for being so largely involved in his incarceration. Even though I knew he was serving time for his own actions and decisions, I just couldn't shake the guilt that I was the one who handed him over to his captors.

Despite the feelings that I struggled with and the hardships Dustin went through during incarceration, I was happy to know that our son was home again and supposedly clean. Now the only question was: could he stay clean?

Later that afternoon my daughter, granddaughter and our son Dustin showed up at the front door. Giving each of them a hug, I couldn't believe how good Dustin looked. Not only did he have the look of life back in his eyes, he had put on about 20 pounds, which his corpse was in desperate need of. As I look back on that day I remember thinking to myself: if only things could stay this way. I also remember thinking how right my brother-in-law was when he pleaded with us to turn Dustin over to the authorities. Having served 12 months behind bars did in fact save our son. It was the best Dustin had looked in more than seven years.

Things seemed to go well for many months. Dustin acquired a part-time job and attended AA and NA meeting via an in-patient program. For the first time in many years, my wife and I felt that there might really be a chance that we'd get our son back.

Despite the huge smiles on our faces, I knew that both my wife and I were thinking that things could fall apart at any minute. After all, "falling apart" had been Dustin's middle name. It can be impossible to shake that feeling of doubt, worry, and suspicion that had come to surround our son. But maybe it is for the best to always keep that mild level of concern on alert. The times my wife and I were most placated and oblivious turned out to be the times we should have been concerned the most. It is like living in a nightmare and being on the verge of waking up, but never being able to reach full consciousness. Having gone through everything we had been through, it was impossible to put full stock in Dustin. It was just too dangerous to, and it may always be that way.

Putting our worries aside as best we could, we watched eagerly as Dustin completed the court's and rehabilitation center's requirements for Dustin to maintain his freedom. Although it took several months, they seemed to pass quickly and before we knew it Dustin was in the transition phase of his rehab program. This meant that in the next little while Dustin would be required to find his own place to live and to also get a full-time job.

As long as our son remained under the supervision of his rehab facility (the Salvation Army) we felt okay in wearing our smiles, but it wasn't long before I received a phone call from Dustin that informed me he was moving in with a friend of his: a former rehab member. "Friends" was always a trouble word when it came to Dustin. Whenever most of his "friends" came into the picture, I lost my son. That news quickly turned my smile upside down. I couldn't bear to think of Dustin going through everything he had already been through again, and dragging us – especially his mother's frail heartstrings – right alongside. Would he really just throw all of his hard work away? It was unbearable to even consider.

At the time I didn't know what it was that had me so worried, but I just knew if Dustin moved in with his new friend that things would change. In my mind it didn't seem like the smartest thing to do: putting two rehab individuals together. Although I tried to remain positive when Dustin told me of his latest decision, I just knew things were about to make a turn for the worst. After all, how or what could two rehabbers do to stay out of trouble. As I look back over Dustin's life, situations such as this had never turned out good. The more I thought about my son's decision the more unsure I got. This just wasn't leaving a good taste in my mouth. Fortunately, he was almost an hour away from me, so I had to develop an attitude of indifference. I thought my skin had grown a few inches from all the emotional calluses I barricaded myself under, but this required another layer of distancing myself from him and refraining from calling him constantly to check in on him.

Despite my worries, Dustin's life seemed to continue on a positive path. He and his friend continued to attend their AA and NA meetings and life seemed to be going well.

It wasn't long before our son applied and received a job at a print shop where he output envelopes. At this point I could only be proud of what Dustin had accomplished. Again, it seemed as though neither my wife nor I should be worrying about Dustin's fight against drugs. He not only had his life going in the right direction, but his appearance was that of a normal healthy individual. At this point, we could only hope that Dustin and his friend would keep doing everything they needed to keep themselves in check and out of trouble.

Although naïve in the beginning, there did come a time when each member of our family became educated to the validating signs and evidence that confirmed whether or not Dustin was on drugs at any given time. Regardless if you are currently dealing with an individual who is a drug addict or not, it is imperative to identify as many signs as you can to help decipher when an individual is embroiled in substance abuse.

A vicious cycle continues to run Dustin and our family. It is a simple cycle characterized by five phases: 1. Dustin asks that we accept him back into our home; 2. We all work together to help Dustin get clean; 3. Dustin stays clean for a short period of time; 4.Dustin falls off the wagon; 5. We kick Dustin back out on the streets. Having delineated this seemingly never-ending sequence, I would like to address stage 4: Dustin falls off the wagon. This is where Dustin proves incapable of confessing that he has slipped up and once again succumbed to drug use and we instead find out it some other hurtful, depressing manner.

Due to the embarrassment and pain it causes, it has been very frustrating to learn that even after collaborating with our son, it is still those people closest to him, innocent bystanders, who become his emotional and physical victims. What only adds to the pain of this is that we often discover his return to sworn-off illegal substances only through extremely turbulent events such as with the pet shop car test drive fiasco or the St. George whirl.

Because you have to assume the individual you are trying to help will not freely admit to you when he or she is using, you must acquire this knowledge yourself. Identifying this usually comes only with experience. Within this repetitive cycle from which I have outlined there will be specific changes - not only in the individual but also in their habits, their associates, and in their daily activities.

For example, the process of compiling this book has taken many years to complete. The reason for this delay is that for each time Dustin falls, so goes the communication, the collaboration, and even the willingness, desire, and ability to move forward. Basically, all progress has come to a halt a number of times.

I have never looked at myself as a perfect person and I know I'm far from it. But, if there are two things I'd like to think I've accomplished before I leave this earth they would be that those who knew me could say, "There's a man who was honest and a man you could trust." Unfortunately, the words "honest" and "trust" are not common values shared by the majority of the world today. What's more, they are two words certainly not valued by an individual hooked on drugs!

Everything a recovering addict says must be questioned. Nothing can be trusted – not their alibis, their excuses, their explanations, or their actions. It is unfortunate to have to mistrust every act and word that comes from your loved one, but it will only help him or her in the long run. Knowingly or unknowingly, establishing trust is an addict's bridge to making a victim out of those closest to them.

It is well worth it to keep a written record of an addict's behaviors and excuses. Then, when you are in entangled in their web of emotional turmoil, you can always double-check yourself or the observations you have made from past experiences. This allows you to step back and think through past actions more clearly. You will be able to analyze their actions better and perhaps even notice certain patterns that develop over time. Including dates and time frames is crucial to this log so you can track things more accurately.

Patterns will emerge and you will learn how you can better help your loved one and perhaps even avoid victimizing yourself to some degree in the process.

Although the cycle of addiction itself will not be broken from merely jotting down a few notes, or noticing certain trends, you can help protect innocent people – particularly your family – by confronting the addict and calling them out on their return to using. Although he or she will brazenly resist your accusations, you must call them out on the drug use and let them know that you know. There must be consequences in place and enforced if they are living in your home. Ignoring their actions, failing to notice them, not wanting to confront them because you are unsure of what to say or worried about maintaining the fragile line of communication that exists are all excuses that make you an ineffective help to your loved one suffering from addiction.

I wish we had noticed much sooner in every relapse Dustin had in our presence. Not just in our home, but in his siblings' homes, or even in his own apartment. I can't blame this all on being an uninvolved parent. Children – or anyone for that matter – are always going to find ways to hide embarrassing secrets from those they want to. That's where being observant comes in. Not overly suspicious of every tiny action or outing, but just establishing the kind of relationship that is conducive to admitting when we have made a mistake. Recognizing that it is okay to ask for help. Dustin would ask for help, but it was always such a last-ditch effort, it made it difficult to decipher how sincere he was. Did he truly want out in those instances, or was it just the heroin talking to keep him alive a little longer so it could destroy him again a month later?

I have concluded that if an addict felt comfortable admitting to a non-user whom they respected and loved each and every time he or she used, it would serve as a moral check to some degree. It wouldn't necessarily conquer the addiction itself, but it would keep them in reality more often. It would make them probe a little more into their reasons for using again. It would be like a safety net that held them to something and prevented them from falling in too deep too fast. Once an addict falls into a relapse, they always fall harder and faster than the time before. That means the climb out is that much more arduous and difficult to achieve unless they have plunged for the final time.

Although Dustin is proof that anyone can change no matter the depth of their addiction, without the proper tools, it is impossible. I wish we had known about these tools. Who knows if we had reached out sooner and trusted experts' advice earlier how much heartache and mess, how many years of drug entanglement, we could have avoided.

Jail and the rehabilitation facility and even the drug court process were incredible tools for our son to begin his genuine recovery. Although it still took years after that, and will always be an ongoing battle, it was his first real starting point. Going through support groups like AA and NA that met daily were tremendously effective at teaching Dustin how to recognize, deal with, and overcome his addiction. What's more, it taught him how to not give up when he slipped up. Having the proper education tools is imperative for addicts to break free from any substance or self-destructive habit.

Likewise, an often overlooked necessity is proper education for the family and other loved ones of the addicted individual. You are most likely reading this book as someone interested in helping an addict or simply to gain the tools to avoid making the same mistakes we did when first dealing with our addict son. There are numerous support groups for families and loved ones of addicts. There are national groups, international groups, and local groups. Although many people have heard rumors of support groups meeting in the basements of various local churches, they don't often take advantage of these because they don't realize how much they could benefit from them. Since they are not the addict, many loved ones don't realize how much knowledge there is to gain from people in their own communities – as well as trained therapists who organize and oversee such support groups. To find a support group in your area, simply conduct an internet search for "Family resources for drug addicts." Several links will be given directing you to statistics, meetings, intervention methods, and local support groups. To find more specific assistance, you can include the city, county, or state in which you live.

The paramount rule of being a caretaker for another person is to take care of yourself first. If you allow yourself to become consumed by the problems of your loved one and neglect yourself, you compromise your capability as a resource for that person who needs you so much. If you can't sustain your own emotional and mental well-being and balance to some degree, you cannot act as a sound anchor for this tumultuous individual. Although my wife and I didn't perfectly follow this advice, we found that when we did take a break from obsessing over the things we couldn't control and focused on grounding ourselves more in reality, on improving our own relationship, on taking care of our own lives and such, we were able to think more clearly and make better decisions when it came time to deal with our son.

14

STEPPING STONES

DUSTIN

MARCH 2008

The vibrations from the speakers gyrate inside my chest and slowly reverberate through the rest of my body. Looking down from the balcony above the concert, the stage is only a small black square with silver uprights at all four corners. Red, blue, and yellow incandescent lights flash consecutively, changing the hue of the entire indoor arena. People around me move in robotic movements under the strobes. It is a strange paradox. My mind is sober, yet I feel like I am high. Low-lying smoke billows across the crowd on the ground floor. Some crazy people are being tossed about like rag dolls to the beat of the drum. I have never understood the appeal of crowd surfing. I am relieved to be in the comfort of my second story seat.

With Rick to my right, the three seats to my left are empty. This makes me smile. It is halfway through the opening band's act and no one has filled these three seats. Just as I reflect on my good fortune, three women come walking down the aisle stairs behind me heading directly towards the empty chairs. They come into the row one by one.

By this time we are all standing trying to see the show as best we can. I try not to be too obvious but as long as I'm going to be stuck sharing my elbow space I want to see what these women look like. Just because I don't want a girlfriend right now doesn't mean I'll pass up the opportunity to check out an attractive woman, especially a woman that will be in such close proximity to me for the rest of the concert.

Checking out the ladies is difficult because of the lighting. As yellow light glints around the room, I try to discreetly glance at my companions, but the lights violently seize into flashes of saturating red and obscuring purple. I am really only able to see the girl standing closest to me on my left. It is almost impossible to miss her long black hair swaying to the deep gyrations of the music and reflecting the psychedelic colors of the strobing lights. She is sexy and tall, especially with whatever heels she is wearing. I wonder if that will be a problem for my 5'10" frame. At least she is skinny like me, so we seem visually compatible in that way. The next thing I notice about her is her hands, or rather what's in them. She is holding a beer. I hurriedly cram the bag of Skittles I'm holding into my pocket. After seeing her beer I don't know what judgments she will pass on me for holding a childish bag of candy. Maybe the three ladies are like undercover Charlie's Angels? Will I be thrown off the balcony? Maybe I'll be mocked by three beautiful women. I don't know for sure, better to limit my vulnerabilities. All I know is that my earlier thoughts about not meeting a woman have vanished. Game on.

Throughout the last three songs, our group has been standing in the row making poor attempts at dancing. Skittle killer girl is constantly bumping and rubbing her hips into me. I don't make eye contact with her because I don't want her to stop. It continues until the opening band is done with their show. Once the lights flicker on for the intermission, we start talking to each other. She tells me about her job as a nurse and where she is from. I tell her I was a needle junkie that did 13 months in jail and just moved out of rehab about a month ago. Okay, maybe I wasn't that open about my life. I just tell her the bare minimum about me, facts that don't incriminate me for who I really am. Had I told her what I really was, she would have outrun Forest Gump trying to get away from my presence. She gives me her phone number and I decide I really will call her. I don't call her the next day though, or the next. In fact, I don't call her for almost three weeks.

As time goes by, things start to get more and more serious between Charlotte and me. We are spending more time together and before too long, I am sleeping at her house more than my apartment. Although things were going well overall, there was one repeated hang-up we just couldn't seem to overcome in the first several months of our relationship. Charlotte was using me and it took months to get to the bottom of it. When I did learn the truth, it drastically changed our relationship.

Charlotte made plenty of money as a nurse. She had her own home in a nice part of town and she bought whatever she wanted. Because she seemed okay financially, I couldn't figure out why she was asking me to do lots of handyman repairs around her home. I didn't mind helping her out, but how she was treating me after I made the repairs was making me increasingly frustrated.

A couple weeks ago she asked me to come over to help her service her swamp cooler for example. Being the willing boyfriend I was, I spent four hours cleaning and repairing the cooler. When I finished she thanked me and left somewhere with her friends. This infuriated me. I felt like she had completely blown me off. I wanted to spend time with her, not just her swamp cooler. And yet, this scenario kept replaying itself with other odd jobs. When I talked to her about her repeated ingratitude and explained that I didn't mind helping her, but I wanted to see her too, somehow, I lost the argument. My resentment festered more and more, and each time I tried to talk to her about, I lost. The clincher came when I found out months later why she wanted me to leave each time, or would pretend to leave with her friends. She needed me gone so she could do cocaine.

I was blown away when I first discovered this. As a recovered addict, I should have been able to see the signs through her deception. I may have been blinded by my emotional connection to her, or my desire for her to not be a shadow from my previous life, or even her professional success. Whatever the reason, I was fooled. If I could be so misled, it is no wonder drug abuse can be so difficult to detect even in the closest of relationships.

Charlotte was a heavy wine drinker when I met her and she had talked about cocaine on numerous occasions. I was just too blind to link the two together. She later told me she thought I was a pushover and that's why she was taking advantage of me. I always thought I was just too nice. All my life I have felt that people mistake my kindness for a weakness. I didn't need that in my life, but because I was a pushover, I stayed with her anyway.

After learning the truth about Charlotte's cocaine habit, we were able to discuss our relationship more openly and made some good progress together. Since then, the past few months have gone really well between us. She seems to respect me more as a partner and we are getting along. I decide to accept her invitation to move in with her. Rick will buy the furniture I acquired while living in our apartment, so it all works out. Charlotte's brother lives in her house too but we get along really well. He is a nice guy and we seem to have a lot in common. All three of us enjoy golfing. We go quite often. We also go on road trips together. We've gone to Wyoming to visit her mom and her aunt and have ventured down to Las Vegas as well. We are planning trips to Mexico and Italy. They still require quite a bit of saving up for, but I'm excited at the thought of it.

One day Charlotte and I get into a discussion about cocaine. By the end of our talk, we both agree to score some this weekend. Somehow, I convince myself that it is okay to shoot up just one more time. The thought of getting some cocaine in my system lights a fire inside me. My stomach flutters with anticipation like when you pause at the apex of a steep drop off on a roller coaster. The rush is so intense I can't stop thinking about it. It wouldn't have mattered if someone told me I would die if I sniffed that cocaine. I still would have done it. Once an addict reaches that decision point, their actions cannot be stopped. I am scared, but that fear is overruled by excitement. It is about to happen. Again.

In the past several months of my relationship with Charlotte, I've noticed a decline in my spirituality level. In fact, it is bordering on extinction. I haven't been to an AA or NA meeting in months. Before I moved in with Charlotte my life seemed like it was under control. But it was only under control with the help of other checkpoints constantly reminding me that I wasn't in control so

I needed to be reminded of that to maintain control. It is a confusing concept as a recovering addict – defining and figuring out who or what is in control of your life and to what extent and when. Self-control becomes such a delicate privilege and one that is easily blurred by freedom. When I moved in with Charlotte, I decided to take full control of my life again. I decided I was ready and I no longer needed all the reminders of what could control my life if I didn't. This is the path where choosing to control my own life without the check of support groups took me. Right back where I was just a few years before: I was teetering on the brink of getting high and preparing to hand my freedom and control over to a much more destructive dictator. I didn't see it that way at the time though. I was convinced that using cocaine just one more time was harmless. I told myself I deserved it. Sound familiar?

I hear Charlotte walk in the door and I know I am about to relapse. I hide those feelings. I burry them deep inside of me so no one can discern my terror. I don't want to frighten them with what I know; I am that excited, or maybe just that delirious to get some cocaine back in my system after so many years.

Charlotte sets out three lines and prepares them into a soft powder with a razor blade. Her brother and I stand by impatiently waiting eagerly for that initial charge into the brain that cocaine gives you when inhaled through the nose. Charlotte goes first, then her brother, then me. It is a feeling I have not forgotten. It takes me back to a place where real life does not exist. I am an empty soul lost between two worlds. My thoughts are at total, intangible peace. Nothing matters. My throat is completely numb. My palms sweat and my heart races. *Can they hear my heart thudding so fast?* It rattles in my ears. The feeling subsides much too quickly and I know why.

We wasted the cocaine by snorting it. I want to shoot it directly into my vein. Since Charlotte is a nurse, she has plenty of insulin syringes, and knows how to tap a vein like no one I have shot up with before. She is a needle professional. She is curious about using needles but she's never tried it before. I know she wants to. What she doesn't realize is that doing so will change her life forever.

I open the package encasing the needle and get it ready. I mixing some cocaine with some water in a spoon and stir it until it dissolves. I draw the mixture into the syringe and pierce my arm. The feeling is too intense, I run to the bathroom and vomit. I walk back into the bedroom and find Charlotte drawing fluid into the hollow point of her own needle. She wants me to help her. This opens a door for her that once opened can never be closed.

Charlotte, like many addicts, took a dangerous leap that day she allowed me to help her shoot up intravenously. Although none of us really saw, refused to see, or were incapable of seeing the fire we lit that day, it turned into a full fledged, out-of-control forest fire mighty quickly. It's these stepping stones in an addict's life that takes us from a normal life to teetering on the brink of reality, our morals completely absolved and our bodies craving just one thing: more. But how does this happen? What are the steps in between point A and Z? Our thoughts are distorted gradually, not stark enough for us to fully realize the gravity of our choices.

Everyone has lines drawn in their mind. Lines they will not cross because they think whatever is on the other side of that line is scary, ridiculous, stupid, or perhaps even mysterious. An addict is no different. We draw lines too. Our lines are drawn in pencil and easily erased apparently instead of drawn with triple-thick permanent marker.

Alexander Pope, an eighteenth century philosophical poet, managed to nail this fact on the head in his *Essay on Man*. Pope eloquently penned:

" Vice is a monster of so frightful mien,
As, to be hated, needs but to be seen;
Yet seen too oft, familiar with her face,
We first endure, then pity, then embrace."

This is the definition and process of addiction. I once thought that smoking a cigarette was ludicrous. Why would smoking some wrapped up crushed plants and other chemicals be appealing? But, I was curious. I thought I would just try it once. I tolerated it and that tolerance turned into indifference until finally I embraced it. Addictions are formed that easily and soon are uncontrollable. But my endurance and pity did not end with cigarettes. I erased that boundary line and drew another one just a little lower. This time, the boundary was marijuana. I promised myself I would never smoke marijuana. It doesn't take long once the initial threshold is compromised to repeat that boundary breaking. All it takes is the knowledge that a friend, a brother or sister, a boyfriend or girlfriend has been experimenting with marijuana and questions start to form in your mind. Your mind creates questions about marijuana, pushing you to try it for yourself, just once, justified by the scientific process of course that first-hand data is the only way to answer those questions. The questions and answers an addicts mind comes up with might look something like this:

Question: How bad is marijuana really?
Answer: Some states have legalized it and others are in the process of doing so, so it can't be *that* bad.
Question: Is it deadly?
Answer: No one has ever died from just smoking marijuana!
Question: Isn't marijuana a gateway drug?

Answer: Maybe for some people, but I don't use heavy drugs!

Seems logical enough, right? These are valid questions with answers that the curious mind has manipulated to allow our boundary line to be ignored. Now that marijuana use is justified, your old line is gone. That's okay though. You know you can draw another- right above cocaine.

Do the lines stop there? No, the lines then become not about what you're using but to what lengths you will go to supply that use. Your moral line becomes thinner and thinner until it is so blurred that it is imperceptible. You are lucky if your mind allows your moral compass to be content with marijuana. Unfortunately, if you are already associating with people who use marijuana, chances are they have several other connections as well and it is only a matter of time before your moral line is sinking into oblivion. Erased, lowered, and redrawn so many times, it becomes so blurred, so far down that it is imperceptible. You become me in the depths of my addiction, roaming the streets, participating in whatever it takes to score another hit – but it certainly isn't anything as mild as marijuana.

Charlotte was walking along a line she had set for herself and it was erased as quickly as a suggestion was made. I don't know if she had become bored, curious, or just incapable of understanding the consequences, but I suspect it was a combination of all three. Once you begin dabbling with addictive substances, they literally possess you and take over any ability you have to reason soundly. That is why reaching out for help – someone or something that is capable of controlling you when you are not – is literally your only option to survive.

I mentioned that Charlotte had another behavior that didn't help her addictive mindset: she drank a lot of wine. In my experiences I have heard many opinions about the difference between alcoholism and addiction. It wasn't until years later that I came to the conclusion that addiction is not a so-called drug problem nor is alcoholism purely an alcohol problem.

During my stints in early sobriety, I was left with a sober Dustin. I still had the same twisted, irrational thoughts but without the drugs. Some call that "white knuckle sobriety" because for most it is all they can do to stay sober and they are miserable and unhappy in their sobriety. I am here to tell you that pure, genuine, and a happy sober life is very possible! In learning this important fact about my addiction it made me realize that without outside help from experienced professionals and counselors, I was sure to fail at long-term sobriety.

Believe it or not, this was a huge discovery for me at that time. It also helped me see that the only difference between an addict and an alcoholic is one likes to smoke or shoot his poison and the other likes to drink it. In other words, the problem is not the drink or the drug it is the brain!

So, why is my brain different than yours or anyone else's? I have heard completely different opinions about this topic from highly specialized doctors and psychologists. Many individuals claim that addiction/alcoholism is a hereditary disease and that it may be passed down from generation to generation. For example, an alcoholic may cite that his father was an alcoholic therefore he is an alcoholic. I have heard one doctor say that addiction is hereditary and I have heard another doctor say it is not hereditary. An entire book could be written on this debate alone so I will make this brief.

It is my opinion that addiction and alcoholism are not strictly hereditary. I believe it is a combination of genes and environment. Our environment can trigger certain genes off and on so to say addiction is simply genetic – I believe that is incorrect. I believe that any single human being can acquire addiction. After all, we as humans have to continually fight the urge to limit the amount of every single thing we enjoy. Whether it is chocolate, coffee, shopping, pornography, sex, bigger homes, more toys, more electronics or mind altering substances. Are you an addict of anything? Try putting your smart phone in a drawer for a couple of days. Try missing your favorite television series for a few weeks. The destructiveness of one addiction compared to another varies significantly. Being hooked on Mountain Dew has completely different implications than heroin obviously. However, when you strip addiction down to its core, you are left with one thing: a human desire to over-indulge. Addiction in any form is merely a synthetic and short-lived attempt to forget about reality.

Two weeks have passed since we did that cocaine. I felt strong enough that I wouldn't need to use any more. *Maybe that was just a one time thing*, I think. I haven't even experienced any mental cravings. *Awesome.*

"I'm home Dustin," Charlotte shouts as she enters the door, kicks off her shoes, and puts her coat and purse away. "Can you come here? I want to talk to you about something."

"Hi, how was work?" I say surfacing from my lounge spot on the couch. It is always good to see her at the end of the day.

"It was good. I had a long day. Some of my patients are so difficult."

"Yeah? Why do you say that?"

"Well, I have this one patient who refused to take her pain medication so she wanted me to take it away from her. It is an old bottle that she has had for months. I didn't want to have to take them all the way back to my office, so I just brought them home with me."

My stomach flutters with a long forgotten urge just thinking that my girlfriend has a whole bottle of painkillers.

"What are they?" I ask as if I don't care one way or the other.

"OxyContin," she reads from the label. I can't help but think she is putting on an act a little bit. "I don't know what to do with them now."

"Just put them in the cupboard for now," I say trying desperately to hide the excitement that is mounting inside me.

There is not one second that I honestly think I won't sniff those pills from the time Charlotte tells me about them. Careful planning to sneak them from the cupboard begins instantly. I can't remember the last time I felt this kind of happiness.

I take a pill from the cupboard within an hour of the orange bottle's arrival. I wait until Charlotte is distracted and I have enough time to enjoy it privately. I carry the pill to the bathroom, crush it into a powder, and inhale it through my nose. I have no plans to slow down until the bottle is gone. I have given into my addiction again without the slightest recognition of what will follow. Once my line has been crossed once, it's like there isn't a line to consider at all.

THE NEXT MORNING

Since I have to leave for work an hour before Charlotte, it gives me plenty of time to sneak two more pills from the kitchen cupboard without her even being awake. As I snatch my loot, I make note of how many pills are left. During my inventory I realize what I am doing and what I am choosing. I have boarded a runaway train that will make no stops. *I am going to die this time,* I think.

I am tired. I have been defeated for the last time. I can't handle what is happening. I don't know how to deal with my weakness towards drugs. I am doomed. If I don't do something, I will be a dead man. Literally. I drive to work in a panic. To deal with the stress of my intense fears and worries, I go into my work's bathroom and crushed up an Oxy on top of the toilet tank. Once I snort the potent powder from the porcelain tank and wipe away the remaining residue with my hand, I am able to smile again. I am numb. My despair vanishes. I exit the bathroom and go to my workstation.

My morning and afternoon bathroom meetings continue for three weeks. I am down 15 pounds and it is easily noticeable. My boss calls me into his office and I know exactly why before he even starts talking. This isn't my first time in this situation. By the end of our meeting, I am without a job. He is merciful though. My boss tells me if I can get clean and stay clean for 6 months, he will give me my job back.

I can only think about what I will tell Charlotte. After a couple days she will wonder why I'm not going to work anymore, so I know I have to come clean with her about what I have done. I am ashamed, nervous and scared. Flashbacks of my failed marriage flicker through my mind on a mental movie reel replaying the intense hurt, the depression, and the anger over and over. I know I have to be honest with Charlotte; she's all I have.

When she gets home from work I sit her down and confess everything. I tell her I need help getting clean. I have already been using for almost a month. I know my withdrawals will be so bad that if I don't have her help, I will cave and find a way to placate my mind.

We make a plan to take a weekend trip to Wendover, Nevada. It is only a 2-hour drive from home and we hope that getting away from everything for a few days will be just enough to get me sober again. Sometimes going to an unknown place that is enjoyable makes the withdrawals seem less intense. Even though much of the withdrawal symptoms are all in the mind, physical diversions like this really can help a person tolerate more pain.

Six hours after arriving in Wendover, I begin to feel my body begging me for more pills. My nose starts running and my body starts to ache. Once the ache reaches my bones, I know I am screwed. I only sleep for 5 restless hours that night. First I wake up in a cold sweat. I am panicked, so I take a scalding hot shower to numb my nerves and break the shivers that cascade through me. I feel better for about 30 minutes.

The next evening is absolute misery. I sleep for maybe 45 minutes out of the entire night. I know we are going home the next morning. At that point, I make my decision. Since Charlotte flushed the remainder of the pills down the toilet, I know I must find some heroin when we return. I have to act like I'm not in so much pain anymore so Charlotte won't suspect anything. I don't want Charlotte to worry about me relapsing. How can I tell her that she has wasted her whole weekend and so much money trying to help me these last couple of days? I can't tell her the truth: my withdrawals are getting the better of me. I don't want to let her down. I know I will, I just don't want to do it. Maybe I can figure a way out before she gets hurt. I will think about that tomorrow.

Once we arrive back home, the pain I felt during the drive here is becoming more tolerable. This isn't my first time experiencing this kind of relief. My brain has plenty of time to know I will feed it what it wants. That very idea relieves some of the pain. We unpack and settle back in and I start concocting my plan to procure heroin.

Charlotte gets a phone call in the midst of my internal conniving. She has to go run to her office to take care of something. My plan just got easier. Two minutes after she walks out the door I bolt for my car. I don't have connections to my dealer anymore or any current phone numbers, but I know it will be easy to find heroin so close to the city. All I have to do is find a homeless man sporting an "Anything helps. God Bless" sign. In my days living on the streets, I knew the game well. Finding a homeless man panhandling for spare pennies is my ticket to heroin. I hate to disappoint any charitable well-wishers in my audience, but let me tell you that homeless people carrying signs around requesting your help don't buy food with that dollar you give them. You are most likely helping them score their next shot of dope.

I drive around downtown for 20 minutes. I know all the panhandling hotspots. Within 45 minutes, I am holding a balloon of black tar heroin. I have to race home to beat Charlotte back. Sure enough, I make it in time. Frantically, I begin searching for her box of insulin needles so I can prepare my heroin. I find one in the junk drawer in the kitchen. By the time I rush into the bathroom and lock the door I am shaking in anticipation. Some of it is the adrenaline from trying to hurry but the rest is from the excitement of knowing I am only seconds away from complete nirvana.

As the needle pierces my skin, every ounce of pain dissipates. I draw back the plunger and watch the transparent cylinder turn to swirls of crimson and brown. With shaking hands, I slam the plunger inwards. A searing heat inundates my being. The shaking stops replaced by an itching, burning flash that overtakes my body and seems to last for hours. It passes in 30 seconds and I feel my legs buckle and break beneath the weight of my body. *Ahhhhhh.*

Once I come to, I shudder at what I know is to come. I try to hide my glimpse of the future in the far corners of my mind. *I am Satan's prisoner again. The only way I will get sober from this one is to die or get thrown in jail.*

2 Months Later

Charlotte and I have both been using cocaine and heroin intravenously consistently over the last two months. Our relationship has taken a turn for the worse. The only thing holding us together is our use of drugs. All we do now is shoot up. Neither one of us trusts the other and it leads to constant arguments. I am to the point where I can't take this life anymore. It's dark and cold and lonely. I am an empty soul. I want out.

I call my dad and tell him what's going on. Fessing up to him brings me back to reality for a moment. I tell him I am thinking about throwing myself in jail. I haven't gotten any new charges yet but I know it won't be long if I don't intervene. The more I play with the idea of throwing myself in jail, the more real it becomes. What other choice do I have? I still owe money to the courts and I'm sure this is my ticket to the only safe haven I know: jail. I decide to make an appointment to see the judge. I plan to explain my situation to him and request to be locked up. Just thinking about going through withdrawals in jail again makes me squeamish. I don't have a choice though. This is a matter of life or death.

After calling the courthouse, the clerk tells me I can't just waltz in and talk to the judge about this matter without an open case. Since I don't have an open case in Salt Lake, I remember that my case should still be open in Utah County where my fines are not paid off yet. I call the Utah County court. This time, the Judge is willing to see me. I decide a written letter to the judge will best explain my situation. As soon as I start getting some ink on my paper, I begin to panic realizing all the outcomes this risky move could strap me with.

What if the Judge decides I need more time in jail than what I'm asking? I mean 21 days in jail should be more than enough time to get through my withdrawals! What if he gives me 6 months? A year? What if I never get out?

Many different ideas course through my head. I start to doubt my plan. Maybe I am making a mistake turning myself over to the mercy of the court system. But a sliver of conscious tells me from deep down inside what is left of my hollow soul that this is my best option – probably my only option – for recovery. I must go through with this. As a puppet to drugs, I was moved involuntarily it seemed by invisible threads willing me this way and that. Now I must summon what is left of my shredded willpower to go through the actions of turning myself in. I have to remove my ability to choose. I prepare myself mentally as best I can for my court day in two days.

Any mental preparation is useless though. My physical and spiritual self know that three weeks of withdrawals will shred every fiber of my being. My only chance of getting through this is to convince myself that it won't be as bad as I think. I am playing a twisted psychotic game with myself. This cannot be good for my long-term mental stability. But I have played this game before. It has never been easy. Focusing on the delusions I create for myself, I begin to plan what I will do when I make it through this.

JUDGEMENT DAY

Charlotte and I exchange bittersweet goodbyes at her house. She has work so my mom and sister have agreed to drive me to the courthouse. Once we arrive, the fear of going back to jail sets in. I can't believe I am really doing this. It feels like an out-of-body experience where nothing is quite real and I don't have full control over my movements and thoughts. What began as a desperate plea on the phone with my father is turning into reality. I am terrified.

I don't want to start my withdrawals any sooner than I have to, so I did what any heroin addict would do: I brought some heroin into the courthouse with me. I excuse myself from my mom and sister and shamelessly admit that I need to use the courthouse bathroom to get in one more shot of heroin. Apparently, this is not a tactful thing to admit. They are appalled and infuriated with my lax contempt. I am numb to the seriousness of the situation though, and no amount of their fury can persuade me to alter my plan. Shoot up. Go talk to the judge. Go to jail. Get clean. Never mess up again. I have simplified the plan in my mind, and I am sure it will work. I am ready to be done with this demon again – just right after this last quick fix.

I quickly find an open stall and lock the latch behind me. I sit on the toilet and take the tools from my pocket. I open the syringe and mix the brown powder in a spoon. I plunge the point into my arm for the last time. Once inside my jutted vain, I slam the plunger inwards. I don't feel much of anything. No high, no itch, no numbness. This dose will only hold off my withdrawals until evening. But for now, at least I can feel nothing. I lick the blood that drips down my arm and throw the flushable items into the toilet. I trash the spoon and needle in the bin outside the stall and walk out of the bathroom.

My mom and sister are waiting for me in the lobby right where I left them keeping their vigil and surely wondering what kind of monster I really am. We file into the courtroom and take a seat towards the back of the room. Being in this room again is all too familiar. The hardwood benches are aligned in neat rows. The window curtains are half drawn so inmates can see only a tiny glimpse of freedom. The jumbo circular state seal hangs ominously above the judge's chambers. Numerous flags stand proud on each side of the judge's elevated throne, their red, white, blue, and gold boasting their allegiance to "liberty and justice for all," casting a shadow over the diminutive podium for the accused to stand awaiting their judgment. Everything about this room makes me uneasy. I am back again. What happened to me? I had been sober for over two years and my life had been going so well. Now I am right back where I was: strung out on cocaine and heroin.

"Dustin John." The Judge's authoritative voice booms through the room. My stomach drops into a pit that slowly starts to move into my throat. I stand up from my seat and walk slowly towards the center podium. "So why are we seeing you here today Mr. John?

"Your Honor, I would like to give you a letter if I may," I say shakily reaching for the folded letter in my pocket.

The bailiff approaches me and takes the letter. He inspects it and hands the letter to the slightly bewildered Judge. He fingers his reading glasses hanging by a gold chain around his neck and situates them low on the bridge of his nose. His brow furrows as he reads the contents of my letter. Silence fills the courtroom waiting for the judge to finish. The anticipation within me swells and I think I might pass out from nervousness. The Judge sets the letter down in front of him and stares into my soul. Finally he speaks.

"You mean to tell me that you are requesting a jail sentence? You want me to throw you in jail?" he questions. His tone suggests that he suspects I have ulterior motives. Maybe he thinks I plan on sneaking drugs into the jail. I can't blame him for his mistrust. I know my request is an odd one, and honestly, I had thought about trying to sneak heroin in with me a number of times. I knew that would defeat my purpose of self-sentencing myself to jail, so I refused to dwell on in too much. I focused on my final shoot up just before the hearing instead.

He has waited for a response long enough. I faintly muster a "yes sir," and the judge provides his verdict.

"I think we can manage that," he responds. "But instead of your requested 21 days in jail, I am going to give you 30 days in jail. On the 30th day, I will bring you back for review with a possible 30 day extension. Are we clear?" he orders.

I was struck with fear by his words. I couldn't fathom doing two more months in jail.

220

"Yes your honor, we're clear," I stammer in mild disbelief.

After the hearing I hug my mom and sister and tell them goodbye. The bailiff and one other officer escort me out of the courthouse to their patrol car. Once we go outside, I ask them if I can have one last smoke before they take me to jail.

"Sure I don't see a problem with that. What you did in there kid, I admire you for that. It must take a lot of courage to go through with this," he says nicely.

"Thanks. It wasn't easy but I know I have to do this or I will end up dead, we both know that right?" I say. He doesn't respond back verbally but gives me a look that conveys care and respect.

That was one of the few times an officer of the law ever treated me like a human being. Not that I deserved it any other time, but it felt good and I respected him a lot for that. I tried my best to enjoy that last smoke. I knew it would be a long while before I had another one. I put my cigarette in the ashtray and the two officers secure me in the back seat of their police car and we drove away.

14

WATCHING FOR SIGNS

DALLAS

MARCH 2008

In the process of compiling this book, there have been a number of times when I have felt that something is very, very wrong. Today is one of those days. Although I am unable to pinpoint the source of my concern, the uneasiness in the pit of my stomach validates that something bad is lurking in the shadows. Whatever the source of this malady, there is a discomforting sensation, a feeling of concern, fear and immediate urgency, which continues to plague me no matter what I do. Sifting through the possibilities, I fear the worst. I have the horrifying suspicion that Dustin is no longer clean.

Although our relationship was obviously tainted by turning Dustin over to the mercy and justice of the law, my wife and I could not be prouder of Dustin's survival of his jail sentence, sobriety, and attitude towards life and of course his successful completion of the rehabilitation program he was enrolled in. Although we don't see him as much as we would like to, our frequent visits confirm that Dustin has made a full recovery and is striving to be an upright member of society.

And yet, as I sit here at my computer reflecting, rewinding and reviewing the multitude of personal conversations between my son, and myself, I can in fact say that several pretty large issues have in recent months challenged my son. Knowing this, I now find myself pondering whether or not the weight on my son's shoulders has become too heavy.

Having said this, I can only hope that I am wrong. Unfortunately, when hit by such a strong sense of fear and immediate urgency in the past, Dustin's return to drugs has proven to be the source of my anxiety.

Although I do not look forward to validating my fear, I know I cannot ignore it. Dustin has been clean for nearly two years, but as our family has learned, once an addict, always an addict. Our son will be the first to tell you that. Although my wife and I have not kept exact records, I'd suspect that one hundred would be a close estimate to the number of times Dustin has fallen off the wagon.

A phone call is the first way to attempt to get to the bottom of this. Establishing an open line of communication with your loved one is paramount. Now, we can't expect to babysit our son for the rest of his life, but I have noticed that when he makes himself scarce and we have a hard time getting a hold of him, he is often entangled in a much bigger problem once again.

Recovered addicts may have their probation officers and other councilors they are required to check in with monthly, but having a loved one checking in on him or her more frequently adds another line of defense. Sometimes it proves to be a saving line.

The day Dustin talked to me about his relapse was a scary day for both of us. I had high hopes of him being finally recovered, as I'm sure he was enjoying the freedom that sobriety brings. I don't understand why he forfeited his freedom when he compromised his sobriety, but like it or not, that's just what he had done.

Dustin's vice has always been going along with other people. It seems like drug use tends to come in a group setting at first, and then the heavier and scarier it becomes, the more individual it becomes. Maybe that's because a group of deceitful, conniving people cannot exist in close company for long before one of them betrays another.

How drugs found Dustin each time he recovered was always a mystery to me. I didn't understand his stupidity. I knew he needed to avoid all contacts and associations from his drug days. But who could warn him about individuals who hid it like he once had that he would become friends with –

even intimate with? As a parent, there was nothing I could do at this point in Dustin's life.

His plan to turn himself over to the courts was interesting if he would indeed go through with it. All I could do was await my wife's report on the Judges' orders for my son.

In his last chapter, Dustin discussed how addicts often draw lines designating their moral boundaries. I would like to discuss another boundary that he has often mentioned. For our purposes, we will call it "The Doctor Line."

Dustin explained to me that he has seen this time and time again within the scope of addiction. Most individuals who use this are people who don't yet know they are addicts, or they just simply will not admit it. Many of them deny it. Perhaps a person gets a serious injury. Maybe a broken appendage, a car wreck, childbirth, or another kind of extensive surgery and they are prescribed narcotic painkillers to help ease their discomfort.

The problem is that narcotic pain pills can only mask the pain for a small period of time. Their chemical makeup does not actually make the pain go away; it only tells the brain that the pain does not exist. The chemicals in the pill attach themselves to the pain receptors in the body and interrupt the pain messages relayed to the brain. Besides interrupting pain receptors, opioid painkillers also have another lovely function. They tell the brain to release a chemical called dopamine. Dopamine relays a message to the brain telling it it is happy. Hence, doped up. After a few hours, the body metabolizes the chemicals and the brain once again starts receiving pain signals. The individual takes another pill and the process starts all over. Over the course of a prolonged prescription, typically a couple of weeks or longer, the brain acclimates to the higher levels of dopamine it has been experiencing. When the prescription runs out and the levels of dopamine fall, the brain craves more. It tells the person that they are unhappy because the dopamine levels are not where they were a few days ago.

As physical withdrawals set in, the individual recognizes the need for more. Once that has been procured, they will start feeling like the original dose is inadequate. They decide to take just a little more than has been prescribed. Maybe it was a tough day. You deserve it, right? The body's tolerance for the medication will continually increase. It will never decrease. The pills are running out faster and faster each month. Time to consult the doctor to explain that the pills aren't quite strong enough and they're running out because it takes a little more than prescribed to have the same effect...

If you notice a friend or a loved one saying and experiencing this type of scenario, you should be concerned. This is "The Doctor Line." Individuals will justify their actions by explaining that: "They are prescribed by a doctor and he says I need them!"

While this scenario is from my own experience, I advise you to confront an individual you are worried about at your own risk. Many people that truly have a prescription drug problem do not realize their own addiction. When confronted, most will deny it. Addiction is a dirty word that no one likes to be categorized by.

15

NEVER SAFE

DUSTIN

JANUARY 2009

"What was I thinking?! Why did I do this?!" I wince to myself as I wipe tears of pain from my cheek. It has been 19 hours since I was in front of the judge and I am already regretting what I did. My red, two-sizes-too-small jumpsuit feels rough against my skin and pinches in uncomfortable places. It had elastic sewn into the fabric about waist high with stiff white letters starched across the back. The only thing that would make my jail garb more uncomfortable is if it were made of itchy wool. They must have used all the wool making the blankets in this hellhole. I just can't believe I am going through this again. During my last sentence, I told myself I would do whatever it took to never return to jail again – much less simultaneously withdrawing.

I guess I am only capable of lies – even to myself. The only truth I know is that nothing I say or think is truth. The irony is mind numbing. Separating my lies from reality is not easy to do. The only hope I have of discerning between the two is having a sober mind. That is another process I will be going through during my stay here. First I must concentrate on overcoming the physical agony upon me.

After surviving the first week, I feel well enough to talk with some of the other cellmates. After telling some guys that I asked to be put in jail, word spread fast. It didn't take long for me to become known as "The idiot." I'm okay with that though. The real idiocy had taken place not days before when I had admitted myself, but months before when I allowed myself to relapse. I didn't much care what anyone inside the jail thought. I am doing this for myself and I know it is my only option to fix my life. I know that when it is all over, I will be glad I did it. Since I've only been in a week, I'm still regretting it. I just need more time.

Charlotte came to visit me a few days ago. It was nice to see her even if it did surprise me with all the turbulence and indifference we had fostered between us in the final months of our relationship. She looked sober and that helped me stay positive. She told me that she would come see me twice a week. I'm happy about that. It gives me something to look forward to, someone in reality to report my progress to. I don't know how much of an anchor she can be, but I will hang onto her for that for now.

3 WEEKS LATER: COURT DAY

The last three weeks have seemed like three months. I am so afraid the judge will sentence me to another month. Charlotte, my mom, and my sister will all be in the courtroom during my reappearance. I know it will be my mother that has the ultimate say in this. I know the judge will ask her if she thinks I am ready. I honestly feel like I am. However, I have to admit that if the Judge had granted my original request of 21 days in jail, I would have relapsed immediately after getting out of jail. I wasn't clear of my withdrawals on the 21st day. This last week has made a huge difference in the way I think and feel. During Charlotte's last visit the other day, she noticed what a huge difference this last week has made. She said I look and sound a lot better now than last week.

I assume I will get to go to the courthouse in person. I am excited to see Charlotte and my family again. But I am wrong. I find out just moments before the hearing that it will be done via video. I am secured in a room inside the jail with a TV and a camera so I can see and hear the Judge and vice versa. Having televised proceedings reduces my anxiety, but it does put a damper on my excitement for freedom and the hope that seeing my loved ones in person would have given me. Finally, the proceedings are under way.

I can't believe it, I have done it! I survived hell once again. I am overjoyed. The judge has deemed me fit to re-enter society. Five hours from now I will be back home with Charlotte. She is coming to pick me up as soon as I receive my release papers. I am thankful I have survived a second time. I am clean and ready to focus on staying that way. I begin to think about the goals I have made for myself during my stay here. Looking forward to the small milestones will keep me on track and prevent me from screwing up yet again.

"Dustin John, roll up your stuff! Your ride is here," I hear the gruff voice through the scratchy cell intercom.

I survey my cell quickly. I don't need to roll up my belongings. I've had my sheets torn off my bed for over three hours now anticipating my freedom. I am ready to smell fresh air. I am ready to go home and live my sober life again. The smile on my face cannot be removed by anyone. Nothing could change my positive, exuberant outlook I had at that moment. Walking through the corridors of the jail and the anticipation of seeing Charlotte is overwhelming. My heart beats out of my chest. I can't wait any longer. When I reach the booking area of the jail, I can see two men in suits on the other side of the glass. Charlotte is nowhere in sight. Panic rips through me. *Where is Charlotte?* One of the men notices me and the change in my demeanor. He whispers something to his partner. His secretive mannerisms make me nervous. *What is happening? Where is she?* From the control room of the jail, the operator releases the mechanical door lock. The loud click rings in my ears. I pull the heavy door open and walk into the lobby. I hope the men are not here for me but for some reason, I know they are. The shorter of the two men approaches me.

"Are you Dustin John?" he asks.

"Yes, yes I am. What is going on?"

"Charlotte isn't coming," he says distinctly. "She was in a horrible accident. She didn't make it. I'm sorry."

Screaming fills my ears. Sweat pours from my face. I can't understand what is going on. My vision blurs as my eyes fill with tears and I can't see anything around me. I sense a fuzzy smear of movement and the sound gets louder and louder. When I finally catch my bearings, I realize what is happening. I am lying on my bed. I am still in my cell.

"Dustin! Get up man! Your ride is here! What is wrong with you?" a voice reprimands me. I finally realize it is my cellmate. I missed the intercom announcement summoning me out of my cell because I was in a deep, obviously stressful sleep. I couldn't believe what had happened. It all seemed so real. It was just a bad nightmare. Charlotte is really here! I am finally going home!

BACK ON TRACK

Being sober again has been the greatest. I have made big plans for my future. I am attending AA and NA meetings on a regular basis again. I have almost been clean for six months and that means I have a job waiting for me. I have also decided to go to college. As icing on the cake, Charlotte's mom and aunt have invited me on a 2-week educational trip with them touring Italy. I don't feel worthy of the trip and I don't think getting sober should be this celebrated. However, I am an addict, I am selfish, and I think I will go. The trip is in three weeks and I will need a passport. I know it takes time to acquire one, so I get working on the process immediately.

Charlotte and I attend AA meetings three or four times a week together. Our relationship this last month has been based around sobriety instead of drugs. We even started meeting with a counselor. We're not required to go to counseling but we both feel better after our talks. There is also a couples NA meeting on Fridays that we attend. I think that is my favorite group. Every time we drive home from that meeting we are both so happy and neither of us can figure out exactly why we feel that way. All we know is we do and so we will continue to go.

While I was getting sober in jail, Charlotte had been working on getting sober on her own. My first evening in jail, Charlotte had an emotional breakdown. She couldn't handle the intense emotions she was experiencing, so she turned to her biggest comfort: cocaine. Charlotte procured a huge amount of cocaine that night. She was home alone and shot up over 10 balloons of cocaine in a matter of a few hours. It is a miracle she didn't die from an overdose.

Charlotte had work the next day. When she arrived, her boss approached her and he could tell something was wrong. Charlotte couldn't hold it in any longer. She told her boss everything she had done. Being a home health nurse and having so much to lose, Charlotte's emotional reserve must have been spent. She just couldn't hide her demon any longer.

Her boss fired her on the spot. Charlotte was a mess once again. The next day, she received a phone call from her employer. They explained that it is illegal to fire an employee if the employee comes forward with the drug problem. Neither Charlotte nor her boss had known that. Charlotte still had her job, but she was now faced with some very stiff legal state requirements. She would now be required to take random drug tests and meet with a drug counselor each month. Charlotte was also placed on probation for four years where she would check in with an assigned probation officer to verify her drug status and intention to be a law-abiding citizen.

I believe the day Charlotte told her boss about her drug abuse was the day she realized that cocaine was much stronger than she was. That was her cry for help. She knew she couldn't do it alone. It was this act of letting go that allowed Charlotte to begin taking control of her life once again.

ITALY TRIP

I am pretty nervous right now. I have never traveled overseas and now I am flying alone. Charlotte, her mother, and her Aunt left the airport 8 hours before me. They will meet up with me after I arrive in Italy; I just hope I don't get lost in the mean time. International travel is a huge mess of unfamiliar places, strict times, and variables you don't want to screw up because you don't know where you'll end up if you do. *What if I accidentally take the wrong flight and end up in some weird country? What if I miss one of my flights? So much could go wrong!* My mind races with all the unknown variables as I try to get comfortable in my cramped middle seat above the airplane's left wing. The last thing I remember is the flight attendant handing me a blanket.

A loud screech pulls me back to consciousness and a sudden jerk lurches me forward in my seat. The noisy engine thrusters echo in my head as the plane touches down.

"All of us aboard Lufthansa Flight 103 would like to welcome you to Dusseldorf," a friendly flight attendant beams over the intercom system.

I guess that is it. *That wasn't so hard.* I can't believe we're already in a foreign country. I slept for almost 11 hours. My back and neck are in knots and my right leg tingles with the sensation of the limited blood flow it must have received from my prolonged seated position. Even though we had landed intact, my body feels like it has barely survived a crash. As the passengers file off the aircraft, I try to shake my aching body. I put on my sunglasses and grab my carryon. I have to navigate the foreign airport and find the customs entryway. The airport is crowded as people rush in all directions. I push my way through the crowds until I spot the entry point. I am nervous. Even though I have nothing to hide, the scrutiny of customs makes me feel like I am breaking the law somehow.

Having uniformed officials question me makes me nervous. I guess I'm so used to being on the wrong side of the law that even when I have nothing to hide, my brain is still trained to be frightened. What if I was an unknowing pawn in an undercover drug smuggling ring? I felt like I was in a movie. My passport is brand new, not a crease or stamp in it. Will customs believe I am really just a carefree tourist? I hand the officer my passport. He inspects it carefully and waves an ultraviolet pen light across one of the pages. He looks back down at it and then looks back up at me. Does my fake smile betray my inner nervousness? Can he tell I am on edge? What's wrong with my passport?

"What is the purpose of your visit?" he questions sternly.

"I'm here on vacation, Sir. We, we are going on a tour of Italy," I stammer.

"Is that right? How long will you be visiting Italy?"

"I will be here for 14 days."

"Hmm," he mumbles.

He does a final scan at the back of my passport and opens it up. He reaches for the approving stamp, but then hesitates and stares at me for a moment. Is he giving me one last chance to confess something?

"Well sir, enjoy your vacation," he finally says stamping my passport.

MILAN, ITALY: THE FIRST EVENING

It is nice to finally be able to relax. I found Charlotte's family at the Milan airport and we all make it to our hotel without a hitch. I am glad to be tagging along with experienced travelers. It is calming to be out of the airports and crowded city areas. There are other families on this tour with us as well. Many of them are friends of Charlotte's mother. We are all staying at the same motels and riding together in a tour bus in the morning. I have met most of them in passing. We're staying in a nice hotel but the towels are only a bit larger than a washcloth. Charlotte, her mom, and aunt go down to the cafe downstairs. They want to drink coffee and watch the sun set on the outdoor patio. I tell them to go without me. I'll be right down after I take a quick shower.

The view from the downstairs patio is gorgeous. A 3-foot tall rock wall encloses the outdoor patio. The rocks are all varying shapes and sizes following no specific pattern. A detailed iron trellis crowns the rock wall created a defining enclosure on three sides. Long wavy vines cover the trellis. Red and purple blooms peek out from the vine curtain. It is all so artistic and bohemian. The roof is half open above revealing a clear sky punctuated by sparkles of starlight. Three large round wicker bowl chairs sit empty in this magical enclosure. If there was anyone here earlier, they have all left by the time I arrive.

I am alone. I sit down in an arched tall-backed wicker chair and close my eyes. I think about my past life and where I was just months before. I am in the middle of paradise right now. I left my life of despair and agony. It is now in the past far behind me and I can see now what life is all about. Look where the freedom of sobriety has taken me already! There are so many things in the world I have yet to experience and the thought of missing out on any of them because of choosing drugs makes me shutter. I can't believe that I would have missed where I'm at right now if I hadn't turned myself over to the courts just months ago. It was one of the hardest things I have ever had to do, but look at the reward! I truly have a new beginning to decide what I will make of my life. It feels so good to know how far away from drugs I am at this moment. This is the farthest I have ever felt from my drug-laden old life. Little did I know that gap was to be shortened, and it was only 10 seconds away.

"Good evening mate! What brings you here?" a thick English accent speaks up intruding on my solitude.

"Good evening!" I reply. I smile at the man's accent. I have never spoken with someone with such a thick British tone. He is in his early thirties and he seems very friendly and eager to chat.

"How would you like to split some English tea mate?" he says.

"Sure! That sounds great. I'll buy!" I offer. It is so easy to make friends here.

I order some tea from the cafe just inside the door and we sit at a booth nearby.

The waitress walks up to our table and sets the tea in front of us. As she walks away my new friend asks, "So, are you American?"

"Yes. Yes I am. I am from Utah," I reply with an awkward smile.

"I would guess when you go home, you're going to tell all your mates that you went to Italy and had English tea with a real Englishman, right?"

I can't help but laugh out loud. His assumption is right. That is exactly what I am going to do. We chat for a few more minutes and then he pops the question.

"Hey mate, I've got a question for ya," he begins as he reaches into his pocket and opens his hand in front of me. "Have you ever seen one of these?"

I can't believe what he is holding before me. I am thousands of miles from home. How can this be? Do I have some kind of enormous target on me that everyone else can see but I cannot? How is it that the first person I have a conversation with asks me if I have ever seen an OxyContin!? Oh you mean my favorite painkiller of all time? Of course I know what it is! An urge comes over me. I want that pill and I want it now! My stomach drops. I feel that familiar empty pit in my stomach. I am completely caught off guard and unprepared to face this pretty yellow pill. I don't want to act like a redneck at a swap meet so I try to play it cool.

"Yeah, that looks familiar. I've heard of 'em," I calmly reply. "Do you want to sell me one?"

By its buttery color, I know it is a 40 mg OxyContin so I know that even a small piece will be more than enough for me. After all, it has been a few months since I have done any and my usual old dose was around 15 mg.

"No I can't sell you any," he says crushing my hopes. His statement devastates me but I try to act like it isn't a big deal. "You bought the tea, so I will just give you some."

He breaks the pill in half and hands me some. I enter a euphoric state with the pill in hand. I can't wait to ingest that pill and feel the numbing effects of it. I don't sniff it this time. I just toss it in my mouth and chew it up. I don't know what my reasoning is for this exactly. I guess I am trying to minimize the damage of my actions – as if that justifies the severity of what I have just done. It won't be as potent ingested orally, but the bottom line is I am in the process of relapsing.

Thirty minutes after chewing up the pill, I have a great idea. I am obviously jacked up, yet I invite my newfound British pal to have dinner with Charlotte

and our group. I don't know how Charlotte or her mom doesn't notice. I am
so high at the dinner table I can't see straight and my pupils are barely larger
than poppy seeds.

I see my British friend at breakfast the next morning. I decide avoid
talking to him – it would only result in another pill. The next day, I tell
Charlotte what I have done.

The rest of the trip goes well. We do a lot of walking, traveling, and moving
from one hotel to the next. After my relapse in Italy, Charlotte and I find an
AA meeting in Rome. It turns out to be a great experience and I learn a major
lesson in my sobriety: relocating or moving to a different area will not keep
an addict sober. Sobriety and geography have no connection. I guess I will
check "get away from the drugs" off my "How to Stay Sober" list. Every time I
tried this route I failed miserably.

6 Months Later

I have been sober since my vacation slip up. I have focused most of my
energy into starting some college courses for Engineering. I never imagined I
was the kind of person who would go to college. Once my life went on a
decade long downward spiral, college always seemed way too far out of
reach. Plus, I figured the rigorous self-discipline of attending class and
completing assignments were nowhere near my skill set. Now that I am
clear-headed, sober, and have gained some confidence in who I am, I am
ready. I am excited at the prospect of doing something with my life.

My college courses have gone smooth so far. I have somehow managed to
get straight A's even with all the arguments at home. Charlotte and I have
been constantly arguing. She claims I am not doing enough with my time and
I claim that nothing would be enough for her. It all boils down to money. She
makes me feel like I am not helping enough financially, which is true. I am
contributing very little monetary increase to our relationship. However, I
tried working full-time and doing school full-time but it was too much for me.
In the beginning, Charlotte was very supportive of my plan to go back to

school and offered to help me through the process. The positive feedback I received only lasted one semester. By the end of that semester, she was making comments to belittle me and made me feel like I wasn't doing my part. I was working as many hours as my boss would give me and I taking 16 credit hours that semester. I was only making enough money each month to make my truck payment, so I wasn't a huge help to her financially. From my stance, I knew I wasn't able to contribute much financially, so I did my best to make up for it. I did the dishes, cooked, and cleaned as much as I could. I am not a huge fan of doing laundry so that was off my contribution list, but I did remodel her entire living room as well as landscape and upkeep our yard. I figured those contributions saved us thousands in labor costs.

No matter what I do though, it's never enough. I have known for a long time this would be a big problem in our relationship. I wish I could have foreseen how big a problem it has turned into. I can't do it anymore. I have to break up with Charlotte.

15

Dreams & Will Power

Dallas

January 2009

I can't explain how proud I am that Dustin was able to successfully pull himself out of the addiction relapse cycle by subjecting himself to some of the toughest help out there: jail. Although it is a roof and food, jail is no fun from his accounts.

It is such a traumatic experience in fact, that Dustin confided in me once that he has had dozens of nightmares dreaming he was in jail. Apparently, those dreams would grip him with horrific terror and felt excruciatingly real. I believe the mental psyche is reaching out during these episodes of what I would say fall into the Post-Traumatic-Stress Syndrome category. Although PTS Syndrome is typically experienced on a regular basis by veterans who have given so much and seen so much for our country, it is a known fact that the brain retains our emotions and can amplify them and recall them in our subconscious.

Dreams are very powerful when an individual is in the drug scene. Dustin has had numerous conversations about this topic with some of his drug associates, and those individuals have verified that he is not alone. On the flip side of terror dreams, these individuals can also experience dreams conveying the euphoria of getting high. According to Dustin, these dreams take an addict through his or her drug routine, but seldom conclude with the addict successfully achieving their high. From these dreams, Dustin would wake up angry, annoyed, and looking for a way to remedy the situation his subconscious had created for himself. Indeed, it is easy to see how these dreams could trigger relapses for those who are not mentally equipped to stave them off.

As Dustin has proven, it is almost impossible for individuals to overcome addiction on their own. That is why they are in the position they are in: they have proved incapable of making choices that would grant their freedom from such binding substances. Dustin has detailed already quite a bit of the benefits of support groups like Alcoholics Anonymous and Narcotics Anonymous. When individuals stick with those programs, they work. They provide the mental, emotional, and spiritual tools addicts need to physically overcome their demons. For a true addict, will power alone can never be enough by inherent genetic composition because they have already introduced such a synthetic substance into their bodies.

Will power is a self-generated matter. It is comprised of self-control and determination. While these characteristics are essential to overcoming addiction and staying sober, the AA and NA programs teach addicts how to develop them, how and when to use them, and when more help is needed.

Dustin always thought he would be like many of the individuals he saw around him on the streets or in jail: homeless, mid-to-late fifties, accomplishing nothing in life, merely existing. To be honest, every time I saw a homeless man with a sign or outstretched hand asking for donations, I saw a glimpse of Dustin. That irony made me sick inside. But I saw Dustin overcome this image. I saw him break free of it. The odds may have been stacked against Dustin, just as they are against many of these other individuals, but the good news is there is hope. There is hope for each of them and their families who want out of addiction but always seem to fall short of continual sobriety.

I had no idea about Dustin's slip-up abroad until the writing of this book, but I can't help but feel proud that he was able to finally exercise his will power in seeking help before a relapse took hold and drug him under once again.

I don't know how often he faces the temptation to check out and give up on his sobriety. It is something he has to fight for, and I know it must take an awful lot of work and courage even digging himself out of the pit he dug for himself, but I know he is working towards goals in his life that he never realized were possible. Sobriety may be difficult to maintain, but as Dustin experiences the freedoms and joys it brings, I pray that will be enough to convince him to never go back.

The human mind is the one of the most complex, powerful, and unpredictable instruments ever studied. This is one reason why people react differently to medications. One individual may have a completely different set of side effects than the next. Because the human mind does not react the same way for every human, you will also have different types and levels of addiction.

I once knew a man who, one day became a smoker. Then he decided he wanted to use chewing tobacco. He continued using tobacco every day for a few years. One day he decided he wanted to quit. And he did. Right then and there. No nicotine withdrawal. No cravings. No anxiety. With a smile on his face, he never looked back. He quit tobacco and it had absolutely no physical or mental control over him.

Is Dustin that kind of person? I have chewed on this question for hours. Why could one guy I knew quit so absolutely, and yet my son seemed fated to struggle through a hellacious battle barely escaping with his life?

This is where a lot of people get confused – including myself. They see that one person who isn't wired with an "addict brain" so they believe that everyone is wired the same way and they will always be in total control over these mind-altering substances. Some people are binge users or drinkers. Let me assure you, it is a dangerous line to walk tampering with these substances thinking you are the one who can remain in control! They comprise a very small minority of addicts out there. Just go to any AA meeting, and you will learn that fact for yourself. These binge users get high or drunk for brief intervals by taking in as much drug or drink as they can in that short amount of time. They may go weeks in between drinking and drugging. Other people, like Dustin, would drink and drug all day, nonstop, as much as he could take until he was about to die.

There is no limit to the variety of addictions and their severity in combination with each unique user's mind. With that being said, there is also no one way to stay sober. Though small in number and very rare, there have been true addicts who have quit for good on their own devices, with no outside help whatsoever.

There is a large majority who, like Dustin, lose total control of their life when they become an active user and/or drinker. I can tell you that I know what has worked for my son and what did not work. If Dustin weren't forced to do rehab, AA, or NA meetings, or group therapy by a Judge, he wouldn't have made it.

Dustin told me that the biggest hurdle for his recovery has been breaking his mindset of promising himself, "Now I will stay sober for the rest of my life." Making that kind of pledge about something you are not in full control of is dangerous. Instead, Dustin has learned the better mindset of: "Today I choose to be sober."

I am so very proud of the accomplishments that my son Dustin has made in these last few years. The difficulties of writing this book for example, have not just been in getting words on paper in a coherent manner, but have specifically posed a threat to Dustin as he has been constantly reminded of his addiction wounds. As his mind has conjured up the blissful feelings of getting high, Dustin has had to lay those urges to experience them once more aside. He has also had to accept that in airing his dirty laundry to the world, he may not be liked so easily. While we all have shadows in our lives we would never want publicized, Dustin has boldly sacrificed his own pride in allowing himself to relive many of his appalling actions in a most public manner. That kind of courage and humility is the mark of a true man. Even now, as my quickly declining health does not have a good prognosis, I can smile knowing my youngest son is now a pillar of hope for others. Dustin has kicked addiction for good; I feel it in my heart and soul.

Surely many people, myself being at the top of the list, want nothing more than to hear Dustin say, and really mean, "I promise I will stay sober for the rest of my life." But really, there is no guarantee in this statement. As we've seen Dustin's chance encounters with relapse and watched him fall victim time and time again to the habits he has already kicked, we cannot help but feel disheartened. However disappointed we feel with his slip-ups, if we believe Dustin cannot recover from his previous vow of sobriety, we condemn him to live out his life as an addict until it takes him to his end.

On the other hand, if he adopts the mindset of taking each day as they come and working each day to choose sobriety, he knows that if something happens one day that causes him to backtrack, he can choose something different the next day. It builds a mental way out for him instead of trapping him within his relapse. Eternal sobriety is an overwhelming ultimatum for a recovered addict. Either they will live or die by such a promise. Although living would be the preferred route, we have to acknowledge the true extent of what addiction is. We know that it goes beyond physical and also tampers with the mental state of an individual. It may not make sense, but the mind has power to make us all do stupid things. Our will power will not always save us from illogical options. It is the same for an addict. He or she may be prone to relapsing despite the therapy and training they have received to help them overcome. But they must understand there is a way out again. This is the only way they will truly overcome for good. The day they assume their recovery is the day they open themself up to temptation. And so, each day for the rest of his life, Dustin must wake up and say, "Today, I choose to be sober."

16

CHOOSING SOBRIETY

DUSTIN

FEBRUARY 2009

My relationship has been over with Charlotte for three months now. I moved back to my hometown and am living close to my family. This is the best thing for me right now. I have missed the small town feel that I grew up in. I have been so removed from it for so long and I love being back here again. Life seems simpler. People seem more genuine. The smell of wheat fields and fresh cut grass fill the air. I've missed the spontaneity of driving down a paved road that suddenly turns into dirt. It's so nice to have the option of taking a back road just to avoid "busy" downtown streets. Having a one-way Main Street. No Stop signs. No gang signs. Bottomless potholes. The quiet whispers of chattering gossip. I have missed it all. I am glad to be back! All my life, my whole family has stayed pretty close to one another geographically. My initial move to Salt Lake was the farthest any member of my family had moved away from one another, except for my stint in St. George. I am back now inside the family nucleus. That is a great feeling.

The only downside to moving back home is that I still work and go to school up in Salt Lake. To help simplify, I transfer to a local community college only 25 miles from home instead of 50. I also decide give my two weeks notice at my job. My boss understands. I am only working enough hours to cover my fuel expenses to drive to work and back. It doesn't make much sense for me to continue working for him and he agrees.

I focus all my attention on my schoolwork. When I'm not studying for a test or doing math problems I play a few hands of Texas Hold'em Poker on the Internet. I was playing it yesterday and I met this woman playing at the same virtual table. She seems really nice. Her name is Maiju. I ask her if she wants to be friends with me on Facebook. She says no. I can't blame her, but I hope I can talk with her again. The glitch with this Maiju girl is she lives in Finland.

It's been two weeks since I first chatted with Maiju. Today I received a friend request on Facebook from her. She wants to be friends after all. I am so excited. I send her a message asking why she decided to friend request me after she originally said no. Her response explains that since I didn't freak out about her denying my request, I passed a preliminary normal test. I guess some men don't take rejection as well and hence they do not pass the normal test. To be fair though, I've also seen the way some men talk to women over the Internet. It is anything but polite and respectful, and if I were a girl, I would be wary of having anything to do with interacting with men online.

Through our virtual correspondence and our Facebook friendship now, I find out a lot more about Maiju. She was born in Finland. She's 25 years old and is the typical Netherlander with blonde hair and beautiful blue eyes. But she is anything but typical to me. She speaks three different languages and uses the metric system. In most cases, using the metric system would a deal breaker. This time, I decide to let it slide. When I asked her how tall she was and she told me in centimeters, it was like some mystery that I was supposed to solve. I had no idea what her centimeters meant in my language. When I told her I was 5'10" I think she thought I would come up to her kneecaps. At this point, I figured it would be useful to find a metric converter so communication between us could be understood a little better.

Luckily, her written English is really good. If I had to try and communicate with her in Finnish, we would have had bigger issues than the metric system. I had no idea Finland had their own language until I met her and I thought Finnish only meant what happened when you were done with something. Maiju has already taught me so much.

We chat on a daily basis. Our time zones are a 9-hour difference. We learned each other's schedule quite quickly. By 3:01 pm today in Utah, it was already tomorrow for Maiju. Once we figured out our available chat times, the rest seemed to come quite easily. We get along so well. Something about her draws me in. She is beautiful and smart and interesting. Most importantly, she has never touched a drug in her life. The thought of actually getting to meet her in person is constantly on my mind. I just don't know if it will ever happen and that makes me sad.

As our relationship progressed from a long-distance friendship to a long-distance crush, I knew Maiju was becoming more afraid of the seriousness of our situation. We like each other a lot and our relationship is progressing more and more. We know the distance between us is a major problem. There are times I feel her pulling away from me in her messages trying to let me down slowly because she knows it is almost impossible for this to ever really work. I understand why Maiju is retracting. I can't blame her for being afraid. I mean, what kind of person exists through a virtual relationship? That's not even considered a healthy behavior by today's emotional and mental standards. At this point in our relationship, I am willing to do whatever it takes to make things work between us. It might sound crazy, but I know she is the woman I have been searching for. She is my other half and she completes me like no one else ever has. I am always able to talk her through our distance issues and the day she told me how many hours it would take her to get to Utah, I knew she was thinking seriously about coming to see me. From that point on, we started planning her first trip to the United States. It is six months away. Having something so solid to plan on makes me unbelievably happy. I can't wait to see Maiju in person; to spend time with her, to get to know, to interact with her face to face. I am ecstatic. Once she purchases her round-trip ticket for a weeklong stay, I begin to plan our week. I want it to be perfect. I want to show her as much as I can during her stay. How else will I convince her to stay forever?

The past six months have been amazing. My relationship with Maiju has only progressed and developed in a positive direction. I am more in like with her than ever. I can't believe she will be here today! Once I pick her up at the airport, we plan to drive straight to Las Vegas. I grab my car keys and walk out my front door. The anticipation and nervousness starts building inside me like never before. *What if she doesn't like me in person?* I take a deep breath, start my car, and focus on steadying my sweaty grip on the steering wheel. *I hope everything goes as planned.*

I pull into the airport terminal and anxiously wait for Maiju to appear in our predetermined waiting spot on the curb. I have only seen pictures of her but I know I will spot her right away. A minute later, there she is, walking towards me, wheeling a pink hard covered suitcase. She is more beautiful than I remembered in her pictures. Her long, straight blonde hair blows slightly in the small wind gusts that swirl around us. Every step she takes towards me, I become more nervous. I am trying my best to hold my composure but her beauty makes me forget how to talk. I get out of the car and walk towards her. As soon as we are close enough, we embrace. This gesture relaxes me enough to mumble a small word despite my nervousness.

"Hi," I say.

"Hello," she whispers in my ear.

I put her luggage into the trunk of the car and open her door.

"It's so good to finally see you in person," I stammer.

"Yes, it is."

"How was your flight?" I ask hoping some conversation will hide the thunderous beating of my heart through my shirt.

"Long!"

"I bet it was! I'm glad you finally made it. You ready to drive to Las Vegas?" I say smiling as we pull away from the terminal.

"Sure!" she replies exuberantly and we're off.

And so our road trip begins. We're not really strangers, but we're not really lovers. We are long-distance friends who want to find out if our relationship is more than that. An adventure to Las Vegas is an ideal testing ground. Time to have some fun experiences together and enjoy getting to know each other more in person. She is nervous about speaking in English with me. I can tell she speaks English just fine, but it isn't her native language and she's never had to speak it consistently before. I can't imagine how different this all must be for her. We solve the communication gap by using paper and pen to speak for the first day or so. The toughest part about that for me is not being able to hear her accent. I love the way she speaks. Her accent is so delicate and the lilt she puts on her phrases make the words different. They become playful and fun, new and wonderful.

I think the hardest part for Maiju is not knowing if I am a serial killer who is going to take her out into the Nevada dessert and bury her in a shallow grave. It took a lot of guts for her to trust that I was the man I portrayed myself to be.

We arrive in Vegas seven hours later, and she is beginning to realize I may be a little crazy, but far from a serial killer. We stay at Treasure Island on the Strip for our two nights in Vegas. I take her to watch the Bellagio water fountains, the M&M Factory, The Coke Factory, and we buy some fun items at the Caesar's Forum Shops in Caesar's Palace.

Our first night there, I am lying on our bed waiting for Maiju to get out of the shower. As I reflect on our relationship over the past several months and then our interactions today, I realize I am falling in love with her. I know it is far too soon but I can't stop myself. I don't want to stop myself. I have to tell her. Maiju is everything I have ever wanted in a woman. I have never been happier in my life. Every aspect of my life feels complete when I am with her. That night, I tell her my feelings. I love her.

We spend two days in Vegas then drive to California. After a 10-hour drive, we finally reach the beach and enjoy stretching our legs and feeling the wet sand between our toes. As we walk along the beach, I find a stick that has washed ashore and use it to carve a large heart in the grainy sand with our initials in it. It is so large you can't read it until we stand cliff-side on our walk back to the car. When I am around her, I feel like I can finally just be myself – and that is a great feeling.

Even though this is her first trip to America and she is technically a tourist, we spend a lot of time in the hotel just talking and watching movies together. The first movie we watch together is the worst movie I think I have ever seen. We both make fun of it through the whole thing. It is so fun just goofing around together.

After three nights in California I realize I have to start planning our return trip. I hate the thought of sending her back on a plane to her home 7,700 miles away from me. It's on the other side of my world – literally! We don't have much time left together. The reality of having to say goodbye so soon breaks my heart like nothing has before. I do my best not to think about it.

We decide to drive back through Las Vegas on our way back to Utah. While we are walking down the strip one last time, I convince Maiju to go up the Stratosphere tower with me and ride the Big Shot thrill ride. It is by far the funnest and scariest ride in Las Vegas. Had she known how scary it really was, she never would have said yes and I never would've been called a bunch of Finnish words I didn't understand.

Maiju is exhausted by the time we return to the car so she sleeps the majority of the ride home. I can't help but glance at her in the passenger seat from time-to-time as I drive and steal glimpses of her sleeping. I know I should keep my eyes on the road, but it is such a beautiful sight seeing her so close to me. I begin thinking about how in love I am with a woman who lives an eternity away. What if we don't see each other again? What if she decides she could never move here? Could I ask her to give up her homeland and move so far from her family and all she has ever known? Could I move there and do the same? I know a long-distance relationship will never work long-term. There are so many people who will tell us we are crazy; that we can never make this work. Right then, at that moment, I realize I don't care what I have to do. I will be with this girl forever. I don't care what other people say. I know she is the one. Once I make that commitment to myself, I know we will be together no matter what stands in our way.

The ride to the airport is torture. I do my best not to breakdown while I'm driving but I am unsuccessful the closer we get. Small tears escape at first, and by the time we drive up to the terminal, I am a gushing mess. As I hold her on the curb, I can't let her go. We both weep as the minutes tick on. I know I have to loosen my embrace around her. She finally releases her hold on me as well and walks away into the airport. I have never felt more heartache than as I watch Maiju leave me. It feels like my heart has been taken to the top of the Stratosphere and let go without any braces or ground beneath. It just keeps falling forever until it smacks the pavement and flattens into a silly putty puddle. I feel completely lost and alone. I only spent one week with her but it feel like she is all I have ever known. Not knowing when I will see her again is killing me inside. I am completely empty, hollowed out by the thoughts of how far away she will soon be.

I drive aimlessly for two hours. Thoughts of getting high flash through my head over and over. Any time I encounter a difficult emotional situation in my life, my mind immediately plays a drug tape highlighting all the problems getting high will solve. Whenever this tape has played through my mind before, I never question it. I immediately just follow the mental advertising I have just played for myself and do whatever it takes to score some narcotic. But today is different. As I consider this option, I actually weigh out the pros: if I get some heroin, the pain of having Maiju leave me will dissipate – for now. Usually, this is where my thought process would stop. Sounds like the obvious solution to me. This time, I let the thought of getting high play through my head and I don't stop the tape there. I play it all the way through to where getting high will take me: being homeless, stuck in Jail, or dead.

None of those options include Maiju. Playing my thoughts all the way through saves me from using that afternoon and consequently relapsing. I realize at that moment, without a doubt, that Maiju is the one.

2 Months Later

My long-distance relationship with Maiju is still very real. We chat every day on the computer. Thanks to our time difference, we also write long messages to each other every day when the other one is sleeping. We talk a little on the phone, but international calls are so expensive we limit those. Video chat makes our relationship possible. Without it, we wouldn't make it through the distance.

For my birthday next month, I am getting the best present I can imagine. I am going to Finland to see Maiju. I have already started packing because I am so eager to see her again. Maiju and I have talked extensively about my past and my issues with drugs. She is so caring and does everything she can to understand. It must be very difficult for her to fully grasp what a monster I am because she has never seen marijuana, let alone heroin. If my addiction history scares her, she doesn't show it. She supports me 100 percent. For that I am grateful. I don't know what I would do without her in my life. How did I get so lucky?

6 Months Later

My trip to Finland a few months ago was amazing! Well, not seeing the sun for two weeks kind of sucked, but everything else was great. I met Maiju's family and her two dogs. Those dogs mean the world to Maiju. The small black one didn't care much for me and he barked at me for the entire time I was there. We took the dogs for walks and Maiju showed me around her hometown. We had a great time.

Leaving her again was heart wrenching. It's difficult when we see each other in person because we know we will have to leave each other again. We hate it so much that we have come up with a plan to fix the unbearable distance.

Maiju and I are working on getting her a VISA so we can live together. It is quite the process and we are far from being done. There are papers and then more papers. After those papers are finished, there is another stack of new papers to fill out. Then you contact the State. You make copies of documents that you have no idea how to get. Make sure they are not only notarized, but they need an Apostle Notary which can't be done without applying for a form through a website that is not on the Internet. Fortunately, this is the easiest way. Since we keep running into roadblocks and loopholes, we decide we need help if we are ever going to finalize this.

We hire a company and pay them a substantial amount to help us. We can't do it without their high-priced help. When I start seeing progress, I can hardly contain my excitement! If everything continues as planned, Maiju will move here in April of next year and by that June, we will be getting married.

MARCH 2012

I just realized that I have not been pulled over or been in trouble with the law in almost three years. The last time I have dealt with the law was when I asked the judge to help me get sober. No speeding tickets, no DUI's, no problems with any legal matters at all. And not just because I'm not getting caught! I am honestly at long last a law-abiding citizen in every aspect of the word.

I am realizing how staying sober pays off in so many ways. At one point in my life in the midst of my addiction battle, I just accepted the fact that I was always being harassed by the police. I thought that was just the way my life was. It was easy to blame it all on arrogant policeman. I now know that is far from the truth. There may be some arrogant officers out there, but the problem was me.

So many good things began to unfold the more sobriety I gathered. First and foremost, if I hadn't stayed sober, I would never have met Maiju. Maiju is a large part of my life that helps me see what I was doing wrong before.

I never wanted to admit who I really was or what I had become. In retrospect, it is easy to recognize that myself as well as all other addicts are extremely selfish people. Recognizing that helped me realize I didn't want to be that. I want to be a caring person who learns from his mistakes and has the ability to improve my life and others'. So many people have helped me on my journey to sobriety, now it is my time to give back to those I have hurt repeatedly. I may not be able to pay back all the financial debts accrued at my expense to my loved ones, but I know I can at least start making amends and righting my wrongs in smaller ways. Being around them and involved with their lives is a good starting place. Talking to them, explaining things in my life, even just writing this book is making up some of those wrongs. Anytime my family needs something, I try to be the first to lend a hand. My monetary value will undoubtedly be anything to brag about, but at least I can be a good person. I think that is what will make all their sacrifices seem worth it in their eyes. Staying sober is the least I can do. As long as I stay sober, I can continue to try to patch up those wounds I created, even if it does take me the rest of my life.

Maiju and I have seen each other two more times in the past eight months. She came back to America for two weeks last September and I went to Finland for three weeks in December. We have grown closer as a couple and our relationship is as strong as ever. I proposed to her on Christmas Eve while in Finland. Luckily she did say yes. That was our first Christmas together. It was the best Christmas of my life.

I just realized the other day though that Maiju and I have never spent more than three weeks together at a time and we are getting married in just a few months. I am not afraid though. I am sure other people thought about this as well but I don't care. I know I'm supposed to be with Maiju regardless of how "different" our relationship has been compared to most who decide to marry.

I just got a job working in the oil industry on the North Slope of Alaska. Even when Maiju moves to America it looks like we still won't be together more than a couple weeks at a time. I will work four weeks in a row, and then come home for two weeks. But since the job pays so well and we will just be starting out, I need to take the job. The US will not allow Maiju to start working over here until she receives her Green Card at least. That will still take another year to complete, so with all these issues in front of us, we know we need all the financial help we can get.

My first work deployment is just days away and since this is the first one, I will be working for six weeks instead of four. This allows me to fly home from Alaska when Maiju arrives in April. I will come home from Alaska and then fly to Chicago the next day. I will meet Maiju at the airport and we will rent a car and drive from Chicago to Utah. It will be a three-day trip. We chose to do it this way because she has all her belonging on the plane, as well as her two dogs. It's going to be a rough flight, especially for Maiju's much bigger, older Finnish Hound.

The last six weeks have been quite the experience for me. I was nervous flying alone to Alaska and training at a place I had never been. I stayed at a motel in Anchorage for the first week of training. It was extremely cold and I was hearing rumors that Anchorage was a beach resort compared to the North Slope.

My boss told me there was a guy flying in from Colorado for the training as well. We opted to share a hotel room and rental car to save some money. I met up with Colorado guy at the airport the next day and got to know him quite well. We had a surprisingly lot in common. First of all, we had the same name. He went by Dusty though so our co-workers could distinguish us. The other shocker was that he too was a recovered heroin addict. He had been sober for two years. I began to wonder if this happened for a reason. Was I supposed to meet this guy? Was he supposed to meet me? I found it very interesting just how parallel our stories were to each other. Our eight-man work crew had been assembled from all different parts of the United States. What were the odds of this guy also being on the crew, and then us being paired up together? When I discovered that Dusty and I had a lot in common, I was relieved. I no longer felt alone. I had someone I could relate too. Starting a new job was never a fun or easy thing for me but meeting Dusty eased a lot of my anxiety.

On our fourth day of training, we had to go to the clinic for our drug screening. I tested negative on all the panels. That was a great feeling. I no longer had to worry about being positive on my drug tests. I had failed so many in the past, I had become used to that failure and disappointment that led to being so depressed and angry with myself and my lack of self-control. Knowing I would come up negative on my drug test was a huge boost to my confidence as well as my sobriety.

After flying from Anchorage to Prudhoe Bay, I came to realize what everyone was saying about North Slope Weather. Cold doesn't even begin to explain wintertime on the North Slope. It was so cold I actually saw a lawyer with his hands in his own pockets!

The Prudhoe Bay Airport is tiny. It doesn't have jet ways for passenger comfort. You walk directly off the aircraft and across the runway into the airport. Well, I wouldn't call it an airport. It's more like a metal Conex with windows.

I didn't know what to expect when I first arrived. When I stepped off the plane and ice started forming on my eyelashes, I wondered if this had been a bad idea. My first paycheck persuaded me that the frostbite was worth it though. Being colder than I've ever been and working harder than I've ever worked was a small price to pay for the little slice of financial security my new job had provided. Just thinking of providing for Maiju in our new life together made it an easy decision to stay.

Now that those weeks are finished and I have worked 45 days straight, I am very ready to meet Maiju in Chicago. I had been counting down the days in Alaska. Once I boarded my plane back to Utah, I started planning the week ahead with Maiju. We have seven days to get from Chicago to Utah and move into our new house I found just before leaving to Alaska. I didn't have time to furnish the home, so Maiju and I will get to have fun picking out furniture, a television, a bed, food and toilet paper together. We have a lot to get done in a short time. When we finish moving into our home, I have to fly back to the Slope for another month leaving Maiju alone in a strange house, in a strange city, in a strange country thousands of miles from anything she knows. I hope she doesn't regret any of this!

I don't care much for the layout of the Chicago O'Hare Airport. It is huge and overwhelming – especially after the simplicity of the Alaska airports! I can't find my way around here. I end up getting lost over and over. Despite the enormity of the airport, my task should be simple. I am looking for a beautiful Scandinavian woman with a house in tow and two barking dogs. They should stick out like me in Mexico.

I pick up our rental car choosing a roomy SUV so we have enough space for the dogs and Maiju's belongings. Once Maiju and I find each other, it's almost 9 pm. We load up the car and travel just outside the city to find a hotel for the evening. My life may look like a helter-skelter mess with all the chaos, but having Maiju by my side once again fulfills me and makes me giddy and content all at the same time.

After four days of driving, we arrive at our new, small home. Maiju has only seen pictures of it before now but I think she really likes it. A natural, wooden porch runs the length of the front of the house with wooden slats lined vertically under a wooden railing. It makes the house feel homey. What little front yard there is is covered in weeds with a scraggly apple tree growing in the middle of the dry dirt. It is a corner lot so the backyard is quite large at least. A rickety wooden barn sits in the backyard and houses a couple of beehives. A peeling wooden fence encloses the backyard. This is great for our dogs. They can run freely without getting loose. Maiju loves it. I am sure our neighbors will love that too – especially at 3 in the morning. Our living room has 10-foot tall ceilings, which is nice and makes the home feel bigger than it really is. The kitchen is on the small side but for just the two of us it will work fine. Maiju jokes that she is living the American Dream now: she has a two-bedroom home, a backyard, and me. We can't imagine a better life for us right now. We are together.

This is a life-changing move for me. This is the first home I have had in over a decade. Having Maiju in my life gives me something tangible to continue to work for. It's sad that I couldn't stay sober years ago. No matter how bad things got, no matter how many times I went to jail, no matter what anyone told me, no matter how poor my health become, no matter how much financial ruin I was in, and no matter how many times death stared me in the face, I just couldn't get and stay sober. The reality is that as soon as addicted individuals accept the truth of their addiction: that it is in fact an addiction and they are not in control of it, the sooner they will be able to allow room for sobriety and healing to occur in their lives.

Now that Maiju is finally here in America, we are ready to finish our to-do list. Maiju moved here on a Fiancé VISA, which means we must get married within 90 days of her arrival. I am okay with that, but it puts a lot of stress to plan our wedding on her – especially because of my work situation. If we fail to make the deadline, she will be deported back to Finland. I am finally making enough money to support myself and Maiju and I don't want to jeopardize that by requesting drastic scheduling changes. We are on a tight schedule for our marriage. I am leaving for Alaska again already and we haven't made any wedding plans yet.

Before we know it, weeks have passed. Returning home from the North Slope, Maiju runs the wedding plans past me seeking my input and approval. We finalize our invitations and send them out. Because we're so crunched for time, only family and a few friends receive the invites in time. June 6th will be the wedding day and it is already May 2nd. There are lots of loose ends to tie up.

Maiju couldn't have been a better bride-to-be. Most American weddings are, well, American weddings. The bride wants everything perfect and grandiose. Thousand dollar cakes and dresses with picture perfect scenery and delicate hors d'oeuvres. They want silk tablecloths with lace ribbons, lustrous centerpieces and fireworks booming and cracking in the background. But not Maiju. She wants to wear blue jeans and a Nirvana T-shirt. For me, she is the ultimate woman. She is impartial to everything except the colors of the wedding. Even then, as long as the blue she was thinking of was close to whatever my mom was showing her then that was fine too. Had it not been for my mom staying up every night, frantically searching websites for different wedding items, the wedding would not have come together. Our wedding theme is half Finnish, half American. My mom somehow found mini Finland and mini USA flags that become the centerpieces. They are perfect. Maiju's mom mailed a number of authentic Finnish items to us to use for decorations. Unfortunately, Maiju's side of the family is unable to attend. We decide we will record the wedding and send it to her family in Finland. At least they can watch the celebration on video.

The days slip away and my two-week break is over. I am on a plane back to Alaska before we know it. The next four weeks on the Slope seems like four years. I can't help but cross off every day that passes. I am like a kid counting the days until Christmas. Sometimes I think it will never come. I will be stuck here forever because time is going so slowly. My anxiety is killing me. But believe it or not, the day finally comes.

Even though it sounded really fun, I convince Maiju to abandon the blue jeans and Nirvana T-shirt for a real wedding dress. She looks amazing in it. So perfect, beautiful and innocent. My sister and her friend do Maiju's hair and makeup. Her hair is pinned up in areas and left down in others. Perfect ringlets flow around her serene face. Her makeup is lightly brushed on and her eyes looked guiltless. She is so amazingly beautiful I can't believe she is going to be my wife. I begin to wonder if Maiju's vision is worse than she thinks. I wonder what she sees in a man like me. Somehow, Maiju is able to look past all my many flaws. I can't understand how she sees beyond them. She is so genuine and pure. She truly loves me, all of me. I don't understand her love for such an imperfect individual as myself, but I'm willing to spend the rest of my life trying to be worthy of that love. I have someone special. I have married my soul mate.

Maiju has shown me what real love in a relationship is all about. Before meeting her I thought I knew love. I was wrong. I would say that I loved, but now I know what love really is. Love does not anger. It does not have jealousy. It does not have selfishness. It does not hold resentments and it does not hate. Love forgives. Love looks past mistakes. Love does not raise its voice and love is necessary to sustain life. Having a disagreement with Maiju and not raising my voice is a foreign concept to me, possibly even un-American. But Maiju has taught me how it isn't necessary to yell or say mean, spiteful things when having a disagreement. Who would have thought?

Looking back at the last 12 years of my life, I am truly grateful for the changes that have taken place. I have gone from a homeless heroin addict who stole from and lied to family and friends, manipulated and injured loved ones and lived an all around horrific life on the streets, to a sober and responsible man who has found the meaning of integrity.

I have a small home with my wife and two dogs and a good job that pays the bills. My family trusts me once again and I work right alongside society.

None of this could have happened had I not made the decision to let go of my life and allow a bigger force to have sway in it. I have proven time and time again that when I try to control the things in my life, I wreak havoc all around me. My sobriety is a daily duty I must maintain. No one can do it for me. Yet, the day I try to do it entirely on my own again will be the day I will lose my freedom from my addiction.

I use my past as a reminder of how bad life will get if I decide to take charge of my life again and allow my pride to tell me I am in absolute control. All I know is that I am sober and I have figured out how to maintain sobriety the hard way.

The one thing I hope for more than anything else is that others can learn from my mistakes so they don't put their families and their self through the same hell that I inflicted on mine. So many times I had completely given up. I had lost all hope. I convinced myself I was going to die with a needle in my arm. Finding just a small piece of hope that was buried somewhere inside my torn soul, I found a way to take my life back time and time again. Putting everything I had into that small piece of hope was all that I had. I feel strongly that that speck of hope came from the unconditional love and belief of my loved ones. It came from their vigilance. I knew that even though I had disappointed them infinitely, they still believed in me. If you are reading this as the support for an addict in your life, I hope you can find that balance and reach the individual whom you must care for so much. If you are reading this as an addict, know that even if you don't feel that hope from anyone else, you just haven't met them yet – or maybe you have and you just don't realize how much you mean to them. It is worth it. If not for the people in your past, then for the people in your future.

I now have my life back and most importantly, my sobriety. There will forever be drugs and alcohol in our world. The "War on Drugs" will never be fought or won by our Governments or our Officials. They will only be fought and won by the affected families and the addicted. Together we can find hope in the war against addiction.

Maiju and I are walking our dogs down the winding sidewalk through our neighborhood. It is a beautiful day. The sun pierces through the singular transparent cloud in the sky. The heat from the sun beats down against my neck and shoulders. I am walking the larger of the two dogs and he pulls me ahead of Maiju who walk the smaller dog. We usually don't walk our dogs near the main road but something told me to take a different route today. Our neighborhood doesn't have any curb or gutter but it does have plenty of unmaintained fields that will someday make a nice housing development. We walk past one of the vacant fields so the dogs can explore and take care of their business.

As we walk out of the field and approach the road, I turn right towards Main Street. Main Street is about the only road in town with a curb and a gutter. We walk further towards the busy road. I am still being tugged ahead of Maiju, so I decide to reign in fido and wait on the curb before crossing the street.

As I stand there waiting for Maiju, a school bus starts coming towards me. As it gets closer, I can't take my sights off of it. The bus pulls right up to the curb and stops directly in front of me. I hear a familiar sound echoing in my mind. The hairs on the back of my neck stand up as the scissor style doors jerk open. The faint smell of hydraulics rips through my senses. Children scamper out of the bus, one by one. I feel afraid to look up at the windows of the bus. I can feel a piercing stare coming from the scratched windows above me. Despite my fears, I lift my head just enough to see the source of my unease. I can't believe what I see. It is a young boy. His hair is so blonde, it almost appears white. He has a small round nose and beams me a half-crooked smile. He looks just like I did 25 years ago. He is waving his hand at me saying hello inaudibly. Smiling. I can't believe what I have just seen. All I can do is grin back at the boy and feel a burst of joy consume me. As the bus pulls away, Maiju approaches me from behind.

"What is it?" Maiju says.

"Nothing. Nothing at all," I smile.

16

Miracles

Dallas

February 2009

Dustin's life has turned around so much in the past few years it is hard to believe he is the same person. In fact, he is not. When Dustin was under the influence on a regular basis, it was not him. It has been wonderful having the real Dustin back in our lives.

The biggest challenges our family faces at this point in our lives is mending the financial distress Dustin's choices have caused us – usually by our own stupidity as we would all too often run to his aid – and establishing real trust with Dustin again.

We are eager to trust Dustin, but we don't want to be victimized again. We have experienced that far too frequently in our lives and I have had enough. Any kind of relationship is established on the common grounds of trust and love. As we have proven, finding the balance between the two can be difficult. In the course of Dustin's sobriety however, we try as best we can to detach the idea of love from the idea of trust.

My wife and I counsel with each other over Dustin's interactions with us and although we are still willing to convey our love and support to him, we make it clear that he understands how to be honest with us. So far, it is going well.

I want to make it clear that what you do or don't do doesn't make another person an addict or alcoholic nor can it make them sober. No matter how much family love and support we gave Dustin, we could never stop him from sticking a needle in his arm. That was his decision and his alone. No one can convince an addict to get high – or to stay sober. It is solely up to them. This may seem contrary to the idea that Dustin put forth some time ago about will power existing in an entirely different part of the brain than addiction. Let me assure you that while you can't check out of addiction with will power alone, will power does play an integral part in opting to avoid addiction, and keeping free from relapsing once sober. We see this manifested through Dustin's choices every day. Exercising that will power to work towards goals in life is what keeps Dustin sober today. As you've seen from his experiences, drugs seem to seek him out. From the OxyContin Chap in Italy to his ex-girlfriend Charlotte, drugs found him wherever he went. It was only through exercising his will power, like avoiding the British man and seeking an AA meeting abroad, or turning himself in to jail, that a recovered addict will stay sober. And it is a conscious decision – a battle of will power – like a muscle that must be strengthened daily in order to be successful.

What we do or don't do makes up much of who we are – it defines us as individuals. Too many times, parents, friends, loved ones of addicts turn inwards wondering what they did wrong. Rest assured, you didn't do anything wrong. That individual makes his or her own choices. Those choices are not caused by any outside source other than the addict themself.

Dustin acknowledges that his childhood was perhaps better than average. He was not molested or beaten. We as his parents were not divorced and tried to model a healthy relationship of trust and love for him to learn from. We love Dustin unconditionally. Dustin told me recently how easy and selfish it would be for an addict to blame his addiction on something or someone other than the source of the addiction. For any addict to refuse responsibility for their own choices – and hence their own outcomes – is selfish and unfair. Blaming other people or circumstances only allows an addict to justify and continue their life choices. Until the addict can be honest with him or herself, they will continue to fall prey to the addiction of their own making.

That being said however, we are no longer a huge influence in Dustin's life. He has found someone who motivates him perhaps far better than we as parents could.

Dustin tells us quite a bit about this Finnish girl, Maiju, he has met online. Although my wife and I have only met her briefly, Maiju has become a loving part of our family's lives. After their marriage, she is around much more of course, especially since we are practically the only people she knows in this country and given the fact that Dustin is still working in Alaska for such long periods of time.

Maiju fits into our family like a fine piece of silken cloth from another country, as if she has been with us for years. Our relationship with her is growing each day, and we can see in her interactions with Dustin that she is full of love, forgiveness, patience, generosity, and simplicity in the things that matter most in life. She is a breath of fresh air for our worn down family that has been through so much. She teaches us the qualities that are missing in most family circles.

One of the most important things that Maiju excels at is her ability to help keep Dustin grounded. Alongside her, his feet remain planted firmly on the ground and she reminds him every day of the deep love she feels for him. I believe Maiju is the catalyst that reminds Dustin of the higher power that he needs to believe in to maintain his sobriety. She makes him remember to enjoy the simple things in his life and appreciate the beauty all around him.

During Dustin's sobriety, it is important that he surrounds himself with good, drug-free individuals. After all, that has been the source of so many of his slip-ups: falling in with the wrong crowd and lacking the self-control to walk away. Dustin has always been well liked by those around him and he typically makes friends easily. It is just getting him to find friends of a drug-free nature that share normal aspirations in life, not just getting high. Unfortunately, as his parents, we have never had the control of this aspect of his life.

You can imagine our relief as parents when we learn that this girl that Dustin has been virtually dating has never tampered with drugs in any way and has no desire to.

I have seen Dustin's experiences in a relationship with another addict more times than I would like. It is hard to treat your child with the respect the law tells you they should have when they become of age when they make such idiotic choices – especially alongside other so-called adults. A relationship comprised of two addicts can be extremely dangerous to each other. It is not impossible for the individuals to stay sober together. We saw in Dustin's relationship with Charlotte how they flourished when they focused on feeding each others' sobriety and encouraged each other to keep going and stay sober. The issue however comes when one of them falls. If one individual slips up, it makes it almost impossible for the other to escape unscathed. Just as sober addicts can boost each other, the opposite is also very real and they can too easily feed each others' fire as well.

For our son to achieve full, and what we can only hope is lasting sobriety, he has had to separate himself from all other addicts before he can progress. Dustin is always weaker than his addiction and he could never get sober on his own. He had to subject himself to incarceration for his healing to begin. That worked two-fold because it separated himself from his drug-user friends, including his girlfriend at the time, and it took away any agency he might have tried to exercise to take him further from or nearer to his vices.

Once an addict can admit their defeat and humble himself or herself enough to realize their addiction is stronger and more powerful than they are, that individual will regain control of their life. Dustin admits that this is one of the most difficult things to realize, and it is even harder to accept. A person cannot be both an addict and in control of their addiction simultaneously. Once Dustin came to that realization, and accepted it, the miracle began to take place.

The miracle I am referring to is evidenced in Dustin's actions and his increasing ability to live his own life. To see the progress Dustin made in his schoolwork, to see his ambitions amplified and his desire to work toward improving his life and creating a stable situation for himself was overjoying to our family. For this transformation to take place in only a matter of years from the hell Dustin had consigned himself to is nothing short of a miracle.

These miracles exist and in fact occur every day. Although we have cited the rampant scourge of addictive substances in this country, there is something stronger than their addictive power. It is difficult to overcome their far-reaching tentacles, but it is do-able. I am a witness to the integral role that loved ones can be in facilitating this miracle. Learning when to help and not help may take a while to master, but we can always show our love for these individuals we care so much about. That miracle of unconditional love goes hand-in-hand with the miracle of sobriety. These miracles take time – often years. They are never finished. Each day I see Dustin living a healthy, normal, drug-free life I consider a miracle.

Epilogue

DUSTIN

Throughout my addiction, I have come to many crossroads. Some have taken me deeper into my addiction while others have aided in my recovery. It is during these critical junctures in time that determine the entire destination of our lives. The years spent writing this book were painstakingly difficult at times, especially during my periods of relapse. Once I reached a point in recovery that I truly believed I had the knowledge and experience to stay sober, I was tested once again. Before my father and I could complete this book, he was diagnosed with a terminal illness. I was powerless to change the course of his disease. As his ailing body waned under the demon that refused to release him, he fought more fiercely than ever to accomplish one last thing in his life: the finishing of this book, our story to the world that some demons can be overcome.

Although he never vocalized it, I have to believe seeing this book completed also held a more sacred promise for my dad. Much like my pathetic attempt at living a successful life, our book was the subject of much hope, hard work, and energy. Who knows how many hours my father languished over his wayward son, how many hours he spent musing of my whereabouts and puzzling over the financial distress I had all too often caused my family. Would there ever be success? Would all of his efforts to raise me, all of the time invested in my manhood, all the love stockpiled in the face of my persistent regression be in vain? I doubted my own ability to prove victorious, and have more than once shuddered at the horrific shadows of my past. I may never be a quantifiable success by society's standards today, but as this book is completed, I know the feeling of victory doubled over.

Like so many that approach the veil of death, Dad became so ill in his last few weeks that he could no longer communicate verbal words. I wanted more than anything to press a published, hard copy of this completed book into his hands, to thumb through it with him, to read the passages of our victory aloud to him by his side, for him to feel the weight of the difference he had made in this world through a few pounds of bound paper sitting on his lap. I never had that chance though. He passed away shortly before this story was finalized.

I don't know what the completion of this story signified more for Dad: if it assured him more of my sobriety, signified that he had indeed made a substantial contribution to society, or just meant that our experiences could now change someone else's life and hopefully prevent or repair the damage of addiction. Whatever exact goal he hoped our finished book would accomplish, he never got to see the finalization of this story in person.

I could spend hours regretting the time I wasted relapsing instead of writing. I could regret the days I tried to type but became distracted instead. I could lament my limitations to finesse my words in time, to organize my thoughts more clearly, to give Dad more to work with before his time was up. But as any journalist working to a deadline, Dad pushed this project along. The closer he came to his end, the more intensely he pushed me and our editor to complete our work. He dedicated himself to making this book a reality. All he wanted was for our story to be told.

Not finishing this book in time for Dad to see it isn't my only regret. The innumerable misdeeds I committed against my father – a man who wanted nothing more than to have his old son back – are also at the top of my remorse list. Each time I let my dad down, each time I violated his trust, or caused him pain was time I spent blotting out an opportunity for joy to fill our lives in the relationship we should have had during the years of my addiction. I won't waste more time agonizing over my shortcomings and listing all the should haves, would haves, and could haves. All I know is that each day I wasn't working toward sobriety was precious time wasted. No one knows when time is up. My dad is considered young by today's standards, and the destroying angel certainly did not pass him by.

The irony is that although I looked this destroyer in the face more times than I can remember throughout my years of drug use, knocking on her door repeatedly, even banging on her door frustrated that she did not answer, the door was never opened. I was never engulfed in her darkness but was instead left to stand on her threshold, wondering when she would save me from having to endure the full pain of emotion and when she would take me from all the problems I had created for myself. Death is not fair, kind, merciful, or just. Death is just death. No respecter of persons, age, ethnicity, culture, or origin. My father, the best man I will ever know who never tampered with death, fell victim to her when I should have taken his place years before.

I have learned that death cannot be reasoned with. Although there are ancient fables of bartering with death, we know that modern medicine is the only tool that can stave off death, but sometimes not even that is enough, and if it ever buys us any time, it is only temporary. Indeed, a decade of my moral insurrection could not be atoned for with a few short years of sobriety and my own recommitment to living a principled life. As death hovered on my family's threshold, she was as ignorant of my pleas to spare my dad's life as when I beckoned for her to take mine years before.

Recognizing my father's love for me, and the time I wasted not building my relationship with him, tears me apart inside. I cannot change my past. However, I can change my future. One thing I learned from my father is that talk is cheap. So as I stand at another crossroad, I realize I can either drown my father's passing with drugs or I can live on.

I choose to live on. I have made it my one life goal to continue on and live as my father did: a well-respected and honest man. I know this is what my father would want from his son. The least I can do for my father and my family is to continue living a sober life, complete this book, and strive to set and reach new goals.

As I have fully disclosed so many of my debaucheries and misdeeds, my moral collapses and times of ethical void, I find myself hiding very little from the world. It is a startling position to find myself in. Knowing that I can now be critiqued and despised by much of society leaves me strangely insecure. And yet, as I finalize these words, I know I have nothing left to hide. That is therapeutic in and of itself. As I have shared with my family the true nature behind so many of my onerous actions, we have cried together, we have languished together, we have held each other more tightly coming to understand what I have experienced, what they have experienced, and what together we have overcome.

Although my father has moved on from this life I feel him with me every day. He will always be a part of me and I want to live my life in a way that will make him smile. And, in the slim chance that you are looking down here keeping a watch on us, I just want to tell you Dad, we did it!

Glossary Of Terms

Words that are used on the street can and do change often. As people discover more and more ways to get high, more slang is invented. This list I have compiled is the words that I have heard used most often. Depending on where you live, the terms that are used may be different. Another way to find the most common "street slang" in your area is by doing an online search. Knowing the most up-to-date slang words involving drugs is invaluable information and will help you fight addiction around you more aggressively and successfully.

ABSCESS

> An abscess is a sore that forms under the skin. This happens to many drug users who use drugs intravenously. Shooting up into the vein will not cause an abscess. If the drug user misses the vein and injects the fluid into the body tissue that is when an abscess can form.

ACID

> Acid is LSD (Lysergic acid Diethylamide.) It alters all senses and causes hallucinations. Other names for acid/LSD are tabs, blotter, and windowpane.

BALLOON

> A balloon is a small water balloon that is used to conceal drugs. Most often heroin and cocaine.

BEANS

> A term for any kind of prescription pill or tablet. Usually pills and tablets that are crushable so the individual can inhale the powder through the nose.

BENZOS'

> Benzos' are benzodiazapines'. Those include Valium, Xanax, Ativan and Rohypnol. Very dangerous when mixed with other opiates/alcohol.

BLACK

> Black is heroin. Heroin can be smoked, sniffed up the nose, taken orally or shot intravenously into the bloodstream. Other names for heroin are antifreeze, black, brown, tar, train, smack, dope, H, and junk.

BUD(S)

> Bud(s) is a term used for marijuana. There are numerous slang terms for marijuana. A few others are weed, green(s), kind, skunk, ace, airplane, 420 (time to smoke), ashes, blaze, burn, spliff, doob(ie), swag.

BUMP

> A single dose of cocaine.

CHASING THE DRAGON

> When heroin is placed on a small square of tin-foil and a heat source is ignited from underneath the foil, the heroin will begin to melt and create smoke. The smoke is then sucked into the lungs with the use of a small straw or tube. When the heroin liquefies, it freely slides about the tinfoil and the smoke has to be chased around; hence the phrase "chasing the dragon."

CHUNK

> A leftover single dose of mushrooms usually in the bottom of a baggie.

COOKER/SPOON

> A cooker or spoon is a devise used to heat up or cook drugs before shooting into the vein. Most often a utensil style spoon is used for this process.

COTTON

> A cotton is the term for "the filter" used when drawing drug mixtures into a syringe. It can be cotton from a Q-tip or even a small piece of a cigarette butt.

CRACK

> Crack is a form of cocaine. When cocaine is "cooked" or "rocked up" and mixed with baking soda it turns into crack or crack rock. Other names include white, nose candy, dust, coke, rails, rich man's drug and powder.

CRUNK

> Crunk means to get high and drunk at the same time. Ex: smoking weed and drinking beer or vodka.

DEXTROMETHORPHAN (DXM)

> A drug in over-the-counter cough suppressants. It has hallucinogenic affects after 900mg. It has many different synonyms. Dex, Candy, Robo, Skittles, and Tussin are a few names used around the four-corners area of the United States.

- Glossary Of Terms -

DOPE

> This word can have multiple meanings in drug slang. I have always used it to mean any type of illegal drug.

DOPE SICK

> A term used for an individual who is coming off of opiates like heroin or morphine.

DOWNER(S)

> A slang term for a substance that have a depressant effect on the central nervous system. In general, downers are sedative-hypnotic drugs, such as benzodiazepines, opiates and barbiturates.

DRUG GAME

> Drug game is a term used for people who are in a drug lifestyle.

FIX

> This word means to ingest drugs in any manner to make withdrawals or cravings go away.

FREE BASE

> Freebase is another way to ingest a drug. It is usually mixed with baking soda and water and then exposed to heat/flame and the smoke that is emitted is then taken into the lungs.

HIT

> To ingest some type of drug into the body.

LOADED

> This word is used to mean someone is high on a mind altering substance.

PAN HANDLE

> Pan handle is the term used for someone begging for money on the streets; usually done with a cardboard sign.

PIECE

> A leftover single dose of heroin.

RELAPSE

> A slip-up or setback in a person's attempt to remain abstinent from drugs or alcohol.

RIG/POINT/NEEDLE/POKE R/ STICK

> These are all terms used for a syringe or needle.

RUNNER

> A person who delivers illegal substance in exchange for money or goods.

SCORE/HOOK-UP/RE-UP

> The exchange of illegal substance for money or goods

SHAKE

> A leftover single dose of marijuana or mushrooms usually in the bottom of a baggie.

SHARDS

> A small single dose sized piece of meth. Piece is heroin. Bump is cocaine.

SHROOMS

> Shrooms usually refer to Psilocybin mushrooms that have psychedelic effects when ingested. Other names for shrooms are caps, mushies, magic mushrooms, or Scooby snacks.

SLANG

> The action of selling large amounts of illegal substances. Ex: He slangs heroin.

SODA

> Baking soda or "soda" is used for cutting cocaine and free basing, as well as for rocking cocaine. Cutting/stomping on cocaine is just making more cocaine by adding extra ingredients like baking soda. When done too many times, bullets may be exchanged. No one wants to pay top dollar for stomped on cocaine. Freebase is mixing water, baking soda and cocaine on tinfoil, spreading it around, letting it dry, then placing a heat source under the foil and inhaling the smoke into the lungs. Cocaine burns terribly on its own and burns the throat and esophagus. Rocking up cocaine is a cooking process that turns powder cocaine into hard little rocks. Once this is achieved, it almost surely must be smoked in a crack pipe. When cocaine is cooked with heat, water and soda in a specific manner, it turns the cocaine into crack. The process is not reversible.

SPECIAL K

> A medication used as an anesthetic. Also called ketamine. It can cause hallucinations and euphoria. Synonyms are vitamin K, horse tranquilizer, and super acid.

SYRUP HEADS

> Users of Dextromethorphan.

TIN FOIL

> Tin foil is used for different drugs. Larger pieces are used for freebasing cocaine. (explained

above) Smaller sizes of tin foil can be used for smoking heroin. (explained above) Another use may be to store drugs.

TOOTER

➢ This is a tube shaped instrument usually made from a writing pen tube or a dollar rolled into a straw shaped tube. It is used for inhaling smoke and/or sniffing crushed up substances.

TRACK MARKS

➢ Scars created from overuse of a needle/syringe on a body part. Scar tissue can build up on the vein and cause the vein to collapse. When this takes place, the IV user must find a different injection area on the body.

TRIGGER

➢ A trigger is any object/place/thing that prompts an addicted individual to think about using a substance.

TURN TRICKS

➢ Selling your body for drugs/money. Prostitution. Sexual based actions.

UPPERS

➢ A slang term for a substance that have a stimulating effect on the central nervous system. Some "uppers" are cocaine, methamphetamines, and caffeine.